Anorexia Nervosa

hope for recovery

To our families:

Eszter, Eva and Andrew

Camilla and my parents

Anorexia Nervosa

hope for recovery

Dr Agnes Ayton

MD MMedSc FRCPsych
Consultant Child & Adolescent Psychiatrist

Hammersmith Press
London, UK

First published in 2011 by Hammersmith Press Limited
14 Greville Street, London EC1N 8SB, UK
www.hammersmithpress.co.uk

British Library Cataloguing in Publication Data: A CIP record
of this book is available from the British Library.

ISBN 978-1-905140-09-1

Commissioning editor: Georgina Bentliff
Designed and typeset by Julie Bennett
Index: Dr Laurence Errington
Production: Helen Whitehorn, Pathmedia
Printed and bound by TJ International Limited, UK
Cover image: © Mark Bolton/Corbis

Contents

Acknowledgements

This book could not have been written without the help and inspiration of many people. First and foremost it has been inspired by sufferers and carers over the course of more than 20 years of clinical practice in the NHS and the independent sector. I continue to learn from patients and families, and I feel privileged that they share their struggles and put their trust in me. I have been struck by the bewilderment people experience when they first encounter anorexia in their lives. This is perfectly understandable: most of us do not anticipate having to cope with illnesses such as this, but when they happen it is important to understand the complete picture. An informed patient or carer is much better equipped to overcome the illness than someone who leaves decisions to professionals alone. I hope that this book will help readers to understand this complex disorder without wasting years of their lives, thereby saving valuable time and reducing unnecessary suffering.

Professor Basant Puri was instrumental in the conception of this work. He suggested to my publisher, Georgina Bentliff, that she contact me and I should like to express my sincere thanks to them both. Georgina has been a great source of support over the years. As someone who has witnessed the effects of anorexia at first-hand, within her own family, she has been both unwaveringly committed to the book and an active contributor

Acknowledgements

to its contents. She has also been extremely patient, which was a practical necessity for a busy consultant psychiatrist like myself, for whom writing a book could be no more than a spare time activity. Her patience has allowed the text to mature over time.

I have learned a great deal from my colleagues at the Royal College of Psychiatrists Eating Disorders Section, and I have tried to cover their work comprehensively in this book. Indeed, I hope that its main strength as a guide for patients and their families is the critical review of the research evidence concerning anorexia that it contains. This should help them to navigate between the certainties and uncertainties of current knowledge, to make informed choices between the services on offer and to avoid the pursuit of quick fixes.

Needless to say, the support and patience of my husband, Dr Andrew Ayton, has been essential. Without his help and emotional warmth this book would not have been possible.

Introduction

It is unclear how many people suffer from anorexia nervosa and related eating disorders. This is a secretive illness: only a fraction of sufferers acknowledge the problem, let alone seek treatment.[1,2] Many endure the condition quietly for years without help, wasting their lives away with a preoccupation with dieting, hoping that the happiness and admiration for which they long will come when their weight has become less than that of everyone else. The tragedy is that often they do not realise until it is too late that anorexia brings devastating isolation with poor physical and mental health.

Even when patients and families decide to seek professional advice, they often find it difficult to get the illness recognised or to access the help they need. In the UK, as in most countries, the first contact is usually with a general practitioner. Studies have repeatedly shown that, for a number of reasons, in primary care the condition is often not recognised or diagnosis is delayed.[3,4]

This should not perhaps be surprising. First, the training of general practitioners does not usually cover eating disorders, apart from a very basic description during undergraduate psychiatric studies. An average family doctor in the UK looks after about 1600-1800 patients, and among them there is unlikely to be more than one patient with a definite diagnosis of anorexia nervosa. Indeed, some general practitioners work for years without encountering a single patient with this condition. Such a level of experience is hardly sufficient to develop expertise in this area; most general practitioners become more interested in common illnesses, such as heart disease or cancer.

Furthermore, general practitioners in the UK have only about 10 minutes allocated for each patient. Allowing any more time would result in unmanageable waiting lists, inefficiency and missed government targets. Unfortunately, patients with anorexia require longer than this. They tend to be frightened and embarrassed to talk about their problems openly; and if they do pluck up sufficient courage to seek help, they may not be able to explain the extent of their difficulties in so short a time. Rather than being open about their eating disorder, they will talk about feeling low, or complain about some physical symptom, such as constipation or not having their periods.[4,5]

To make matters worse, full physical examination has ceased to be a routine procedure in modern medical practice. Apart from the issue of time efficiency, doctors have become increasingly concerned about potential complaints and litigation, particularly against male doctors examining unclothed female patients. Clothes may disguise even severe malnutrition, and anorexia nervosa can easily go undetected during the first consultation if a physical examination is not carried out. Far too often the patient will leave the surgery disappointed, with nothing more than a prescription for an antidepressant, a laxative or the pill (to help with the lack of periods). Many do not return, unless the condition worsens significantly and their families press them to do so.

Parents and patients often report a time lag of several months between first making contact with health services and diagnosis. This is similar to the delay in the recognition of schizophrenia; and in both conditions, delaying treatment can be detrimental.

The situation is similar in other countries. Studies from the US[6] and continental Europe suggest that only a fraction of eating disorders are recognised and consequently receive treatment at primary care level. Managed care, which is driven by the financial interest of the large insurance companies, allows only limited services for patients with anorexia nervosa, leaving patient and family to sort out the problem.

In the UK, the specialist services for eating disorders are patchy at best. Although the Royal College of Psychiatrists has laid down clear guidelines for the provision of specialist services in the NHS, these are not necessarily followed by the cash-strapped Trusts. Eating disorders have never been regarded by any government as high on the list of priorities. Sadly, this is mainly because patients with these conditions do not pose a danger to the public, just to themselves, and they are generally law-abiding citizens.

This book has been written with the aim of guiding patients and their families to a better understanding of anorexia. It offers information about services and treatment options with the hope that sufferers will find the inspiration to set out on the road to recovery. It is all too often the case that patients and family members learn about anorexia by trial and error, thereby wasting valuable time and suffering unnecessary anguish.

This book aims to be comprehensive, with information relevant to all age groups and both sexes, and for families and carers as well as patients. This is necessary for a number of reasons. Anorexia is often a chronic disorder, starting in adolescence, but also affecting adulthood. The separation of adolescent and adult issues is somewhat artificial. People make the transition from adolescence to adulthood at different paces, and many anorexia sufferers lag behind their peers in this respect. Child and adolescent mental health services differ from adult services in terms of service organisation and philosophy. This can be confusing and it is important to understand these differences. Furthermore, about one in 10 sufferers is male, and it is particularly difficult to find information for them. I discuss issues specific to males as I go along.

In addition to providing information about the illness and treatment options, this book also offers practical self-help advice for patients, and families. As many sufferers choose not to seek professional help, or cannot access it, self-help may be the only way forward for them. The good news is that some people are able to get better without professional help,[7-9] usually by taking advantage of the support and help offered by loved ones. Families and friends can be very effective in helping a person with anorexia. However, first-time experience of the illness can be bewildering and extremely painful for families. Parents and siblings often feel guilty, attributing blame to themselves, and this can have a paralysing effect. I hope that the book will help to dispel these feelings, freeing up positive energies in the family that can assist the sufferer in making changes.

For those who cannot succeed on their own, it is important to know how to ask most effectively for help, and how to assess the quality of services on offer. A well-informed patient is more likely to be able to recognise the dangers of anorexia and to access appropriate services. The same applies to families who are desperate to help their loved ones.

The information in this book may also be helpful for professionals working in educational settings and primary care, including general practitioners.

References

1. Keski-Rahkonen A, Hoek HW, Susser ES, Linna MS, Sihvola E, Raevuori A et al. Epidemiology and course of anorexia nervosa in the community. *American Journal of Psychiatry* 2007; **164(8)**: 1259-1265.

2. Hoek HW. Incidence, prevalence and mortality of anorexia nervosa and other eating disorders. *Current Opinion in Psychiatry* 2006; **19(4)**: 389-394.

3. Bryant-Waugh RJ, Lask BD, Shafran RL, Fosson AR. Do Doctors Recognize Eating Disorders in Children? *Archives of Disease in Childhood* 1992; **67(1)**:103-105.

4. Ogg EC, Millar HR, Pusztai EE, Thom AS. General practice consultation patterns preceding diagnosis of eating disorders. *International Journal of Eating Disorders* 1997; **22(1)**: 89-93.

5. Becker AE, Thomas JJ, Franko DL, Herzog DB. Disclosure patterns of eating and weight concerns to clinicians, educational professionals, family, and peers. *International Journal of Eating Disorders* 2005; **38(1)**: 18-23.

6. Walsh JME, Wheat ME, Freund K. Detection, evaluation, and treatment of eating disorders - The role of the primary care physician. *Journal of General Internal Medicine* 2000; **15(8)**: 577-590.

7. Ben-Tovim DI, Walker K, Gilchrist P, Freeman R, Kalucy R, Esterman A. Outcome in patients with eating disorders: a 5-year study. *The Lancet* 2001; **357(9264)**: 1254-1257.

8. Woods S. Untreated recovery from eating disorders. *Adolescence* 2004; **39(154)**: 361-371.

9. Perkins SJ, Murphy R, Schmidt U, Williams C. Self-help and guided self-help for eating disorders. *Cochrane Database of Systematic Reviews* 2006; **(3)**.

Chapter 1

What is anorexia nervosa?

It would be easy to assume that everyone in the Western world is on a diet. Supermarkets are full of diet products, lifestyle magazines provide regular dietary advice, and there is always a diet book on the bestsellers list. The weight and diet of celebrities are discussed on a weekly basis in the media, and the majority of female stars follow one diet or another at different phases of their lives. Some of them promote or support various weight loss regimes, which involve either dieting or exercise; and by doing so they not only supplement their income, but also enhance their celebrity status. If a celebrity puts on weight, it makes international news, usually with derogatory or pitying comments. If she loses weight, it usually goes unnoticed unless the weight loss is severe. Even then, the most common attitude reflects Mrs Simpson's famous comment: a woman can 'never be too rich or too thin'. Men are not exempt from this scrutiny, although they are less often targeted by public comments about their weight and shape. The self-imposed starvation of stars is depicted as glamorous in glossy magazines, and young people who aspire to the same lifestyle are easily seduced into following their example. Celebrity eating disorders have become common, although only a few who suffer from them are prepared to discuss this openly in public. Being thin is desirable, but at the same time, the consequences of becoming too thin have become a modern taboo.

Nevertheless, the media are not solely responsible for this phenomenon. Ultimately, they discuss weight, shape and diet because the public's appetite for these matters is insatiable.

Dieting and fitness are multi-million-dollar industries. The problem is that dieting does not work in the vast majority of cases. Despite the phenomenal business success of the diet industry, the weight of the general population has been growing. Since the mid-20th century, it has become increasingly difficult to maintain a normal weight. In the richest countries, there is an abundance of high-energy foods, while the level of physical activity has reduced dramatically as a result of technological advances and changing lifestyles. As a result, the risk of obesity has soared (in the US and the UK more than 50% of the population is overweight or obese).[1] The trends are changing frighteningly fast: for example, in Europe, the prevalence of obesity has trebled since the 1980s. Developing countries and the poor are no longer exempt: by the beginning of the 21st century, the rate of obesity had approached 100% in some Pacific Islands.[2] Childhood obesity has also become a growing problem worldwide, even in countries like Japan, where obesity rates have traditionally been low.[3]

As dieting has become part of normal life, the risks of taking it to extremes are overlooked. Unfortunately, this is true not just of the press, but also of the health profession. In some vulnerable people, dieting can get out of control and lead to full-blown anorexia nervosa.[4, 5] Although dieting in itself is not sufficient to cause anorexia, without dieting the illness does not occur. Nobody knows why it is – when the majority of us give up dieting long before the weight loss becomes severe – that people with anorexia nervosa just cannot stop. It is a devastating illness, which usually lasts for years and can be life threatening. Sadly – and precisely because dieting is so common – most sufferers and families do not initially recognise the severity of the problem. More often than not, initial comments about the weight loss, from friends and family, are positive and this can reinforce dieting in vulnerable people.

Symptoms and features

What is the difference between 'normal' dieting and anorexia nervosa? Anorexia nervosa cannot be diagnosed by means of a blood test or a scan. Instead, doctors rely on the consensus of a somewhat artificially drawn-up collection of symptoms and signs.

There are two main diagnostic systems used by doctors and health care organisations throughout the world. The World Health Organisation (WHO) developed the International Classification of Diseases (ICD-10), whilst the American Psychiatric Association introduced the Diagnostic and Statistical Manual for Mental Disorders (DSM-IV). There are only minor differences between the two systems in the definition of anorexia nervosa (see Table 1). By their very nature, these diagnostic systems describe the illness in a technical fashion. In this chapter, I shall explain the main issues behind the technical terms and the characteristics of the illness.

Table 1. Diagnostic criteria for anorexia nervosa

	DSM-IV[6]	ICD-10[7]
1.	Refusal to maintain body weight at or above a minimally normal weight for age and height (85% of expected); or a failure to make expected weight gain during a period of growth, leading to a body weight of less than 85% of expected	There is a weight loss, or in children, a lack of weight gain, leading to a body weight at least 15% below the normal

2.	Intense fear of gaining weight and becoming fat, even though underweight	The weight loss is self-induced, by avoidance of fattening foods
3.	Disturbance in the way in which one's body weight or shape is experienced, undue influence of body weight or shape on self-evaluation, or denial of the seriousness of the current low body weight	There is a self-perception of being too fat, with an intrusive dread of fatness, which leads to a self-imposed low weight threshold
4.	In females who have had their first period, amenorrhoea, or no periods without hormone treatment (the absence of at least three menstrual cycles)	A widespread endocrine disorder, in women manifested as amenorrhoea (no periods), and in men as a loss of sexual interest and potency
	Subtypes: a) restricting; b) binge-eating/purging	

Low body weight

The core feature of anorexia nervosa is deliberate weight loss, and the maintenance of abnormally low body weight. This feature is essential for the diagnosis. People who diet, but without losing so much weight that they become clinically underweight, may still suffer from an eating disorder, such as atypical anorexia, or bulimia (conditions that will be discussed later); but not from anorexia nervosa.

What is an abnormally low body weight? This is an important question, as many patients and their families are not necessarily clear about the answer. People with anorexia nervosa have a strong desire to be thin, but they usually do not believe themselves to be abnormally underweight. Concerned comments from friends or family are either ignored or perceived as the positive result of the hard and painful process of disciplined weight loss. Alternatively, and worse, some sufferers believe that others are simply lying when they express concerns about their frail figure. Objective information can help sufferers and their families to recognise the danger. Low weight is one indicator of the severity of the eating disorder, just as abnormal liver functioning is an indicator of the severity of alcoholism. It shows that the body is already damaged.

In the two main diagnostic systems, (ICD-10 and DSM-IV) 'abnormally low body weight' is defined as below 85% of normal weight. Like any number, this is somewhat artificial, but it is based on normal distribution of weight for height in the population. As with IQ, the average healthy body weight according to a person's age and height is 100%. Anything too far away from average is regarded as abnormal (in statistical terms, below or above a standard deviation of 2). According to UK growth chart data, 85% of normal weight is equivalent to body mass index (BMI) 18.5 in a 20-year-old female, and 19 in a 20-year-old male. (See below for how this is calculated.) This database contains information for the normal development of both sexes from birth to age 20. After this age, the body finishes development and any changes will be the result of lifestyle or illness.

Table 2. Body mass index for adults (WHO guidelines)

	BMI
Obese	30 or higher
Overweight	25-29.9
Normal weight	20- 24.9
Thin (borderline)	18.5-20
Underweight	Less than 18.5

BMI is easy to calculate: it equals a person's weight in kilograms divided by height in metres squared (BMI=kg/m^2).

Example:
A 20-year-old woman is 164 cm tall and weighs 54 kg
Her BMI = 54/(1.64 x 1.64) = 20

BMI 20 is a slim but healthy body weight, at the lower end of the normal range. BMI is often used in the general medical literature to measure risks associated with obesity, and people above a BMI of 25 are advised to lose weight on medical grounds (Table 2). If you are an adult and your BMI is between 18.5 and 20, you may or may not be healthy. Small proportions of adult women (mainly of Asian origin) have regular periods and are fertile at this weight, but many are not. If your BMI is below 18.5, you are clinically underweight according to WHO definitions. Research shows that this low body weight is associated with increased mortality at the population level – clear evidence that this weight is unhealthy.[8] The upper end of the normal limit (BMI 25) has been criticised: men with large muscles (rugby players, for example) can be heavier than this without having an ounce of unnecessary fat on their bodies.

In children or adolescents, BMI is not a good substitute for percentage of normal weight, because normal body shape and composition change during development. For example, while a BMI of 14 would be perfectly fine for a seven-year-old, it would be dangerously low for a 14-year-old. The different developmental pathways for males and females complicate the picture still further. For this reason, it is not as easy to calculate normal weights for young people under 18 as it is for adults. However, national norms for childhood development are available for various countries and they can be obtained from the specialist medical literature or from the web – for example, at: http://www.cdc.gov/growthcharts/. Using these norms, the percentage of normal body weight can be calculated. This is a more

accurate measure for children and adolescents, but the calculation is difficult without relevant software. Some public websites provide this facility in order to help parents assess the nutritional status of their children: http://shop.healthforallchildren.co.uk/pro.epl?DO=USERPAGE&PAGE=Calculator
http://www.healthforallchildren.co.uk

Unfortunately, the diagnostic systems also give a lower figure (BMI 17.5) for the diagnosis of anorexia nervosa, which is confusing for patients as well as professionals. In fact, this number is equivalent to 80% of average healthy weight for an adult woman. The reason for this discrepancy is that the BMI of 17.5 is the result of a different calculation of normal weight. Instead of using the average weight according to WHO definitions (BMI = 22.5) as 100%, the lowest figure for normal (BMI = 20) is assumed to be 100% (Table 2). It is regrettable that this inherent inconsistency exists within the current diagnostic categories.[9] One can only hope that this will be corrected in the next revision of the DSM and ICD.

Although using this lower criterion ensures that the diagnosis of anorexia nervosa is probably the most reliable of all psychiatric diagnoses, at the same time it also excludes many patients from the full diagnosis, who suffer from the illness. Indeed, this gives the false impression to some patients that a BMI just above 17.5 is fine. This is not the case. For example, most females cannot have periods at this level, and the low oestrogen levels in the body are associated with an increased risk of osteoporosis, depression and so on. A BMI of 18.5 also appears in the WHO definition of human nutritional states as the cut-off point for Grade 1 malnourishment, and there is good scientific evidence in all races to support this.[10] Unfortunately, websites exist that glamorise the extremely low BMIs of certain celebrities, thereby giving the false impression that chronic starvation is a personal choice required for success, rather than a health risk. The reliability of these sites is, of course, highly questionable.

Intense fear of putting on weight

The fear of being or becoming fat is another central feature of anorexia nervosa. At the beginning of the illness, friends and family usually regard this as normal. Many people believe that in the context of the high risk of obesity in modern times, everybody is worried about becoming fat. This, of course, is not true; the fear of getting fat is not overwhelming for people without an eating disorder. Otherwise, the average weight of the rest of the population would not have grown so much during the last two decades. There are other things that are much more important in life, such as family, friends, career and pleasure.

In anorexia, the fear of fatness becomes overwhelming: it is an all-consuming preoccupation, which interferes with normal functioning in life. It intrudes into all activities, except perhaps academic work and cleaning, both of which can become increasingly obsessional. This occurs to such an extent that many patients feel that they would rather be dead than fat. Associated with this is the belief that being fat is disgusting, and that only thin people can find success and happiness. Unfortunately, the media – and, indeed, supermarkets – constantly reinforce this belief. Anorexia sufferers take this to the extreme, by wanting a totally fat-free body.

The intensity of fear in anorexia is different from other common fears. Most people with fears – such as of heights or public speaking - experience a reduction in the fear if they face the cause and practise challenging it. People can learn that their fears are irrational and unhelpful, and can conquer them. For some reason, in anorexia the fear of fatness and fear of eating are extremely tenacious and do not subside as easily as other fears. There may well be a biological difference in the way that people suffering from anorexia respond to stress, but it is not certain whether this is due to the starvation itself or whether people who are at risk of anorexia are more likely to experience intense fear for some other (e.g. genetic) reason. The combined intensity and tenacity of this fear is one of the main reasons why anorexia is so difficult to treat.

Biologically, humans cannot function normally without a significant amount of body fat. At least 22-25% of body fat mass is needed for regular menstrual cycles and normal fertility.[11] This is one of the reasons why some female athletes with normal BMI develop amenorrhoea (periods stop). Intensive training uses up the normal body fat mass and turns it into muscle, with negative hormonal consequences. Human females are not designed by evolution to be 'fat-free'. There is a good reason for this: producing and bringing up a child requires a huge amount of extra energy from the mother. It would simply be unsafe to be fertile during times of food shortage.

Adult males and children generally have lower body fat stores than adult females, but for this very reason they are more vulnerable to the effects of starvation. Ultimately, being fat-free is incompatible with life. Fatty tissues are found everywhere in the body, and have vital roles. For example, the brain's dry weight is more than 50% lipid,[12] and the bone marrow that produces our blood cells is mainly fatty tissue.

Many people with anorexia do not realise these facts, or, even when they do, they find it difficult to accept them. They have an intense desire to avoid fat in both their bodies and their diet, at whatever cost. In the most severe cases, the fear of being fat can reach delusional intensity: some sufferers will not even kiss their loved ones for fear of gaining fat through touching other people with their lips. Others will not use moisturisers or lipstick for the same reason. In extreme cases, patients cannot touch fatty foods or even approach a kitchen or restaurant, the fear of being contaminated by fat – through their skin or by breathing in the air – being too great.

As I have said before, this extreme fear of becoming fat is one of the reasons why it is so hard to help a person suffering from anorexia. It is not possible to recover from the condition while keeping one's weight abnormally low, and weight restoration is not possible without increasing the body's fat stores. To make it even more difficult, in the short term, any excess energy is stored in the form of fat tissue, and it takes several months for the body to rebuild other tissues such as bone and muscle from this energy reserve. This inevitable physiological mechanism makes weight restoration very difficult for anorexia sufferers. They usually believe that family members and professionals are against them, because they want them to do the very thing that they fear the most: to put on weight, which inevitably increases their fat stores. It is important to remember that this means no more than returning to full physical health. Professor Lacey from St George's Hospital in London has suggested that we should rename the fear of fatness in anorexia, a fear of normal weight, and indeed this might help to avoid the confusion.

Despite the intensity, the fear of fatness is not fundamentally different from any other fear: it can only be overcome if the sufferer is determined to face that fear until it disappears. In anorexia, this process takes a long time, but it can be successful.

Body image disturbance

In addition to their fear of fatness, patients with anorexia believe that they *are* fat. This symptom is particularly poignant when the person is in fact severely underweight. Paradoxically, body image disturbance can get worse with further weight loss. For loved ones, body image distortion is particularly difficult to understand. Their desperate attempts to help the sufferer appreciate the seriousness of their predicament often fall on deaf ears. A significant proportion of patients change their style of clothing in an attempt to hide their body, which they believe to be fat despite being malnourished. Many start wearing baggy, dark clothes, and avoid exposing their body as much as possible, for fear that other people might see how fat they are. In severe cases, they believe themselves to be fatter than anyone else, and experience serious panic in the company of slim people – to such an extent that going out into public places becomes impossible.

To understand body image distortion, it is helpful to consider that the estimation of one's own body size is notoriously difficult.[13] Most obese people believe that they are slimmer than they really are,[14] while normal or even thin people worry about being overweight[15, 16] or being fat in certain areas of their anatomy. This discrepancy occurs because we judge the bodies of other people differently from our own. While we assess other people's size mainly by sight, this is not easily achieved with ourselves. We can see only certain parts of our bodies – mainly the front from below the neck. Other parts can be viewed only in mirrors or photographs, which present two-dimensional images. People are often surprised to see photo or video images of themselves; they feel different from the inside from what they can see from the outside. Our own body size can also be estimated in other ways: by pinching the skin, by putting on clothes of certain sizes, or by stepping on the scales. We are also aware of things happening inside our bodies – such as the feeling of being bloated or hungry, energetic or weak – and all of this information tells us whether we are fine or not.

Anorexia sufferers do not feel fine because of the chronic starvation they inflict on themselves. However, feeling hungry is often interpreted as an indication of greediness, which needs to be controlled as much as possible. Sometimes, patients spend an enormous amount of time checking their bodies – by looking into mirrors, or by pinching the skin to feel the fat-layer under the skin (which does not disappear totally until the very last stages of starvation).[17] It is as if they were not sure about their bodies. It may be difficult for anorexia sufferers to make sense of their predicament: that, on the one hand, they feel fat, while, on the other, they are hungry or are being told that they are too thin. Pinching the skin may confirm the anorexic belief: 'I can pinch my skin, therefore I am fat; so I must continue to lose weight.' Checking body weight obsessively can be another manifestation of the problem. Many sufferers check their weight daily or even more than once a day, not realising that there is a normal fluctuation of body weight, and that the difference can be as much as 2 kg in a day.

Believing that they are fat, sufferers continue wanting to lose weight, setting lower and lower targets for themselves. Body image distortion also explains the intense guilt patients experience regarding eating. If you are a sufferer reading this book, you will recognise this feeling. If you are a friend or family member, consider this: how would you feel about eating, if you were convinced that you were enormously overweight? Patients report feeling greedy, guilty and bad.

When the illness becomes severe, it is sometimes only by depriving them of responsibility for their diet that patients' guilt can be relieved. This is the reason why even seriously ill patients can gain weight in specialist hospitals. The treatment team takes responsibility for the necessary dietary intake, and as a consequence, the sufferer no longer feels so guilty about eating. Alternatively, having clear professional advice can help parents take control over their child's dietary intake without entering into unbearable conflict.

Often, body image distortion is specific to certain parts of the body. Many young women, to achieve an ideal female figure, would like to have less fat on their stomach and hips, and more on their breasts. Until recently, diet and exercise were the only ways to change body shape; but with the advent of cosmetic surgery, this has now changed.

In my own clinical practice, during the last few years, an increasing number of anorexia sufferers have expressed a desire to have breast implantation, to make their bodies look more feminine, while wishing to have no fat elsewhere. This new surgical option adds a further dimension to the body image disturbance in anorexia: sufferers are unhappy about having fat in certain places, but they wish to have it (in the form of an artificial implant) elsewhere. I can only hope that the regulators of the plastic surgery industry will introduce appropriate ethical safeguards to prevent this becoming a new disorder with surgery-related risks. In starvation, the breasts shrink (or, in adolescents, they stop developing), so the best solution to the problem is to allow the body to recover to normal weight; and, as a result, breast size will improve through the effects of normal hormonal activity.

Body image disturbance interferes with normal functioning in life only if body shape is regarded as more important than anything else. For most people without an eating disorder, being thin is valued less highly than other personal qualities. For example, the majority of healthy women would regard being a good mother, wife or lover as more important than being as thin as possible. Similarly, most young men value other qualities more highly than thinness, such as being strong, smart and sexually potent. Young people are perhaps particularly preoccupied with personal attractiveness, because this is the time of life when relationships are formed, and the competition for attractive mates is intense. We shall come back to this later. But other qualities are also valued, such as being popular, smart or friendly. Furthermore, most people value their health highly, and try to avoid activities that are clearly harmful, particularly if there is potential damage to their fertility.

In anorexia, sufferers become preoccupied with their weight and shape to such a degree that they regard these as the most important qualities in themselves as people. Sometimes, this is because these are the easiest things to control in their lives, but it would be wrong to assume that this is the only reason. In starvation, the focus of attention shifts away from the outside world towards the body. In anorexia, there is a further tension between hunger and wanting to lose weight. The hunger is a painful reminder of the goal of wanting to lose weight, and the body is continuously examined with the anorexic magnifying glass. Any perceived imperfections help the sufferer to continue with the starvation, despite the body's desperate signals for nutrition. In some cases, this focus on the detail is not just the result of the anorexia itself, but seems to be a specific problem with information processing, not dissimilar to autistic spectrum disorders.[18, 19]

Hormonal abnormalities

Chronically low weight is associated with widespread hormonal abnormalities. Sex hormones shut down, and stress hormones increase. The body, at this stage, is functioning on high alert. In adult females, the normal menstrual cycle is lost, and adult males lose their libido. Children and adolescents suffer a delay in growth and sexual development. These symptoms reflect the body's effort to save energy for the maintenance of life, and clearly signal that something is seriously wrong. Regular menstrual cycles are a good indicator of healthy weight in females above the age of 13 to 14 years. The cessation of periods is a direct communication from the body that there is not enough energy in the system. Testicular atrophy (shrinkage) and the loss of sexual interest are an equivalent consequence of starvation in males.

The link between the return of periods and healthy weight is so strong that many specialised services use this information to estimate minimum healthy weight for individual patients. Research shows that at 100% of normal weight the return of periods is almost 100%, while only a small proportion of females who have 85-87% of normal weight (BMI around 19) can have regular periods.[20, 21]

Sex hormones have a profound effect on the body and mind, not just on the sexual organs. Males with low testosterone levels are at high risk of osteoporosis (brittle bones), muscle wasting and depression. Females lacking oestrogens also develop osteoporosis, breast atrophy and depression. In both sexes, the abnormally low hormones further increase the negative effects of starvation, resulting in a downward vicious circle.

The emergence of these symptoms usually poses a dilemma for the person trying hard to keep her/his weight low. The majority of young women are alarmed by the realisation that they might become infertile, or that they are not as healthy as their peers. Men are usually deeply troubled by the loss of libido and of sexual performance, while children are concerned about being short, or not developing as well as their peers.

Other hormones are also affected. Low thyroid function is a common consequence of starvation, resulting in slow metabolism, feeling cold, and developing coarse dry hair and skin.

The reality of negative health consequences is important in helping sufferers to confront their condition: they can be powerful motivators for change. This is similar to the smokers' experience when they first develop smoking-related diseases, such as heart disease or lung cancer. It is difficult to persist with behaviour that is clearly harmful, and many people decide to change before it is too late. Sadly, others ignore all warning signs, and despite the evidence of negative effects on their health, continue regardless of the consequences.

Artificial hormones in contraceptive pills can mask the hormonal deficits in anorexia nervosa: periods will continue when the pills are stopped for a week in a month, regardless of the body's health status. The consequent regular blood loss will further deepen the nutritional deficiencies in underweight women who, due to the pill, continue with their periods. For this reason, it is preferable to use other forms of contraception if needed. Artificial female hormones also have their side effects, and instead of helping, contribute to the health risks of anorexia in the long term.

Abnormal eating behaviours

The US diagnostic system (DSM-IV) distinguishes between two types of anorexia based on eating behaviour: 'restricting' and 'bingeing and purging'. In both types, there is a major change in eating behaviour. Initially, most patients cut down their intake of foods that are regarded as fattening. Various dietary fads during the last 100 years have regarded foods that have high energy density as fattening; latterly, the focus has moved onto meat, dietary fats, carbohydrates, and various food combinations, such as the Zone diet or the Atkins diet. Cutting out food is called 'dietary restriction' by the health profession, and it simply means the reduction of food intake. Anyone who has ever tried to diet knows how hard it is to eat less than your appetite dictates. Although 'anorexia' in Latin means loss of appetite, patients suffering from anorexia nervosa do not lose their appetite until the malnutrition is severe. The conflict between the body and the mind leads to strange eating habits as a way of coping with the urge to eat and the overwhelming desire to lose weight. Many patients claim to follow certain 'healthy' diets, and this line of reasoning is used to ensure avoidance of higher energy foods. For example, after the beginning of the illness, a significant proportion of sufferers become vegetarian or vegan.[22, 23] In Western societies, being vegetarian has become fashionable in the last 30 years. Indeed, it is often regarded as a healthy personal choice, so family members or friends may find it difficult to challenge. Unfortunately, the risk of anorexia and the prognosis are worse if the patient follows a vegetarian diet, [22, 24, 25] and there are biological reasons for this, which will be discussed later.

Many patients avoid eating with other people. The intense

fear of fat, and the guilt, make mealtimes an ordeal even when eating alone. It is still worse to maintain the pretence, in front of others, that everything is fine. Young people, afraid that their parents will make them eat more, try to avoid having meals with the family. As the illness progresses, patients may take hours cutting up their food into little pieces; they may spoil the food with salt or excessive spices; or paradoxically, they may eat very fast. These are the results of chronic starvation, which have been observed in severely malnourished people during famines, as I will discuss later.

In severe starvation, people often become obsessional about food. They may formulate rules for eating. These may involve having meals only at certain times; or allowing only a certain number of calories; or developing compensatory behaviours to ensure ongoing weight control, such as various forms of exercise, vomiting or using various medications. These rules may convey a false sense of security and control, which make the self-induced starvation more tolerable. By this stage, sufferers think about little else other than food and weight loss, with devastating consequences for the quality of their lives and relationships.

Some become preoccupied with cooking for other people. This behaviour serves several goals. Cooking allows time with food, which can relieve hunger in the short term. It also creates a superficial impression that there is nothing wrong, and allows social interaction with others. Often friends and family members interpret this as a positive sign, but it is not necessarily the case. Not being able to eat with your friends and family when hungry is highly abnormal. Sometimes feeding other people becomes almost a hostile act – as if it served the purpose of trying to fatten up everyone else.

Self-induced vomiting can develop as a way of coping with the guilt surrounding eating. This can occur after binges or after normal or even small meals, if the meal is perceived to be too big. Professor Fairburn and his group at Oxford University recommended that a distinction be made between objective binges, when the amount of food intake would be large for anyone (a whole loaf of bread, for example), and subjective binges, when the amount seems big only to the sufferer. In anorexia, subjective binges are more common. For example, eating a few apples can result in intense guilt and resort to compensatory behaviours, such as exercise or vomiting. Some patients use other purging methods, such as laxatives, slimming pills or hormone tablets, all of which increase the physical damage to the body and the risk of death by causing dangerous electrolyte imbalance. Others use smoking cigarettes or illicit substances to reduce appetite, which can worsen the health consequences.

Purging is a poor prognostic sign in anorexia. Self-induced vomiting is very unpleasant, and usually people with more complex problems use this strategy. They are more likely to have a history of sexual or physical abuse, depression, and more physical complications, such as dangerous electrolyte disturbance. The mortality rate is higher in this group, so it is very important to stop this behaviour before it is too late.[26]

Other eating disorders

Although this book focuses on anorexia nervosa, it is important to understand the similarities and differences between this condition and other eating disorders. For scientific purposes, it is essential to have strictly defined categories, so that research that is carried out all over the world can be compared.

Eating disorders in adults are divided into three categories:
1. Anorexia nervosa;
2. Bulimia nervosa;
3. Eating disorder not otherwise specified (EDNOS), including binge-eating disorder.

However, the reality is more complicated: there is significant continuity and overlap between eating disorders. Furthermore, many childhood eating disorders do not fit neatly into these current categories.[27] An expert team led by Professor Lask has developed an alternative diagnostic approach for childhood eating disorders, but this has not yet been accepted by the main diagnostic systems.

Bulimia nervosa

Bulimia nervosa was first described as a distinct eating disorder in 1979.[28, 29] This condition seems to have newly emerged in the context of affluent societies, with plentiful food, and focus on a slim ideal weight. One of the most famous and outspoken sufferers was the late Princess of Wales.

Bulimia nervosa is characterised by regular bingeing that is associated with an overwhelming sense of loss of control over eating, and is followed by various compensating behaviours, such as vomiting, laxatives and exercise, to achieve weight loss (even if it is just a temporary loss of water, such as is the case with using laxatives). For the full DSM-IV diagnosis, these behaviours need to occur at least twice a week in frequency and have to occur continuously for at least three months. Patients' self-evaluation is also very much influenced by body shape and weight, but in contrast with patients suffering from anorexia nervosa, bulimic patients are not clinically underweight. This is the main diagnostic difference. Some regard bulimia as an 'unsuccessful' version of anorexia in people who cannot tolerate hunger and chronic starvation. However, having normal weight significantly reduces the risks associated with anorexia, and explains the much lower risk of mortality in bulimia compared with anorexia.

There are two subtypes of bulimia. Patients with 'purging type' engage in self-induced vomiting or misuse laxatives, diuretics and enemas, while patients with 'non-purging type' use other compensatory behaviours, such as fasting or excessive exercise. Underweight people who engage in bingeing and purging are diagnosed as having either anorexia nervosa 'binge-eating/purging type'; or 'eating disorder not otherwise specified' (EDNOS) if one of the main diagnostic features of anorexia is missing.

Eating disorder not otherwise specified (EDNOS)

People do not fit into neat little boxes, as defined by expert committees of the various medical diagnostic systems. The EDNOS category was introduced to allow a clinical diagnosis for those patients who have significant eating problems, but do not meet the full diagnostic category of anorexia nervosa or bulimia. For example, a few women may continue with their periods even if their weight is below 85% of healthy weight, so do not qualify for the strict diagnosis of anorexia. One could also argue that the lack of periods is a redundant diagnostic item,[30, 31] as it simply reflects the severity of the malnutrition rather than being specific to anorexia nervosa. Patients who have all the symptoms of anorexia but are still above the cut-off point of 85%, would also fall into the EDNOS category. Some patients who lose 20-30% of their body weight rapidly as a result of an eating disorder can become dangerously ill, despite still being within the 'normal' weight range for the general population. This is particularly true of children and adolescents, or males of any age, whose initial weight was higher than normal before the eating disorder began. Alternatively, patients with chronic anorexia nervosa may just manage to maintain body weight minimally above 85%. These patients are likely to be severely ill, with significant detriment to their health and life, but do not strictly fulfil the diagnostic criteria. To make it even more confusing, if clinicians use the alternative cut-off point of a BMI of 17.5 for the diagnosis, even more patients are excluded from the anorexia nervosa category. Given that the current

DSM-IV diagnostic criteria render anorexia nervosa a very rare disease, and EDNOS the most common, it would make much more sense to use a BMI 18.5 as the cut-off weight for anorexia nervosa. As we have seen before, this would be equivalent to 85% of average healthy adult weight according to WHO criteria (BMI: 22.5).

A significant proportion of children and adolescent sufferers restrict their diet and become dangerously underweight, but do not suffer from body image distortion and do not necessarily want to lose weight. Selective eating, food phobias and fear of choking are all more common in childhood than in adulthood. Under DSM-IV criteria, all of these would be diagnosed as EDNOS. Professor Lask has distinguished 'food-avoidance disorder' and 'pervasive refusal syndrome' to categorise these young patients. It is uncertain whether these conditions are a variant of severe depression, or a combination of depression and childhood eating disorders.

The current EDNOS category also includes patients with bulimic symptoms who binge fewer than two times a week. To confuse matters even further, the DSM-IV includes binge-eating disorder under the EDNOS category, although in clinical practice this diagnosis is accepted as a separate category. These patients are on the opposite end of the spectrum: they are usually over-weight.

Not surprisingly, EDNOS is the most common eating disorder (as much as 20 times more common than anorexia nervosa in some studies) as it includes a wide range of eating-related problems. Unfortunately, it is also the least studied, as, unlike anorexia or bulimia, it is not regarded as a scientifically robust category.

Experts in the field have called for a change to correct this anomaly.[32-34] One solution would be to remove the current inconsistencies in the weight definition. A more radical alternative would be to have three main separate categories of eating disorder depending on the weight of the patient: underweight (anorexia and atypical anorexia), normal weight (bulimia), and overweight (binge-eating disorder). This classification of eating disorders would reflect the health risks associated with underweight and overweight in eating disorders.

The ICD-10 system is slightly different. It includes a category called 'atypical anorexia nervosa', which applies to people who have most of the features of anorexia, but do not quite fit into the strict category. For example, according to ICD-10, patients above BMI 17.5, or without the drive for thinness, would be classified as atypical anorexia nervosa. This makes the ICD system more consistent than the DSM.

Diagnostic categories: do they matter?

Although there are significant differences between the various diagnostic categories, there is also a significant overlap. Patients suffering from anorexia and bulimia share the same intense preoccupation with weight and shape, and they value themselves according to these concerns above anything else.

The most important difference between these two disorders is weight, and the nature of the eating behaviours. Patients with bulimia do not suffer from chronic and severe malnutrition, and generally they are in better overall physical health than patients with anorexia. They are also easier to treat psychologically. Christopher Fairburn's team have researched psychological treatments of eating disorders at Oxford University for more than 20 years. They have shown that psychological treatments, such as interpersonal therapy and cognitive behavioural therapy, can be effective in the treatment of bulimia,[35] but this is not the case in patients with anorexia who are significantly underweight. The reasons for this difference are not clear, but it is possible that the severe starvation of the brain interferes with normal thinking processes, and the patients are less able to use psychotherapy effectively.

However, people do change, and there is significant movement between the various diagnostic categories over time. This observation has been confirmed by research from Switzerland.[36] The researchers followed up 55 patients with various eating disorders for three years. If the first diagnosis was anorexia, about 50% still had the full symptoms of anorexia after three years, 9% had developed bulimia nervosa, 20% EDNOS, and only 22% of them had recovered. On the other hand, only 5.6% of bulimic patients had developed anorexia nervosa, and 33% had recovered. A recent, larger study[37] followed up 216 women with a diagnosis of anorexia nervosa or bulimia nervosa for seven years. During this time, more than half the women with anorexia nervosa crossed over between the restricting and binge eating/purging anorexia nervosa subtypes. Although one-third crossed over to bulimia nervosa, these patients were likely to relapse into anorexia nervosa again. Women who began with bulimia nervosa, on the other hand, were unlikely to develop anorexia nervosa at all.

The recovery rates of EDNOS and bulimia seem to be better,[38] whilst anorexia associated with bulimic symptoms (purging subtype) has the highest mortality rate and the poorest prognosis. These differences in recovery rates suggest that the existing diagnostic categories do represent eating disorders of differing severity.[39]

Summary and self-diagnosis

As we have seen, there is significant overlap and continuity between various eating disorders. Diagnosis has some practical value, as it confirms to patient and family (as well as the health services) that the problem has gone beyond 'normal' dieting. Answering the following questions may help self-diagnosis.

Your weight and hormones:		
What is your BMI (as calculated from your weight (in kg) and height (in m) at present?		
Are you clinically underweight? (See the guidelines above)	Yes	No
Have you experienced any changes in your hormonal functions? (Females: loss of periods; Males: loss of erection and loss of sexual interest; Both: feeling cold, or tired?)	Yes	No
Your fears and beliefs:		
Do you worry about your weight and shape?	Yes	No
Do you fear being fat or consuming fats in your diet?	Yes	No
Do you think that you are fat even when other people tell you otherwise?	Yes	No
Do you think that being thin is more important than anything else in your life?	Yes	No
Your eating behaviours, and weight control:		
Have your eating behaviours changed? (see list below)	Yes	No
• Do you restrict your diet?	Yes	No
• Do you try to avoid certain foods to control your weight?	Yes	No
• Do you calorie count?	Yes	No
• Do you eat secretly or avoid eating socially?	Yes	No
Do you use exercise to control your weight?	Yes	No

How many times a week and for how long?	Twice or more	Less than twice
Do you binge?	Yes	No
How many times a week?	Twice or more	Less than twice
Do you make yourself sick?	Yes	No
How many times a week?	Twice or more	Less than twice
Do you use laxatives or any other substances in order to control your weight?	Yes	No
How many times a week?	Twice or more	Less than twice
Do you use enemas to control your weight?	Yes	No
How many times a week?	Twice or more	Less than twice

The diagnosis is anorexia nervosa:
- If you are clinically underweight as a result of deliberate weight loss;
- If you continue to believe that you are fat, even when other people and the figures tell you that you are underweight;
- If you are preoccupied with your weight and shape most of the time;
- If your periods have stopped or if your libido has been lost;
- If your eating habits have changed. (If you also binge and purge, you have the purging subtype.)

The diagnosis is EDNOS if not all of these criteria are met, and bulimia nervosa if you are not underweight but use various methods to control your weight and binge or purge at least twice a week.

Diagnosis is the first step to recovery. If you do not believe that there is something wrong, why would you want to change? Furthermore, the most effective way to access help is to make an appointment and tell your doctor that you suffer from anorexia (or one of the other eating disorders). Ask for advice about local services and for a physical examination. Most doctors respond positively to direct communication from patients or carers, and they should not be offended by your self-diagnosis. An informed patient can use the health care services more effectively.

The full physical examination (including the measurement of weight and height in your underwear) is very important for both you and the medical practitioner to assess the level of immediate danger and the potential long-term consequences of the illness. Do not be afraid to ask for it. You can just say that you want to understand how your health has been affected. Remember, there is no blood test for anorexia. Therefore, a normal blood test does not exclude the diagnosis, and it does not mean that you are safe and well. I shall discuss this in more detail in chapter 6.

Sometimes, if the illness is recent, the doctor may send you away trying to reassure you that all will be well. The lack of recognition of an eating disorder can be as high as 80% during the first GP consultation.[40] This is a very frustrating experience for families, especially for mothers, who usually are the first to recognise the problem and work hard to persuade the patient to seek help in the first place. It is also very confusing for the patient. Do not despair, and do not give up seeking help. If this happens to you or your family member, you still have various options: you can find another doctor, or simply go back within a few weeks. Usually, by the second consultation there will be a more helpful response.

References

1. Shell ER. *The hungry gene: the science of fat and the future of thin.* London: Atlantic Books; 2002.
2. World Health Organization. *Obesity: preventing and managing the global epidemic.* Geneva: WHO; 2000.
3. Matsushita Y, Yoshiike N, Kaneda F, Yoshita K, Takimoto H. Trends in childhood obesity in Japan over the last 25 years from the National Nutrition Survey. *Obesity Research* 2004; **12**(2): 205-214.
4. van den Berg P, Neumark-Sztainer D, Hannan PJ, Haines J. Is dieting advice from magazines helpful or harmful? Five-year associations with weight-control behaviors and psychological outcomes in adolescents. *Pediatrics* 2007; **119(1)**: E30-E37.
5. Hsu LKG. Can dieting cause an eating disorder? *Psychological Medicine* 1997; **27(3)**: 509-513.
6. American Psychiatric Association. *Diagnostic and statistical manual of mental disorders.* Washington, DC: American Psychiatric Association; 1994.
7. World Health Organization. *ICD-10 Classification of mental and behavioural disorders.* Geneva: 1993.
8. Thorogood M, Appleby PN, Key TJ, Mann J. Relation between body mass index and mortality in an unusually slim cohort. *Journal of Epidemiology & Community Health* 2003; **57(2)**: 130-133.
9. Thomas JJ, Roberto CA, Brownell KD. Eighty-five per cent of what? Discrepancies in the weight cut-off for anorexia nervosa substantially affect the prevalence of underweight. *Psychological Medicine* 2009; **39(5)** :1-11.
10. Gu DF, He J, Duan XF, Reynolds K, Wu XG, Chen J et al. Body weight and mortality among men and women in China. *Journal of the American Medical Association* 2006; **295(7)**: 776-783.
11. Klentrou P, Plyley M. Onset of puberty, menstrual frequency, and body fat in elite rhythmic gymnasts compared with

normal controls. *British Journal of Sports Medicine* 2003; **37(6)**: 490-494.

12. Piomelli D, Astarita G, Rapaka R. A neuroscientist's guide to lipidomics. *Nature Reviews Neuroscience* 2007; **8(10)**:743-754.

13. Chang VW, Christakis NA. Extent and determinants of discrepancy between self-evaluations of weight status and clinical standards. *Journal of General Internal Medicine* 2001; **16(8)**: 538-543.

14. Madrigal H, Sanchez-Villegas A, Martinez-Gonzalez MA, Kearney J, Gibney MJ, de Irala J et al. Underestimation of body mass index through perceived body image as compared to self-reported body mass index in the European Union. *Public Health* 2000; **114(6)**: 468-473.

15. Chang VW, Christakis NA. Self-perception of weight appropriateness in the United States. *American Journal of Preventive Medicine* 2003; **24(4)**: 332-339.

16. Stevens C, Tiggemann M. Women's body figure preferences across the life span. *Journal of Genetic Psychology* 1998; **159(1)**: 94-102.

17. Mountford V, Haase A, Waller G. Body checking in the eating disorders: Associations between cognitions and behaviors. *International Journal of Eating Disorders* 2006; **39(8)**: 708-715.

18. Lopez C, Tchanturia K, Stahl D, Booth R, Holliday J, Treasure J. An examination of the concept of central coherence in women with anorexia nervosa. *International Journal of Eating Disorders* 2008; **41(2)**: 143-152.

19. Zucker NL, Losh M, Bulik CM, Labar KS, Piven J, Pelphrey KA. Anorexia nervosa and autism spectrum disorders: Guided investigation of social cognitive endophenotypes. *Psychological Bulletin* 2007; **133(6)**: 976-1006.

20. Key A, Mason H, Allan R, Lask B. Restoration of ovarian and uterine maturity in adolescents with anorexia nervosa. *International Journal of Eating Disorders* 2002; **32(3)**: 319-325.

21. Sobanski E, Hiltmann WD, Blanz B, Klein M, Schmidt MH.

Pelvic ultrasound scanning of the ovaries in adolescent anorectic patients at low weight and after weight recovery. *European Child & Adolescent Psychiatry* 1997; **6(4)**: 207-211.

22. O'Connor MA, Touyz SW, Dunn SM, Beumont PJ. Vegetarianism in anorexia nervosa? A review of 116 consecutive cases. *Medical Journal of Australia* 1987; **147(11-12)**: 540-542.

23. Klopp SA, Heiss CJ, Smith HS. Self-reported vegetarianism may be a marker for college women at risk for disordered eating. *Journal of the American Dietetic Association* 2003; **103(6)**: 745-747.

24. Martins Y, Pliner P, O'Connor R. Restrained eating among vegetarians: Does a vegetarian eating style mask concerns about weight? *Appetite* 1999; **32(1)**: 145-154.

25. Neumark Sztainer D, Story M, Resnick MD, Blum RW. Adolescent vegetarians – A behavioral profile of a school-based population in Minnesota. *Archives of Pediatrics & Adolescent Medicine* 1997; **151(8)**: 833-838.

26. Steinhausen HC. The outcome of anorexia nervosa in the 20th century. *American Journal of Psychiatry* 2002; **159(8)**: 1284-1293.

27. Nicholls D, Chater R, Lask B. Children into DSM don't go: A comparison of classification systems for eating disorders in childhood and early adolescence. *International Journal of Eating Disorders* 2000; **28(3)**: 317-324.

28. Russell GFM. Thoughts on the 25th anniversary of bulimia nervosa. *European Eating Disorders Review* 2004; 12(3):139-152.

29. Russell G. Bulimia Nervosa – ominous variant of anorexia-nervosa. *Psychological Medicine* 1979; **9(3)**:429-[?].

30. Grave RD, Calugi S, Marchesini G. Is amenorrhea a clinically useful criterion for the diagnosis of anorexia nervosa? *Behaviour Research and Therapy* 2008; **46(12)**: 1290-1294.

31. Attia E, Roberto CA. Should amenorrhea be a diagnostic criterion for anorexia nervosa? *International Journal of Eating Disorders* 2009; **42(7)**: 581-589.

32. Fairburn CG, Cooper Z. Thinking afresh about the

classification of eating disorders. *International Journal of Eating Disorders* 2007; **40**: S107-S110.

33. Fairburn CG, Cooper Z, Bohn K, O'Connor ME, Doll HA, Palmer RL. The severity and status of eating disorder NOS: Implications for DSM-V. *Behaviour Research and Therapy* 2007; **45(8)**: 1705-1715.

34. Zimmerman M, Francione-Witt C, Chelminski W, Young D, Tortolani C. Problems applying the DSM-IV eating disorders diagnostic criteria in a general psychiatric outpatient practice. *Journal of Clinical Psychiatry* 2008; 69(3): 381-384.

35. Fairburn CG, Jones R, Peveler RC, Hope RA, Oconnor M. Psychotherapy and Bulimia-Nervosa – Longer-Term Effects of Interpersonal Psychotherapy, Behavior-Therapy, and Cognitive-Behavior Therapy. *Archives of General Psychiatry* 1993; **50(6)**: 419-428.

36. Milos G, Spindler A, Schnyder U, Fairburn CG. Instability of eating disorder diagnoses: prospective study. *British Journal of Psychiatry* 2005; **187**: 573-578.

37. Eddy KT, Dorer DL, Franko DL, Tahilani K, Thompson-Brenner H, Herzog DB. Diagnostic crossover in anorexia nervosa and bulimia nervosa: Implications for DSM-V. *American Journal of Psychiatry* 2008; **165(2)**: 245-250.

38. Herzog DB, Dorer DJ, Keel PK, Selwyn SE, Ekeblad ER, Flores AT et al. Recovery and relapse in anorexia and bulimia nervosa: a 7.5-year follow-up study. *Journal of the American Academy of Child & Adolescent Psychiatry* 1999; **38(7)**: 829-837.

39. Birmingham CL, Touyz S, Harbottle J. Are anorexia nervosa and bulimia nervosa separate disorders? Challenging the 'transdiagnostic' theory of eating disorders. *European Eating Disorders Review* 2009; **17(1)**: 2-13.

40. Hach I, Ruhl UE, Rentsch A, Becker ES, Turke V, Margraf J et al. Recognition and therapy of eating disorders in young women in primary care. *Journal of Public Health* 2005; **13(3)** 160-165.

Chapter 2

Who suffers from anorexia nervosa?

Historical perspective

Is anorexia nervosa a modern illness or did people suffer from it in the past? This is not just a hypothetical question of purely academic interest. It is important for understanding the condition now and for helping those who suffer from it or who may be vulnerable. If anorexia is a new form of mental disorder which did not occur before during the history of humankind, could it be a lifestyle choice, like a modern fashion accessory? Alternatively, could there be something new in the modern environment that triggers anorexia in vulnerable people?

The idea that anorexia nervosa is simply a lifestyle choice is popular in some circles. Some patient groups advocate this explanation, particularly on the pro-anorexia websites.[1, 2] The media, and even some professionals, subscribe to this view, and this has significant consequences for the treatment philosophy and options available. In this reasoning, anorexia nervosa is a personal choice, therefore it does not need to be treated. Alternatively, it needs to be treated only if the patient wants help, regardless of the severity or risk to life. The number of people who have died because of such attitudes towards treatment is unknown, but, sadly, it could be substantial. This view can be incredibly confusing and frustrating for family members, who can sometimes feel like they have hit a brick wall when desperately searching for help for their loved one. Trust your common sense: people should not die of starvation, regardless of whether or not it is self-induced.

Moving on to the second possibility, there might be something new and harmful in the modern environment and lifestyles that can trigger anorexia in people with certain vulnerabilities. This would not be unprecedented, as environmental factors have always had an impact on human health. Most known illnesses have been around throughout the history of humankind, but their frequency can change radically depending on environmental factors. Very few diseases remain the same in frequency across different cultures and over centuries. The ones that do are usually those caused by rare genetic errors, but even simple single gene disorders, which are supposed to be 'entirely' biological, can become more prevalent due to social and cultural influences. For example, rare genetic disorders are much more frequent in cultures that encourage marriages between first cousins. Research by the BBC found that while British Pakistanis account for 3.4% of all births, they also account for 30% of all British children with rare recessive genetic disorders because of the practice of arranged marriages between relatives. This observation shows that cultural practices can increase even the risk of 'pure' genetic illnesses.

Environmental factors have an even greater influence on common diseases. Poor hygiene and poor nutrition have been responsible for many illnesses and epidemics during human history, whilst today smoking and sedentary lifestyles cause very different public health problems. Activity levels have gone down, and access to highly palatable and energy-dense foods has increased tremendously during the last 40 years or so. During this time, the rate of obesity has reached unprecedented levels. Could something similar be happening in the case of anorexia? Let us consider the historical information about anorexia and related disorders first.

It is difficult to be absolutely certain whether people suffered from anorexia-like illnesses in the past, as self-induced starvation was not necessarily understood as a mental disorder. We need to bear in mind that the current diagnostic classification systems are only a few decades old.

Descriptions of mentally disturbed behaviour in general are limited in written historical records, although there are some famous examples of depression and post-traumatic disorders in the Bible. There are also a few historical descriptions of starving saints, both male and female.[3, 4] One could argue that probably the first description was St John the Baptist – although religious scholars would contest this assumption vigorously. Other prominent religious figures, who ate minimal amounts and were reported to be significantly underweight, were the 13th-century princess St Margaret of Hungary, who died at age 28, and the 14th-century St Catherine of Siena, who died at 33. Interestingly, both of these women also severely harmed themselves as part of religious penitence, and lived a celibate life. Catherine of Siena publicly acknowledged that her inability to eat was 'an infirmity, not an ascetic practice at all'. This suggests that she was aware that her dietary restriction was not simply driven by religious beliefs.

There are folktales in all cultures describing people who stopped eating, usually due to some sort of heartache. Although folktales were fictional by their very nature, they drew on real life scenarios to teach the next generation. If these stories are anything to go by, a significant proportion of these self-starving people died in the past, but others recovered, usually when they found love.

If anorexia developed in historical times, it might have been labelled as something else: religious devotion,[5, 6] a broken heart, wasting illness, weakness of the mind, or even a physical illness such as 'consumption' (tuberculosis). To make matters more complicated, poor nutrition increased the risk of tuberculosis or other infections, so some people might have developed a physical illness due to their self-starvation, without anyone realising the original cause of the problem. It is possible that anorexia sufferers in modern times live longer simply because of vaccinations and antibiotics.

However, if we look at the modern diagnostic criteria, one of the main features of typical anorexia was missing in these historical cases. The reason for the extreme dieting was religious or emotional, rather than preoccupation with weight and shape. The starving saints might have had abnormally low body weight, hormonal abnormalities, abnormal eating behaviours, fear of fatness and even body image distortion (as a sign of greed or gluttony). Nevertheless, as far as we can tell, the person's self-evaluation was not unduly determined by their weight and shape in historical cases. Similarly, the folk tales do not describe a person who wants to be thin above all else. In modern clinical practice, these historical descriptions of a starvation illness might receive a diagnosis of 'eating disorder not otherwise specified' – EDNOS (according to DSM-IV, or atypical anorexia nervosa using ICD-10 criteria) – but not the full diagnosis anorexia nervosa. However, it is important to note that the proportion of patients with eating disorders who fulfil *all* diagnostic criteria for anorexia nervosa is in the minority even in modern times.[7-9]

It is also essential to remember that the manifestation of most psychiatric disorders is strongly influenced by the cultural belief systems of the times. For example, in other conditions, such as in psychosis, the content of delusions varies depending on the mainstream beliefs of the society that the individual inhabits. Psychotic patients in the 19th century were preoccupied with the devil, evil spirits or witchcraft; nowadays technical and cinematic preoccupations (such as the internet and aliens) are more common. Why should eating disorders be different? It is possible that preoccupation with weight and shape, and self-evaluation driven by thinness, are more likely to arise in an environment where the risk of obesity is high.

The first recognised medical record of self-starvation (for psychological reasons) was made in 1689 by an English physician, Richard Morton, who described 'a Nervous Consumption' caused by 'sadness, and anxious cares'. This description showed a remarkable insight into the nature of the disorder, and it still stands up to scrutiny. People do not go through the agony of self-starvation if they are happy and satisfied with their lives. Dr Morton recognised this feature of the illness. He was also the first to describe the condition in males.[10, 11]

In 1807, Goethe wrote a novel about the teenage Ottilie, who died of self-starvation. It has been argued that this might have been the first literary description of anorexia nervosa as we understand it.[12] The capture of the problem in a novel suggests that self-induced starvation for emotional reasons must have been prevalent in the general public at the turn of the 19th century.

There have been only a few historical descriptions of potential male eating disorder sufferers; one notable exception was Franz Kafka, the writer.[13] However, he also suffered from tuberculosis, so it is difficult to be absolutely certain whether he had an additional eating disorder or not. He died young due to self-starvation.

By the 19th century, the modern description of anorexia nervosa had started emerging. One of the most famous examples was Empress Elisabeth of Austria, a celebrated beauty, who feared becoming overweight, and so restricted her diet and exercised excessively, resulting in weight loss and malnutrition.[14] She was regarded as 'severely ill' at the time, but a diagnosis was not given, possibly due to her status. There are several similar case reports in the French and English scientific literature as well. Charles Laségue (1873) described the condition as 'a hysteria linked to hypochondriasis', and Sir

William W. Gull (1874)[15] described it as 'a perversion of the ego', and he introduced the term 'anorexia nervosa'. The prominent French psychiatrist Pierre Janet described the first purging patient in 1898. These doctors understood the illness to be a purely psychological disorder.

In contrast, in Germany in 1914, the German physician Morris Simmonds proposed that a physical cause, 'pituitary insufficiency', was the explanation of the severe weight loss in some of these patients. This gland is the main regulatory centre of hormonal functions in the brain, and it is essential for survival. In 1937, the English endocrinologist Harold Leeming Sheehan described a similar picture in a woman, which was the result of damage to her pituitary gland during childbirth. Consequently, many patients who would be diagnosed as having anorexia nervosa today were diagnosed as suffering from Simmonds' or Sheehan's disease in the first part of the 20th century in Europe, and the popularity of these diagnostic terms survived into the 1970s.[16] There are still reports in the medical literature describing patients initially thought to have anorexia nervosa who are later diagnosed with various brain tumours, including of the pituitary gland,[17-20] but these are extremely rare. However, the existence of these rare cases confirms the link between brain pathology and anorexia, indicating that biology is an important factor for the development of the illness.

Non-European cultures

Historical information about potential cases of eating disorders in non-European cultures is even more limited. However, fasting and self-starvation are practised in most religions, not just in Christianity. For example, Indian Jain monks advocated self-starvation for a period of 12 years. It is difficult to be certain whether this is sufficient evidence of a potential eating disorder in historical times in Asia. At the time, it was regarded as self-sacrifice for religious reasons, similar to the self-starvation of Christian saints. Fasting is also an integral part of Hinduism and Islam. One could argue that fasting (voluntary dietary restriction) is an almost universal practice in religious groups across the globe. There are very few notable exceptions to this rule; the Sikhs are one.

The idealisation of a thin body shape is by no means unique to European cultures. Ancient Egyptian sculptures and images always depicted beautiful women as thin, with a narrow waist. Similarly, thinness is valued in Far Eastern cultures, such as China and Japan.[21] There is one well-documented historical description of anorexia in Japan in the 18th century. This case provides evidence that eating disorders can arise independently of Western culture.[22]

It is often said that historical depiction of beauty in Indian images emphasises women's full breasts and hips, and this is viewed as an alternative to female beauty in European cultures. This is not so simple. These Indian images of idealised women always portray them with a narrow waist, and they are not that different from modern sexually provocative images of young European women. One could argue that there are hardly any cultures on the planet with a preference for obesity in young women.

I am unaware of any historical description of potential African cases. Maybe the frequent famines in Africa did not favour the emergence of self-induced starvation, but the reasons for these ethnic differences are not completely understood.

Modern population ('epidemiological') studies

Epidemiology is the study of the occurence of diseases in the general population. It is one of the main pillars of modern medical science. Epidemiological studies are very important in the understanding of many illnesses. They measure the need for healthcare, and they can also provide clues about the nature and cause of diseases. For example, if there is a change in the pattern and presentation of an illness over time, or if an illness is more common among people with certain lifestyles, this can highlight important opportunities for prevention and new interventions. The recent changes in the law regarding smoking in enclosed public spaces in several Western countries resulted from epidemiological research: the evidence that smoking causes harm to smokers and those in their environment had become irrefutable.

To understand the numbers quoted in various epidemiological studies, it is helpful to explain the methodological definitions briefly. The occurrence of diseases can be captured in different ways.

1. The measurement of **prevalence** refers to the number of sufferers in the general population. This can be either
   a. **point prevalence**, meaning the number of sufferers at any point in time,
   b. or **lifetime prevalence**, meaning the number of people suffering from the illness at any time during their lifetimes. (Lifetime prevalence is always higher than point prevalence.)
2. **Incidence** means the number of new cases in a year.

Unfortunately, it is difficult to conduct good quality studies to estimate the true prevalence and incidence of eating disorders. The only way this would be possible would be if researchers systematically measured the weight and height of a large number of people in the general population and enquired about their beliefs regarding weight, shape and eating habits using one of the well-established questionnaires or clinical interviews. Because anorexia nervosa is relatively rare, a high quality study to determine its true **incidence** would involve interviewing and examining hundreds of thousands of people. It would be impossible to persuade everybody, particularly individuals not in contact with health services, to participate in such a study. Furthermore, there would be a strong possibility that people not wanting to reveal their eating disorder would simply refuse to participate in such studies, and therefore the true picture would always remain hidden despite all efforts. For these reasons, the majority of studies trying to estimate the incidence and prevalence of anorexia nervosa use some sort of methodological short cut.

Most epidemiological studies of anorexia nervosa rely either on:

- Medical records and databases;
- Detailed surveys of specific populations (mainly young girls and women in education); or
- Using self-rating questionnaires provided by a large number of participants from the general population.

All of these approaches present their own methodological problems, making comparisons between different studies difficult. For example, information from medical records is dependent on available medical services, diagnostic traditions, and cultural and economic factors relating to treatment-seeking in different countries. Data from specific groups – such as ballet dancers or college students – cannot be generalised to everybody. The use of different age groups in studies also makes comparisons between epidemiological data from different countries difficult. Surveys using self-rating questionnaires rely heavily on voluntary participation and openness from participants, and people with eating disorders often deny their problems.

Despite these methodological complications, there are some consistent findings in the scientific literature: prevalence seems to be significantly higher in Western countries. The majority of anorexia sufferers are young females, but all ages can be affected to a lesser extent. A substantial minority – about 10% – of clinical samples are male. Interestingly, a recent population-based study in the US found that the reported lifetime history of anorexia had a female-to-male ratio of 3:1.[23] However, other studies have produced very different results. For example, using a different methodology (evaluating the information on the UK General Practice Database), Currin *et al* found a 12:1 female-to-male ratio for anorexia nervosa.[24] These contradictory findings may simply mean that men are less likely to seek medical help, or, if they do, they are less likely to be diagnosed with anorexia. There is also some evidence that the illness may be more transient in men, and this would also explain the differences between clinical and community samples.[25] However, the illness is certainly more common among young females.

Anorexia nervosa is a relatively rare disease, affecting about one to two people in a thousand (or in young females about 0.2-0.5%) in various Western countries.[23, 26-29] The incidence (number of new cases per year) in the UK is about 4.7 per 100,000, but with much higher levels amongst young women between the ages of 10 and 19 years (around 35 per 100,000).[24]

There has been no clear evidence of a significant increase in the incidence or prevalence since the 1980s in Western countries (unlike, for example, the trebling obesity rates),[30] suggesting that there has been no new environmental factor since then that might contribute to the development of anorexia nervosa. This finding has been confirmed in several countries. For example, a recent large study of twins in Sweden demonstrated an increased lifetime prevalence of anorexia nervosa in people born after 1945. The overall prevalence of anorexia nervosa was 1.20% and 0.29% for female and male participants respectively.[28] The ratio of females to males in this study was about 4:1.

There is an ongoing debate in the scientific literature about whether the illness is becoming more common. Although the mass media often state that this is indeed the case, current scientific evidence does not support this view.

Non-European countries and ethnic groups

The prevalence of anorexia seems to be lower in traditionally non-white countries. However, the quality of epidemiological studies supporting this is mixed at best. Most relevant studies rely solely on information from medical records, and can therefore detect cases only if the sufferers concerned present themselves for treatment and are diagnosed as having an eating disorder. Given the recognition of eating disorders is known to be poor at primary health care level, and the wide variation in medical services between countries, these studies probably reveal only the tip of the iceberg.

Studies in Japan have demonstrated a lower prevalence than in Caucasian populations.[31, 32] However, anorexia nervosa has become more common in Japan in recent decades, suggesting that there are new environmental factors at play there. There is good quality public health evidence that both obesity and extreme thinness have increased in Japan in the last 25 years.[33-35] However, this gives only an indirect suggestion of the proportion of patients with eating disorders. Although these changes are usually attributed to cultural influences, it is worthwhile considering that globalisation has had a major effect on diet and physical activity too.

There have been very few African cases described.[36-39] Interestingly, this is also true of women of African origin living in Western countries.[40-44] The risk in mixed-race populations, however, seems to be higher.[45, 46]

Some authors argue that the different levels of prevalence may be caused by a lack of cultural sensitivity in the various screening tools used to identify eating disorders in non-European populations.[47] In particular, body image distortion is a rarer feature of eating disorders in the Far East (such as Hong Kong), whereas physical symptoms are common.[48-52] However, this may simply mirror the historical picture in Europe a hundred years ago. As discussed above, before the 19th century, body image distortion was a far less common feature of self-induced starvation. It has been observed that second-generation Asians living in the UK and US also show less fat phobia,[53, 54] but there is some indication that the preoccupation with weight and shape may be increasing in Asian patients.[55]

Age at onset

Anorexia mostly affects young people.[26, 56] The illness usually starts around adolescence, but it can also emerge in early adult-hood. In contrast with bulimia and binge eating disorders, it is rare for it to start late in life.[57] This characteristic of anorexia nervosa is particularly poignant: it devastates the physical health and the quality of life of young people in the prime of their lives.

A recent 20-year long-term study of body weight, dieting and disordered eating in women and men found that women's weight perception and dieting frequency decrease over time from adolescence to mid-life, whereas men's weight perception and dieting frequency increase. Marriage and motherhood are associated with this reduction in disordered eating.[58] Marital dissatisfaction, on the other hand, increases the risk of unhealthy dieting and body dissatisfaction in women, and can precede the onset of anorexia in some cases.[59, 60] The few cases starting late in life that have been described in the scientific literature were associated with bereavement and interpersonal difficulties.[57]

Particular groups and occupations

It is well documented that certain groups are at high risk of eating disorders. For example, ballet dancers, models and actors are more likely to develop eating disorders, including anorexia.[61-64] It is commendable that the fashion industry has started a discussion about the ethical issues around employing 'size zero' models, following the tragic deaths of a number of young models recently. However, at the time of writing this book, there is no universal agreement on the solution to the problem, and the wafer-thin images of pre-pubertal models continue to dominate the catwalks and glossy magazines.

The 'female athlete triad' has been described in sports people, and manifests as a combination of disordered eating, lack of periods and osteoporosis (weak bones).[65] The high-risk sports for eating disorders fall into the aesthetic category where a 'perfect' body is expected, such as in gymnastics or ice-skating, or sports in which low body fat is advantageous, such as cross-country and marathon running.[66] Male athletes are most at risk of developing eating disorders in sports in which there is a focus on weight or thin body shape, such as wrestling, horse racing, or aesthetic sports.[67-70]

In the 1970s, higher social class was regarded as a risk factor for anorexia nervosa, but more recent studies have shown a reduction in this association in Western countries. It is possible that the abundant availability of food in combination with the desire to keep a thin body shape is more important for the development of the illness, with the effect of social class being minimal.

Males

Although the risk of anorexia nervosa is higher in females, boys and men are not immune. Interestingly, atypical eating disorders, such as 'selective eating' (very limited food choices), are more common in boys than girls before puberty. These are often related to developmental disorders, such as autism spectrum disorders, or to severe anxiety. However, very few of these eating problems develop into anorexia nervosa after puberty.

As already discussed in this chapter, about 10% of people

with anorexia known to health services are male. On the other hand, large community-based epidemiological studies have recently shown that as many as 30% of participants reporting a lifetime history of anorexia were male, but only a minority sought treatment. Eating disorders are associated with women and this may be an impediment to seeking treatment for men.[71] John Prescott's disclosure of his bulimia could be a typical example of this situation.

However, even if as many as 30% of sufferers were male, the imbalance towards the female sex is most extreme amongst psychiatric disorders. Interestingly, there is some evidence that homosexuality/bisexuality is a specific risk factor for eating disorders (particularly bulimia) in males.[72, 73] According to a recent study, attending a gay recreational group is significantly related to eating disorder prevalence in gay and bisexual men.[74] The reason for the higher prevalence in non-heterosexual males[75] is unknown at present.[76, 77] In some cases, the drive for weight loss may be an expression of the rejection of male sexuality, such as in men with gender identity disorders.[78, 79]

The motivation for initial weight loss is usually different for men than for women.[80] Preoccupation with a muscular but 'fat-free' body is more common, sometimes resulting in excessive exercise and steroid abuse.[81, 82] This is consistent with male sexual attractiveness, but paradoxically, these strategies damage normal sexual functioning. Biologically, abnormally low weight does not allow muscle building, not just because of lack of nutrients, but also because testosterone levels fall during starvation. The low testosterone does not just affect libido and sexual performance, but also the body's ability to build muscles. Steroids illicitly used for muscle building also interfere with normal sex hormone production, and can be harmful in the long run.

Illicit substance misuse has also been associated with anorexia in males, for a number of reasons. Firstly, amphetamines, heroin and cocaine all reduce appetite. Secondly, some underlying personality traits may present a risk for both conditions.[83]

Research on anorexia in boys and men is limited.[84] This is mainly because only a small proportion of clinic populations are male, so it is very difficult to recruit sufficient numbers of male participants into studies. Furthermore, the majority of research studies concerning anorexia nervosa exclude male patients from recruitment or the analysis in an attempt to keep the methodology simple. The Minnesota Semi-Starvation study, which will be discussed later, included only male participants. Hence, this study has provided invaluable information about the consequences of self-induced starvation in males.

Medical complications are more common in men than women during starvation.[85] However, a recent study in Sweden showed that the long-term recovery rate of men hospitalised for anorexia was good.[86] The same research group has also shown that the outcome of eating disorders in females has improved in Sweden (in contrast to many other countries).[87, 88] These findings may be true only for the Swedish population, due to the effective screening programmes and early intervention in this country's highly developed and equitable healthcare system. Finnish researchers also found better outcome for males in terms of weight restoration, but additional psychological problems were common.[25]

Co-existing mental health problems (co-morbidity)

Epidemiological studies have highlighted the link between anorexia nervosa and other mental health problems, mainly depression and anxiety disorders, including obsessive compulsive disorder.[23, 89-92] The co-occurrence of anorexia with these other mental health problems is consistent across research studies. However, the nature of this association is not entirely clear. It has been known since the seventeenth century, that people do not starve themselves for prolonged periods of time if they are happy and relaxed to start with. This has been confirmed by a recent study showing that the risk of developing eating disorders is higher in young people who have developed anxiety disorder or depression at an early age.[93] On the other hand, acute starvation can cause depression and irritability, and prolonged malnutrition has a severe impact on the brain and mental health.

There is, however, evidence that even if people recover from anorexia, the risk of depression and various anxiety disorders is higher than in the general population.[88, 94] There is some evidence that anorexia and depression share a common underlying basis.[95]

Alcohol and drug abuse can also occur, particularly in chronic cases. The association with alcohol abuse is probably related to the high level of anxiety accompanying anorexia, as some patients use alcohol as a way of dealing with anxiety. Others use various illicit substances, such as amphetamines or cocaine, to reduce their appetites.[96] Both of these are highly dangerous strategies, as they worsen the patient's physical and mental health, and increase the risk of mortality.[97]

Over the last few years, there has been an increased recognition that a small but significant proportion of anorexia patients have autistic features, which include rigid thinking, poor interpersonal skills and a tendency to get lost in the details, instead of seeing the bigger picture.[94, 98, 99] Researchers have raised the question of whether these deficits are more common in anorexia than previously thought. This is an exciting new area of research as it may lead to a deeper understanding of anorexia in the future.

Summary

In summary, self-induced starvation is not entirely new to modern times. It has been around for at least a few hundred years in European cultures, possibly even longer. Cases of religious self-induced starvation have been described in other cultures as well, including India and Japan. Fasting is common practice in most religions. However, the meaning of self-imposed starvation has changed over time, from the religious to preoccupation with weight and shape. This could simply be due to the increased risk of obesity in recent times.

Modern epidemiological evidence suggests that self-imposed starvation occurs mainly in white ethnic groups, in societies where food is available in abundance. On the other hand, if food is not abundant, the reason for self-imposed starvation is much more likely to be altruistic than egocentric. The risk of preoccupation with thinness increases with the risk of obesity, and this may explain the change in the presentation of the illness over the centuries. It is not known why certain groups, such as African people, have a lower risk of developing anorexia nervosa.

The majority of sufferers are young females, but there is a substantial minority of males. The beginning of the illness is most commonly around adolescence. Certain groups and occupations are associated with a higher risk of developing the condition.

Recent research has suggested that there was an increase in the number of people suffering from anorexia until the 1950s, but since then the prevalence has been stable. Sufferers are at a high risk of developing other mental disorders, such as anxiety and depression, even after recovery from anorexia.

Reference List

1.   Abbate DG, Gramaglia C, Piero A, Fassino S. Eating disorders and the Internet: cure and curse. *Eating and Weight Disorders* 2006; **11(2)**: e68-e71.
2.   Norris ML, Boydell KM, Pinhas L, Katzman DK. Ana and the Internet: A review of pro-anorexia websites. *International*

Journal of Eating Disorders 2006; **39(6)**: 443-447.

3. Walker Bynum C. *Holy Feast and Holy Fast: the religious significance of food to medieval women.* Berkeley: University of California Press; 1987.

4. Bell RM. *Holy anorexia.* Chicago: University of Chicago Press; 1985.

5. Vandeth R, Vandereycken W. Food refusal and insanity: sitophobia and anorexia nervosa in Victorian asylums. *International Journal of Eating Disorders* 2000; **27(4)**: 390-404.

6. Bemporad JR. Self-starvation through the ages: reflections on the pre-history of anorexia nervosa. *International Journal of Eating Disorders* 1996; **19(3)**: 217-237.

7. Fairburn CG, Bohn K. Eating disorder NOS (EDNOS): an example of the troublesome "not otherwise specified" (NOS) category in DSM-IV. *Behaviour Research and Therapy* 2005; **43(6)**: 691-701.

8. Abbate-Daga G, Piero A, Gramaglia C, Gandione M, Fassino S. An attempt to understand the paradox of anorexia nervosa without drive for thinness. *Psychiatry Research* 2007; **149(1-3)**: 215-221.

9. Zimmerman M, Francione-Witt C, Chelminski W, Young D, Tortolani C. Problems applying the DSM-IV eating disorders diagnostic criteria in a general psychiatric outpatient practice. *Journal of Clinical Psychiatry* 2008; **69(3)**: 381-384.

10. Silverman JA. Richard Morton, 1637-1698. Limner of anorexia nervosa: his life and times. A tercentenary essay. *Journal of the American Medical Association* 1983; **250(20)**: 2830-2832.

11. Pearce JMS. Richard Morton: Origins of anorexia nervosa. *European Neurology* 2004; **52(4)**: 191-192.

12. Bhanji S, Jolles FEF, Jolles RAS. Goethe's Ottilie – an early 19th-century description of anorexia-nervosa. *Journal of the Royal Society of Medicine* 1990; **83(9)**: 581-585.

13. Fichter MM. [Franz Kafka's anorexia nervosa]. *Fortschr Neurol Psychiatr* 1988; **56(7)**: 231-238.

14. Vandereycken W, Abatzi T. [The anorectic life of Empress Elisabeth of Austria (1837-1898). Slenderness cult of the Habsburg family]. *Nervenarzt* 1996; **67(7)**: 608-613.

15. Vandereycken W, Vandeth R,. Who was the first to describe anorexia nervosa: Gull or Lasegue? *Psychological Medicine* 1989; **19(4)**: 837-845.

16. Habermas T. [Anorexia nervosa in German medical literature 1900 to 1945. The role of anorexia nervosa in the origin of psychosomatic medicine]. *Sudhoffs Arch* 1992; **76(1)**: 37-62.

17. Lin L, Liao SC, Lee YJ, Tseng MC, Lee MB. Brain tumor presenting as anorexia nervosa in a 19-year-old man. *Journal of the Formosan Medical Association* 2003; **102(10)**: 737-740.

18. Winston AP, Barnard D, D'Souza G, Shad A, Sherlala K, Sidhu J et al. Pineal germinoma presenting as anorexia nervosa: Case report and review of the literature. *Internal Journal of Eating Disorders* 2006; 39(7): 606-608.

19. Sokol MS, Fujimoto CK, Jackson TK, Silberberg PJ. Anorexia nervosa and brain tumor in a 14-year-old girl. *CNS Spectrums* 2006; **11(9)**: 669-673.

20. Kopp W, Rost F, Kiesewetter S, Deter HC. The fatal outcome of an individual with anorexia nervosa and Sheehan's syndrome as a result of acute enterocolitis: A case report. *International Journal of Eating Disorders* 2010; **43(1)**: 93-96.

21. Singh D, Renn P, Singh A. Did the perils of abdominal obesity affect depiction of feminine beauty in the sixteenth to eighteenth century British literature? Exploring the health and beauty link. *Proceedings of the Royal Society B-Biological Sciences* 2007.

22. Nogami Y. Eating disorders in Japan: a review of the literature. *Psychiatry Clinical Neuroscience* 1997; **51(6)**: 339-346.

23. Hudson JI, Hiripi E, Pope HG, Kessler RC. The prevalence and correlates of eating disorders in the national comorbidity survey replication. *Biological Psychiatry* 2007; **61(3)**: 348-358.

24. Currin L, Schmidt U, Treasure J, Jick H. Time trends in eating disorder incidence. *British Journal of Psychiatry* 2005; **186**: 132-135.

25. Raevuori A, Hoek HW, Susser E, Kaprio J, Rissanen A, Keski-Rahkonen A. Epidemiology of anorexia nervosa in men: A nationwide study of Finnish twins. *Plos One* 2009; **4(2)**.

26. Keski-Rahkonen A, Hoek HW, Susser ES, Linna MS, Sihvola E, Raevuori A et al. Epidemiology and course of anorexia nervosa in the community. *American Journal of Psychiatry* 2007; **164(8)**: 1259-1265.

27. Kjelsas E, Bjornstrom C, Gotestam KG. Prevalence of eating disorders in female and male adolescents (14-15 years). *Eating Behaviour* 2004; **5(1)**: 13-25.

28. Bulik CM, Sullivan PF, Tozzi F, Furberg H, Lichtenstein P, Pedersen NL. Prevalence, heritability, and prospective risk factors for anorexia nervosa. *Archives of General Psychiatry* 2006; **63(3)**: 305-312.

29. Wade TD, Bergin JL, Tiggemann M, Bulik CM, Fairburn CG. Prevalence and long-term course of lifetime eating disorders in an adult Australian twin cohort. *Australian and New Zealand Journal of Psychiatry* 2006; **40(2)**: 121-128.

30. Hoek HW. Incidence, prevalence and mortality of anorexia nervosa and other eating disorders. *Current Opinion in Psychiatry* 2006; **19(4)**: 389-394.

31. Tsai G. Eating disorders in the Far East. *Eating and Weight Disorders* 2000; **5(4)**: 183-197.

32. Nakamura K, Yamamoto M, Yamazaki O, Kawashima Y, Muto K, Someya T et al. Prevalence of anorexia nervosa and bulimia nervosa in a geographically defined area in Japan. *International Journal of Eating Disorders* 2000; **28(2)**: 173-180.

33. Matsushita Y, Yoshiike N, Kaneda F, Yoshita K, Takimoto H. Trends in childhood obesity in Japan over the last 25 years from the National Nutrition Survey. *Obesity Research* 2004; **12(2)**: 205-214.

34. Takimoto H, Yoshiike N, Kaneda F, Yoshita K. Thinness among young Japanese women. *American Journal of Public Health* 2004; **94(9)**: 1592-1595.
35. Inokuchi M, Matsuo N, Takayama JI, Hasegawa T. Prevalence and trends of underweight and BMI distribution changes in Japanese teenagers based on the 2001 National Survey data. *Annals of Human Biology* 2007; **34(3)**: 354-361.
36. Eddy KT, Hennessey M, Thompson-Brenner H. Eating pathology in East African women – the role of media exposure and globalization. *Journal of Nervous and Mental Disease* 2007; **195(3)**: 196-202.
37. Fahy TA, Robinson PH, Russell GFM, Sheinman B. Anorexia-nervosa following torture in a young African woman. *British Journal of Psychiatry* 1988; **153**: 385-387.
38. Szabo CP. Eating attitudes among black South Africans. *American Journal of Psychiatry* 1999; **156(6)**: 981-982.
39. Buchan T, Gregory LD. Anorexia-nervosa in a black Zimbabwean. *British Journal of Psychiatry* 1984; **145(SEP)**: 326-330.
40. Striegel-Moore RH, Dohm FA, Kraemer HC, Taylor CB, Daniels S, Crawford PB et al. Eating disorders in white and black women. *American Journal of Psychiatry* 2003; **160(7)**: 1326-1331.
41. Mulholland AM, Mintz LB. Prevalence of eating disorders among African American women. *Journal of Counseling Psychology* 2001; **48(1)**: 111-116.
42. Taylor JY, Caldwell CH, Baser RE, Faison N, Jackson JS. Prevalence of eating disorders among Blacks in the national survey of American life. *International Journal of Eating Disorders* 2007; **40**: S10-S14.
43. Chao YM, Pisetsky EM, Dierker LC, Dohm FA, Rosselli F, May AM et al. Ethnic differences in weight control practices among US adolescents from 1995 to 2005. International Journal of Eating Disorders 2008; **41(2)**: 124-133.

44. Fernandes NH, Crow SJ, Thuras P, Peterson CB. Characteristics of Black treatment seekers for eating disorders. *International Journal of Eating Disorders* 2010; **43(3)**: 282-285.

45. Hoek HW, van Harten PN, Hermans KME, Katzman MA, Matroos GE, Susser ES. The incidence of anorexia nervosa on Curacao. *American Journal of Psychiatry* 2005; **162(4)**: 748-752.

46. Katzman MA, Hermans KME, Van Hoeken D, Hoek HW. Not your "typical island woman": Anorexia nervosa is reported only in subcultures in Curacao. *Culture Medicine and Psychiatry* 2004; **28(4)**: 463-492.

47. Becker AE. Culture and eating disorders classification. *International Journal of Eating Disorders* 2007; **40**: S111-S116.

48. Cummins LH, Simmons AM, Zane NWS. Eating disorders in Asian populations: a critique of current approaches to the study of culture, ethnicity, and eating disorders. *American Journal of Orthopsychiatry* 2005; 75(4): 553-574.

49. Yates A, Edman J, Aruguete M. Ethnic differences in BMI and body/self-dissatisfaction among whites, Asian subgroups, Pacific islanders, and African-Americans. *Journal of Adolescent Health* 2004; **34(4)**: 300-307.

50. Hsu LKG, Lee S. Is weight phobia always necessary for a diagnosis of anorexia-nervosa? *American Journal of Psychiatry* 1993; **150(10)**: 1466-1471.

51. Wardle J, Bindra R, Fairclough B, Westcombe A. Culture and body-image – body perception and weight concern in young Asian and Caucasian British women. *Journal of Community & Applied Social Psychology* 1993; **3(3)**: 173-181.

52. Khandelwal SK, Sharan P, Saxena S. Eating disorders – an Indian perspective. *International Journal of Social Psychiatry* 1995; **41(2)**: 132-146.

53. Tareen A, Hodes M, Rangel L. Non-fat-phobic anorexia nervosa in British South Asian adolescents. *International Journal of Eating Disorders* 2005; **37(2)**: 161-165.

54. Lee HY, Lock J. Anorexia nervosa in Asian-American adoles-

cents: do they differ from their non-Asian peers? *International Journal of Eating Disorders* 2007; **40(3)**: 227-231.

55. Lai KY. Anorexia nervosa in Chinese adolescents – does culture make a difference? *Journal of Adolescence* 2000; **23(5)**: 561-568.

56. Nielsen S. The epidemiology of anorexia nervosa in Denmark from 1973 to 1987: a nationwide register study of psychiatric admission. *Acta Psychiatrica Scandinavica* 1990; **81(6)**: 507-514.

57. Beck D, Casper R, Andersen A. Truly late onset of eating disorders: a study of 11 cases averaging 60 years of age at presentation. *International Journal of Eating Disorders* 1996; **20(4)**: 389-395.

58. Keel PK, Baxter MG, Heatherton TF, Joiner TE. A 20-year longitudinal study of body weight, dieting, and eating disorder symptoms. *Journal of Abnormal Psychology* 2007; **116(2)**: 422-432.

59. Kiriike N, Nagata T, Matsunaga H, Tobitani W, Nishiura T. Married patients with eating disorders in Japan. *Acta Psychiatrica Scandinavica* 1996; **94(6)**: 428-432.

60. Markey CN, Markey PM, Birch LL. Interpersonal predictors of dieting practices among married couples. *Journal of Family Psychology* 2001; **15(3)**: 464-475.

61. Bettle N, Bettle O, Neumarker U, Neumarker KJ. Adolescent ballet school students: their quest for body weight change. *Psychopathology* 1998; **31(3)**: 153-159.

62. Ringham R, Klump K, Kaye W, Stone D, Libman S, Stowe S et al. Eating disorder symptomatology among ballet dancers. *International Journal of Eating Disorders* 2006; **39(6)**: 503-508.

63. Ravaldia C, Vannacci A, Zucchi T, Mannucci E, Cabras PL, Boldrini M et al. Eating disorders and body image disturbances among ballet dancers, gymnasium users and body builders. *Psychopathology* 2003; **36(5)**: 247-254.

64. Bettle N, Bettle O, Neumarker U, Neumarker KJ. Body image and self-esteem in adolescent ballet dancers. *Perceptual and*

Motor Skills 2001; **93(1)**: 297-309.

65. Manore MM, Kam LC, Loucks AB. The female athlete triad: Components, nutrition issues, and health consequences. *Journal of Sports Sciences* 2007; **25**: S61-S71.

66. Filaire E, Rouveix M, Bouget M, Pannafieux C. Prevalence of eating disorders in athletes. *Science & Sports* 2007; **22(3-4)**: 135-142.

67. Baum A. Eating disorders in the male athlete. *Sports Medicine* 2006; **36(1)**.

68. Sundgot-Borgen J, Torstveit MK. Prevalence of eating disorders in elite athletes is higher than in the general population. *Clinical Journal of Sport Medicine* 2004; **14(1)**: 25-32.

69. Byrne S, McLean N. Elite athletes: effects of the pressure to be thin. *Journal of Science and Medicine in Sport* 2002; **5(2)**: 80-94.

70. Pietrowsky R, Straub K. Body dissatisfaction and restrained eating in male juvenile and adult athletes. *Eating and Weight Disorders-Studies on Anorexia Bulimia and Obesity* 2008; **13(1)**: 14-21.

71. McVittie C, Cavers D, Hepworth J. Femininity, mental weakness, and difference: Male students account for anorexia nervosa in men. *Sex Roles* 2005; **53(5-6)**: 413-418.

72. Kaminski PL, Chapman BP, Haynes SD, Own L. Body image, eating behaviors, and attitudes toward exercise among gay and straight men. *Eating Behaviour* 2005; **6(3)**: 179-187.

73. Russell CJ, Keel PK. Homosexuality as a specific risk factor for eating disorders in men. *International Journal of Eating Disorders* 2002; **31(3)**: 300-306.

74. Feldman MB, Meyer IH. Eating disorders in diverse lesbian, gay, and bisexual populations. *Internal Journal of Eating Disorders* 2007; **40(3)**: 218-226.

75. Bramon-Bosch E, Troop NA, Treasure JL. Eating disorders in males: a comparison with female patients. *European Eating Disorders Review* 2000; **8(4)**: 321-328.

76. Procopio M, Marriott P. Intrauterine hormonal environment and risk of developing anorexia nervosa. *Archives of General Psychiatry* 2007; **64(12)**: 1402-1408.

77. Raevuori A, Kaprio J, Hoek HW, Sihvola E, Rissanen A, Keski-Rahkonen A. Anorexia and bulimia nervosa in same-sex and opposite-sex twins: lack of association with twin type in a nationwide study of Finnish twins. *American Journal of Psychiatry* 2008; **165(12)**: 1604-1610.

78. Winston AP, Acharya S, Chaudhuri S, Fellowes L. Anorexia nervosa and gender identity disorder in biologic males: a report of two cases. *International Journal of Eating Disorders* 2004; **36(1)**: 109-113.

79. Hepp U, Milos G, Braun-Scharm H. Gender identity disorder and anorexia nervosa in male monozygotic twins. *International Journal of Eating Disorders* 2004; **35(2)**: 239-243.

80. Ata RN, Ludden AB, Lally MM. The effects of gender and family, friend, and media influences on eating behaviors and body image during adolescence. *Journal of Youth and Adolescence* 2007; **36(8)**: 1024-1037.

81. Benninghoven D, Tadic V, Kunzendorf S, Jantschek G. Body images of male patients with eating disorders. *Psychotherapie Psychosomatik Medizinische Psychologie* 2007; **57(3-4)**: 120-127.

82. Kanayama G, Barry S, Hudson JI, Pope HG. Body image and attitudes toward male roles in anabolic-androgenic steroid users. *American Journal of Psychiatry* 2006; **163(4)**: 697-703.

83. Abbate-Daga G, Amianto F, Rogna L, Fassino S. Do anorectic men share personality traits with opiate dependent men? A case-control study. *Addictive Behaviors* 2007; **32(1)**: 170-174.

84. Vandereycken W, Vandenbroucke S. Anorexia-nervosa in males – a comparative-study of 107 cases reported in the literature (1970 to 1980). *Acta Psychiatrica Scandinavica* 1984; **70(5)**: 447-454.

85. Siegel JH, Hardoff D, Golden NH, Shenker IR. Medical complications in male-adolescents with anorexia-nervosa.

Journal of Adolescent Health 1995; **16(6)**: 448-453.

86. Lindblad F, Lindberg L, Hjern A. Anorexia nervosa in young men: A cohort study. *International Journal of Eating Disorders* 2006; **39(8)**: 662-666.

87. Lindblad F, Lindberg L, Hjern A. Improved survival in adolescent patients with anorexia nervosa: A comparison of two Swedish national cohorts of female inpatients. *American Journal of Psychiatry* 2006; **163(8)**: 1433-1441.

88. Steinhausen HC. The outcome of anorexia nervosa in the 20th century. *American Journal of Psychiatry* 2002; **159(8)**: 1284-1293.

89. Calderon R, Vander Stoep A, Collett B, Garrison MM, Toth K. Inpatients with eating disorders: demographic, diagnostic, and service characteristics from a nationwide pediatric sample. *International Journal of Eating Disorders* 2007; **40(7)**: 622-628.

90. Walters EE, Kendler KS. Anorexia-nervosa and anorexic-like syndromes in a population-based female twin sample. *American Journal of Psychiatry* 1995; **152(1)**: 64-71.

91. Bulik CM, Thornton L, Pinheiro AP, Plotnicov K, Klump KL, Brandt H et al. Suicide attempts in anorexia nervosa. *Psychosomatic Medicine* 2008; **70(3)**: 378-383.

92. O'Brien KM, Vincent NK. Psychiatric comorbidity in anorexia and bulimia nervosa: nature, prevalence, and causal relationships. *Clinical Psychology Review* 2003; **23(1)**: 57-74.

93. Sihvola E, Keski-Rahkonen A, Dick DM, Hoek HW, Raevuori A, Rose RJ et al. Prospective associations of early-onset Axis I disorders with developing eating disorders. *Comprehensive Psychiatry* 2009; **50(1)**: 20-25.

94. Berkman ND, Lohr KN, Bulik CM. Outcomes of eating disorders: a systematic review of the literature. *International Journal of Eating Disorders* 2007; **40(4)**: 293-309.

95. Wade TD, Bulik CM, Neale M, Kendler KS. Anorexia nervosa and major depression: shared genetic and environmental risk

factors. *American Journal of Psychiatry* 2000; **157(3)**: 469-471.

96. Herzog DB, Franko DL, Dorer DJ, Keel PK, Jackson S, Manzo MP. Drug abuse in women with eating disorders. *International Journal of Eating Disorders* 2006; **39(5)**: 364-368.

97. Keel PK, Dorer DJ, Eddy KT, Franko D, Charatan DL, Herzog DB. Predictors of mortality in eating disorders. *Archives of General Psychiatry* 2003; **60(2)**: 179-183.

98. Zucker NL, Losh M, Bulik CM, Labar KS, Piven J, Pelphrey KA. Anorexia nervosa and autism spectrum disorders: Guided investigation of social cognitive endophenotypes. *Psychological Bulletin* 2007; **133(6)**: 976-1006.

99. Gillberg IC, Rastam M, Wentz E, Gillberg C. Cognitive and executive functions in anorexia nervosa ten years after onset of eating disorder. *Journal of Clinical and Experimental Neuropsychology* 2007; **29(2)**: 170-178.

Chapter 3

What causes anorexia nervosa?

While historical and epidemiological studies can tell us who suffers from anorexia, they cannot tell us what causes the illness. Sufferers and family members often search for one simple answer to this question. Over the last hundred years, many theories have been proposed to explain the origins of the illness. This suggests that there is no simple answer.

The common popular view is that anorexia is caused by cultural factors, such as the idealisation of a thin body shape for young women in Western cultures. This sounds a reasonable explanation at first, but on closer examination it cannot be the sole cause. Yes, it is true that most Western women try some form of weight loss or weight control at least once in their lives. But why is it that 99% of us who start to diet will fail, while only a small minority will develop anorexia? And why does anorexia often run in families?

At the present time medical science cannot answer the question, 'What causes anorexia nervosa?' Initially, this can be difficult for sufferers and their families to accept as we all would prefer simple explanations. However, many other illnesses, such as type-2 diabetes, heart disease and most cancers, do not have a single cause. They result from a complex interaction of genetic predisposition, family traditions, stress, diet, lifestyle and perhaps even other factors that we are not aware of. For example, it has recently been suggested that the plastic packaging of food may be a contributory factor in the development of some cancers. Anorexia is similar to these illnesses. Searching for a simple answer is futile. It can even be harmful, as people often end up in an endless search for blame rather than focusing their energies on achieving positive changes.

Perhaps the best way to understand the causes of anorexia is to think about factors that might make certain people vulnerable to the development of the illness. These may be identified as:

- Factors which predispose to the condition
- Factors which trigger the condition
- Factors which maintain the condition

All of these categories are influenced by several biological, psychological and social components. Let us examine the first two initially. I will discuss maintaining factors in the next chapter.

Predisposing or vulnerability factors

Cultural factors

As we have seen in Chapter 2, anorexia nervosa is more common in Western countries. For this reason, it is sometimes regarded as a 'culture-bound syndrome' by some psychiatrists. This term is used to describe mental disorders that occur only in certain cultures, and are therefore thought to have essentially cultural origins. This line of thinking goes as follows: 'The thin shape of young women is idealised in Western countries. At the same time, there is an increasing risk of obesity, driving more and more people to diet in these countries, resulting in a higher rate of anorexia nervosa.'

It is unquestionable that living in this cultural environment can have a powerful effect on some vulnerable young people. Given the increased risk of childhood obesity, several countries' governments have developed public education programmes about healthy eating and exercise aimed at schoolchildren. For this reason alone, even young children have become more concerned about their weight and shape.[1, 2] With the introduction of new government policies in the UK and elsewhere, the pressure on young people to stay thin is likely to increase.

However, the origin of the illness is unlikely to be entirely cultural. As discussed in Chapter 2, if this were to be the case, there would have been an ongoing increase in anorexia in parallel with the increase in obesity over the past 20 years. There is no evidence that this has happened. In fact, the rate of anorexia in the UK has remained remarkably stable over this period, despite the substantial increase in both obesity and bulimia nervosa during this time. Furthermore, certain ethnic groups are less likely to develop anorexia nervosa than Caucasians. As we have seen, African women rarely develop anorexia. This is not just true for women living in regions of Africa where food is scarce, but for those living in Western countries too.[3, 4] Given that second-generation Africans tend to adopt Western lifestyles, this difference between ethnic groups does not support the idea that the illness can be caused entirely by cultural or even lifestyle changes. Otherwise, there would have been an increased risk of anorexia in the second generation of immigrant women of African origin in the UK compared with the first generation. Such a trend can be observed in a number of other illnesses in immigrant groups. For example, the risk of obesity and type-2 diabetes is higher in Asians and Africans living in the West compared with those living in their countries of origin.

The fact that this does not happen with anorexia indicates that cultural and environmental influences in themselves are insufficient to cause the illness. Maybe this can be explained by evolutionary pressures. In certain populations, which have originated from harsh environments and have been decimated by repeated famines, genes that predispose to obesity and diabetes have become more common, whilst genes which predispose to anorexia have been selected out, as they would have impaired the survival and reproduction rates of those people who had them. When, after many generations, individuals from these populations emigrate to rich countries, the abundant availability of food increases their risk of obesity, but not of anorexia, because the biological vulnerability in that population is only there for obesity. Future genetic research may answer this question.

Family factors

It is known that anorexia can run in families. Is this because of genetic or cultural factors, or difficulties in parenting?

The family is an important mediator of culture. Children growing up within their family learn their parents' social and cultural values, their parents' attitude to food, weight and shape. They usually develop similar tastes in food and dietary habits. Some families value food very highly, particularly if it is expensive in relation to income. Other families make an extra special effort to keep their diet 'healthy', and they exclude certain 'bad' foods from their diet. In addition, they might focus on exercise to keep their bodies healthy and their figures trim. Children learn these attitudes towards food, weight and shape, just as they learn everything else from their parents.

These are important factors that might make certain young people vulnerable to developing an eating disorder. For example, there is research evidence to show that mothers who have suffered from anorexia nervosa themselves have more problems feeding their children than mothers who have never had an eating disorder.[5-7, 8] This can happen in a very subtle but consistent way. For example, such a mother may try to exclude certain foods from the family's diet because they are not 'healthy'; she may be overly concerned about the size of food portions; or she may simply not join in with family meals, thus giving the message to growing children that eating should be restricted and controlled.

In clinical practice, it is relatively common to see a young anorexia sufferer with a mother who is very slim herself, but not necessarily ill. When the growing daughter reaches the same size as her mother at the age of 15 or 16, she may panic and decide that she needs to lose weight, as she cannot possibly be larger than her middle-aged mum. Sometimes, this is about fear of growing up, but sometimes it is competition: 'I need to be thinner and prettier than my mum.' Or: 'If Mum wants to be thin at her age, I must be thinner than her, because I am younger.'

The family often unwittingly reinforces this belief, by emphasising the desirability of a slim body shape. Adolescent girls are sensitive to weight-related teasing by their family members, especially by their fathers.[9, 10] The father's preference for a thin body shape can be very important for young women.

Another common scenario that can lead to weight loss in the daughter is if the father leaves the family for a thinner (and usually younger) woman. In this situation, the adolescent daughter might conclude that being thin is more important for a woman's happiness than anything else in life, and starts dieting.

This illness-associated behaviour may be inadvertently reinforced by parental behaviour in this situation too, as it is likely that the father's attention will shift back towards the first family if a child becomes seriously ill. This may give the daughter false hope that her self-starvation could save the family from disintegration, and she will become too frightened to give it up before it is too late. Competition is also a potential factor here: the daughter feels that she needs to be thinner and prettier than the new love interest in her father's life. Similarly, even adult women respond with weight loss and eating disorders if there is a breakdown, or the threat of a breakdown, within their relationship.[11]

On the other hand, there are many families under similar

circumstances whose children respond differently, and do not develop anorexia. It is important to bear in mind that almost 40% of marriages end in divorce, yet less than 1% of adolescent girls develop anorexia, and the rate of adult-onset anorexia is even lower. Conversely, there are many families whose children develop the illness without any of these issues in the background. Therefore, clearly, there must be additional vulnerabilities. Some of these may be of biological origin and some may be psychological.

Psychological factors

The predisposing psychological factors of anorexia can only reliably be identified in what are called 'prospective longitudinal studies'. This methodology requires the researchers to screen a large number of people from a young age, and compare the initial characteristics of those who later develop anorexia nervosa with those who do not. As it is a relatively rare disease, this type of study would require many thousands of volunteers, who would need to be willing to participate in research over many years. Not surprisingly, these studies are rare, as they are very expensive. One such study included 11,000 English children followed up from birth.[12] Out of these, 101 had developed anorexia nervosa by the age of 30 years. (Of these, 95% were females.) Only a few risk factors were identified. These included female gender, feeding problems in the first six months of life, under eating and poor self-esteem in childhood. The observation of early feeding problems as a risk factor indicates that something may be different in terms of the appetite regulation of people who are vulnerable to anorexia. Good maternal mental health and normal maternal 'body mass index' (BMI) were protective.

In a study of 30,000 Swedish twins, 'neuroticism' (which was also shown to be under considerable genetic influence) was found to be a risk factor for the later development of anorexia nervosa.[13] However, many people who have neurotic features (such as extreme anxiety or difficulty overcoming emotional disappointments) early in life, can learn to cope with these problems without ever developing any psychiatric illness, so the development of an eating disorder is not easily predictable.

As the diagnosis of 'eating disorder not otherwise specified' (EDNOS) is much more common than anorexia, it is easier to identify general risk factors for disordered eating rather than anorexia itself. Many of these are general; only a few differentiate between anorexia, bulimia and EDNOS. Common findings in longitudinal studies (that is, studies over time) are female gender, white ethnicity, early childhood eating and tummy problems, increased weight and shape concerns, negative self-evaluation, various traumatic life experiences, and general psychiatric problems. Poor self-esteem, perfectionism, low mood and difficulties with relationships all seem more common in anorexia.

The other method of researching psychological factors is to ask patients and their families to describe what the person was like before the onset of anorexia. This approach is less reliable, as people may remember problems selectively with the benefit of hindsight. For example, a mother is more likely to remember problems with the child who becomes ill than with the healthy ones. Nevertheless, sufferers and their families commonly report perfectionism as a personality trait before the onset of anorexia.[14] This has also been confirmed in a large twin study, so these findings seem robust.[15]

Recent research has also highlighted problems with information processing.[16, 17] These problems include focusing too much on details instead of being able to see the bigger picture, difficulties with emotional recognition and autistic traits. It is too early to state with confidence that people who are vulnerable to anorexia have specific problems with information processing before the onset of their illness, or whether this is mainly a result of starvation. Still, this is an interesting development, as it may explain why some young people are more vulnerable to developing anorexia than the rest of the population.

Biological factors

Various biological factors contribute to the vulnerability to, and development of, the illness. These are partially genetic, and partially environmental, including the individual's diet itself. Let us start with the genetic research first.

Genetic factors

Anorexia nervosa tends to be several times more common among the biological relatives of sufferers.[18, 19] When a disease runs in families, it is not always easy to tease out what is the result of the family's environment, habits, diet (or any other aspect of the shared experiences) or genes.

The most commonly used method for differentiating environmental from genetic factors is to study twins. This method uses the comparison of identical and non-identical twins as a special opportunity for the exploration of genetic and environmental causes. Identical twins share 100% of their genes, whilst non-identical twins share only 50%. Both also share the same family environment, but not necessarily the same experiences and environments outside the family. In the simplest case, when a condition is entirely caused by a genetic fault without any environmental contribution, identical twins would share 100%, whilst the non-identical twins would share only 50% of the risk. Such single gene diseases tend to be rare. Alternatively, if a condition is caused entirely by the family environment, then the risk is the same for both identical and non-identical twins. If, however, a condition is caused by an environmental risk outside the family, then the illness will affect only the exposed person. In reality, there is a complex interaction between genes and environment, but these examples help to show how twin research can elucidate the underlying causes of illnesses.

Reviewing the results of twin studies in anorexia nervosa in 1999, Professor Fairburn's team found that estimates for the heritability of anorexia nervosa ranged as widely as from 0% to 70%.[20] This was mainly due to methodological problems, such as small numbers of people participating in the studies. On reflection, this was not entirely surprising; there are very few countries in the world that have sufficiently large twin registers to include the number of patients with anorexia necessary for reliable statistical analysis.

Although the lack of consistency between studies was disappointing, this also meant that anorexia was unlikely to be caused either entirely by genes or entirely by environment. If this were the case, the results would have been much more consistent between earlier studies.

A recent, population-based study of Swedish twins was large enough to overcome the previous methodological problems. Cynthia Bulik and her team reviewed about 30,000 twins in the Swedish Twin Registry born between 1935 and 1958. These twins underwent screening for a range of disorders, including anorexia nervosa. In this study, the genetic heritability of anorexia nervosa was estimated to be 56%. Of the risk, 38% was attributable to the individual's environment, and only 5% was explained by shared environment in the family.[13] Another longitudinal twin study confirmed these findings and showed that the role of genes emerges during adolescence.[21] This can be observed in clinical practice. Even if there is a family history of anorexia nervosa, the illness usually develops in adolescence and not in childhood. Modern genetic science has shown that this is possible on a molecular level. Not all genes are active all of the time; some of them are 'expressed' only during certain periods of development, or under certain environmental circumstances. This also means that some disorders with a genetic background can be prevented or improved by manipulating environmental factors, such as diet, for example.

To put the results of these recent studies simply: the risk of anorexia nervosa is determined approximately half and half by genetic vulnerability and the individual's environment. The term 'environment' in this context encompasses many factors, ranging from personal experiences to the physical environment. This includes diet, infections and anything else that is specific to the person. The shared family environment (which is the same for all the children in the same family) plays only a small part in the development of the disorder. Of course, it needs to be taken into consideration that siblings can have very different life experiences within the family even if they are born to the same parents, so teasing out the non-shared environmental factors can be impossible in individual cases. However, these findings provide the most powerfully reassuring evidence for parents that it is not their 'fault' if their child develops anorexia nervosa. The illness is down to a combination of genetic vulnerability, and effects of the individual's environment and experiences. The observation that the illness tends to run in families is mainly due to genetic factors.

Molecular genetic studies

During the last 10 to 15 years, significant efforts have been made to identify genes that might contribute to the development of eating disorders, including anorexia nervosa. At the time of writing (2010), molecular genetic studies are inconclusive.[22] This lack of consistency suggests that multiple genes are likely to be involved, possibly each with a small effect. Either there are multiple genetic errors that can trigger the same vicious circle resulting in anorexia nervosa, or there is an unfortunate interaction between many genes and the environment, or possibly all of these factors contribute to the illness.

Because the cause of anorexia is not known, geneticists have either been looking at random parts of the human genome, or have tried to investigate genes that are known to have a role in appetite regulation or the development of various other mental disorders, such as depression. Different research groups have found links between anorexia and certain variants of neuro-transmitter systems. However, at the time of writing, there have been no studies that have been consistently replicated.[23-25] It is likely that molecular genetic research will accelerate during the coming decades, as genetic techniques are developing rapidly. Further large studies are already under way.[26]

While it is disappointing that there are no clear answers about the genetic basis of anorexia yet, this is similar to the state of science for the majority of other illnesses. For example, the causes of most cancers are unknown. It also means that it is pointless to blame the genes of either side of the family. The anorexia sufferer is unlucky, by having a combination of genes and circumstances that predispose to the illness. It is nobody's fault.

Background diet

You may be surprised to learn that background diet is a potential biological risk factor for anorexia nervosa, as this is not usually discussed as a possibility. However, dietary factors can contribute to the emergence of many diseases by disturb-ing various biological systems in the body. One well-known example is the high level of salt intake in Western countries, which increases the risk of high blood pressure and heart disease. Or, historically, gout was a common disease of wealthy people due to their high meat and alcohol consumption.[27]

Modern Western diet is far removed from the natural food stuffs to which we have become adapted during millennia of human evolution, and this means that our bodies do not nec-essarily cope well with these recent changes. Easily available high-energy dense foods have been linked to the risk of obesity. Clearly, obesity is the result of genetic vulnerability, which is widespread in the population, combined with sedentary lifestyles and modern diet. Could it be that certain aspects of the modern diet are similarly harmful to individuals who are susceptible to anorexia nervosa?

Vegetarianism, for example, has been found to be associated with anorexia and its poor outcome.[28-33] Some people do move to a vegetarian diet to hide their anorexia, but this is not the full explanation for the association. Vegetarian diet is often promoted as a healthy alternative lifestyle, which reduces the risk of obesity and heart disease. However, there is no epidemiological evidence that strict vegetarianism reduces overall mortality from common diseases, nor that it increases longevity.[34] The longest living populations on the planet are the Norwegians, the Japanese and some Mediterranean groups. All of them consume large amounts of fish, vegetables and fruit, but they are not exclusively vegetarian. In large population-based studies vegetarians tend to be slimmer, but they also have a higher rate of mental health problems, particularly depression and eating disorders.[31, 35]

The simple biological fact is that human beings are omnivores (adapted to eat a mixed plant and animal-based diet). The evidence for this is all over our gastrointestinal system: starting with our teeth, through to the stomach and intestines. There are various essential nutrients that we need to obtain from foods of animal origin, because our bodies cannot manufacture them. Consequently, dietary deficiencies can easily occur in vegetarianism. These include the shortage of omega-3 fatty acids, calcium, iron, zinc, iodine, vitamin D, vitamin B12, riboflavin, and essential amino acids.[36-38]

These essential nutrients play important parts in the normal function of the nervous system. It is possible that the lack of some of these nutrients can increase the vulnerability to anorexia, by increasing the risk for depression, or interfering with appetite regulation. Teenagers are particularly at risk of developing dietary deficiencies as their knowledge of nutrition is usually limited, so if they are vegetarian, they are more likely to consume a diet lacking essential nutrients. Adult vegetarians often take nutritional supplements to complement their diet. I will explain the relevance of omega-3 fatty acids and zinc deficiency next.

Omega-3 fatty acids

It has been known for about 80 years that certain poly-unsaturated fatty acids (PUFAs) are essential and necessary for normal development and brain function. This means that humans cannot make these fatty acids in their bodies, but have to obtain them from their diet in the same way as various vitamins (Table 3).[39] In this respect, these PUFAs are different from other lipids in the diet, such as mono-unsaturated (found in almond and olive oil) and saturated fats (in lard, or palm oil), which can be made by the body. PUFA deficits are highly likely to develop in anorexia, given the prolonged and severe restriction of dietary fat intake.

PUFAs are divided into two main groups: omega-6 fatty acids and omega-3 fatty acids. Omega-6 fatty acids are commonly found in meat and various commercial vegetable (including soy and corn) oils. Omega-3 fatty acids are obtained from oily fish, seaweed, and fresh, green leafy vegetables. Flaxseed is the most easily accessible vegetarian source of omega-3, but the human consumption of flaxseed has never really become popular due to its taste. If consumed at all, it is likely to be through eggs from hens fed on flaxseeds (which are easily available in British supermarkets).

It has been suggested that only the two parent fatty acids (LA and LNA) are truly essential, and under normal circumstances the other fatty acids can be manufactured by the human body. However, this process of manufacture is limited by a number of factors which include starvation, various nutritional deficiencies and the presence of trans-fatty acids in the diet.

Table 3. Dietary sources of fatty acids

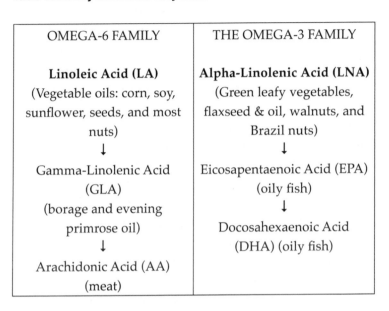

OMEGA-6 FAMILY	THE OMEGA-3 FAMILY
Linoleic Acid (LA) (Vegetable oils: corn, soy, sunflower, seeds, and most nuts) ↓ Gamma-Linolenic Acid (GLA) (borage and evening primrose oil) ↓ Arachidonic Acid (AA) (meat)	**Alpha-Linolenic Acid (LNA)** (Green leafy vegetables, flaxseed & oil, walnuts, and Brazil nuts) ↓ Eicosapentaenoic Acid (EPA) (oily fish) ↓ Docosahexaenoic Acid (DHA) (oily fish)

Although the minimal daily requirement has not yet been established, prolonged dietary deprivation of LA and LNA is incompatible with life.[40]

Omega-6 deficit is highly unlikely to develop even in anorexia, as omega-6 fatty acids are abundant in modern foods, and they are also included in various nutritional supplements. In contrast, omega-3 deficit is a modern problem. The current US guidelines[41] recommend four three-ounce portions of oily fish per week (approximately 400 g/week). In Western countries, very few people have this amount in their diet, in contrast with historical times, when the Church prescribed fasting days. On these days only fish could be consumed, and records from the medieval period show that people who lived then did consume fish three to four times per week.[42]

The instability of omega-3 fatty acids also means that they do not fit well with modern food manufacturing and distribution, as they deteriorate very quickly and can spoil the taste of food if not fresh. Furthermore, unlike most vitamins, these molecules continue to break down even in frozen foods. As a result, modern Western diet has become much lower in omega-3 fatty acids than it was during most of our evolutionary history.[43] It is estimated that traditional diets included a 1:1 ratio of omega-6 and omega-3 fatty acids until the beginning of the 20th century. The modern food industry of today has shifted this to a 20:1 ratio. There are many reasons for this change. In Europe and North America fish consumption has reduced with the decline in the Church's influence on diet, whilst meat, soy and corn oil consumption has increased to previously unprecedented levels. Historically farmers fed animals on grass in the summer, and frequently used flaxseed cakes as animal feed in the winter, resulting in higher omega-3 content, not just in meat, but also in milk and eggs. These days, animals are mainly fed on corn or soya, and because of these practices, meat, milk and eggs are higher in their omega-6 content than they were even a hundred years ago. It has been proposed that this new imbalance of these biologically active fatty acids has resulted in the increase in a number of common diseases, such as various chronic inflammations, heart disease, depression and related mental health problems.[44-46]

Omega-3 deficit is associated with low metabolic rate, growth retardation, dry skin, depression, muscle weakness, impairment of vision and learning ability, poor motor coordination, immune dysfunction, and heart problems. All of these problems can be observed in cases of severe anorexia.

Over the past few years, a number of products have appeared on the market to compensate for the loss of omega-3 PUFAs in modern foods, but omega-3 consumption has remained relatively low.[45] The higher rate of depression and mental health problems amongst vegetarians may also be related to their lower omega-3 intake. This is because access to a wide variety of fresh leafy vegetables, seaweed, or sprouting seeds is limited in supermarkets, and modern vegetarianism is heavily reliant on soya bean, corn and dairy-based products, all of which are high in omega-6. High soy intake may be a good idea as part of a high fish-based Japanese diet, but it may not be so beneficial for the Western teenager, who does not eat fish or seaweed, and does not gather fresh wild herbs for food to complement their high omega-6 intake.

Epidemiological studies over the past two decades have shown that increased fish consumption is associated with reduced morbidity and mortality (disease and death) from a number of common illnesses, such as cardiovascular disease, some cancers, depression and even suicide.[41,47,48] Fish consumption is beneficial for all parts of the body, including the brain, for many reasons other than high omega-3 content, as fish and seafood are low in saturated fats, and rich in vitamin D, the vitamin B group, calcium, potassium and iodine. However, omega-3 fish oil supplementation has been shown to be helpful in several medical conditions, including heart disease,[49,50] auto-immune disorders,[51,52] and even in cancer-related weight loss and wasting.[53-56] All of these conditions are associated with a higher risk of depression and related symptoms. It has also been suggested that there may be a common underlying mechanism involving inflammation and the body's use of fats (lipid metabolism).[57] Based on this hypothesis, omega-3 PUFA supplementation has been tested in clinical trials and has been found to help in several psychiatric disorders, most consistently in depression,[58-62] self-harm and aggression.[63-66] There is increasing evidence to suggest that one of the components of fish oil (eicosapentaenoic acid: EPA) has the most significant mood-elevating and stabilising effect.

There is a possibility that low intake of omega-3 essential fatty acids plays a part in anorexia.[67] It is notable that the risk of anorexia is lower in countries where fish consumption is traditionally high, such as Japan, where the incidence of the illness has been increasing alongside the adoption of Western foods. Patients with anorexia avoid dietary fats for long periods of time. However, the role of dietary fat deprivation in causing anorexia has not really been explored, which is strange to say the least. There have been only a few studies examining PUFAs in anorexia nervosa.[68-71] To form a clearer picture, it would be necessary to study PUFA levels at different stages of the illness, and their relationship to dietary intake.

There is a strong possibility that dieting at first corrects the high omega-6 to omega-3 ratio by reducing omega-6 intake.[70] Western patients with anorexia nervosa initially cut down on high-energy foods, such as cakes, biscuits, crisps and junk foods. By doing so, they reduce their intake of both trans-fatty acids and omega-6 and may thereby improve the omega-6 to omega-3 PUFA ratio, resulting in improved mood, skin condition and resistance to infections.

This would be consistent with anorexia sufferers reporting that when they start dieting they feel better. In addition to the changes they experience in body shape, the biological effects of the improved fatty acid ratio on the brain may also contribute to this feeling. However, if the dietary restriction continues, PUFA reserves become depleted. Omega-3 reserves are likely to be depleted sooner than omega-6 because of the modern Western diet. This may have a negative effect on mood. The sufferer will start feeling worse, but remember that initially, dieting had a positive effect. However, further dieting will lead to the deepening of anorexia and depression. Unfortunately, during re-feeding in Western countries, there is a high risk of consuming too much omega-6 while omega-3 PUFAs are further depleted. Vegetarians are even more at risk, as vegetarian sources of omega-3 are limited. Patients requiring artificial feeding are also vulnerable, as most artificial feeds have a 6:1 omega-6 to omega-3 ratio and no long-chain PUFAs (except one preparation, ProSure). This low omega-3 intake might also explain the deterioration in mood during weight restoration. Customarily, this has been regarded as an 'understandable' psychological response, because of the fear of fatness. However, the brain's physical response to these nutritional factors should also be considered. Given the effect of omega-3 PUFAs on mood, there is a strong possibility that the depletion of omega-3 stores contributes to the vulnerability to, as well as the maintenance of, the vicious circle of low mood and self-induced starvation in anorexia.

Several features of anorexia, including known risk factors, epidemiology (level of occurrence in the general population), co-morbidity (presence of other mental health problems) and mortality also indicate the possibility of PUFA abnormalities. For example, there is a higher risk of self-harm, depression and suicide, and all of these are associated with low omega-3 intake. Furthermore, around 50% of deaths associated with anorexia are caused by heart rhythm abnormalities, and given that fish oil supplementation is helpful in stabilising heart rhythm,[72] it is possible that this would reduce the risk of mortality in anorexia too.

My own clinical observations have suggested that EPA supplementation during weight restoration can speed up recovery of mood and escape from anorexic preoccupation,[73, 74] with the exception of those patients who have significant obsessive symptoms. However, large studies to confirm or refute this possibility have not yet been carried out due to lack of funding. This may change in the next decade or so.

Zinc deficiency

Zinc is another essential micronutrient that may be important for some patients with anorexia. This mineral is a component of over 300 enzymes in the body, which are necessary for normal growth, immune functions and reproduction. It is also necessary for the generation of new nerve fibres (neurons) and new connections between nerve cells, which enable learning. Zinc is commonly found in meat and seafood, therefore vegetarians and vegans have a low intake.[38] For vegetarians who eat eggs and/or dairy products, zinc intake usually meets daily recommended doses,[75] but if people have a restricted vegetarian diet, this is not the case.[76] Zinc deficiency has been well documented in anorexia, and it is not necessarily easily resolved by weight restoration.[77]

Interestingly, zinc deficiency shares some of the symptoms of anorexia nervosa, such as loss of appetite, loss of subcutaneous fat tissue, growth retardation, depression and dry skin.[78] Similarities between zinc and PUFA deficiencies have been described in both animal and human studies. This is because they are complementary in several physiological functions.[79] PUFAs are important in zinc absorption, whilst zinc deficiency impairs the conversion of essential fatty acids in the body.[80] Zinc may also have a role in PUFA absorption from the gut, so PUFA deficiency symptoms develop more rapidly if the diet is also deficient in zinc. This can easily occur in vegetarians who tend to have low intake of both of these essential nutrients.

It is possible that a diet low in zinc also predisposes people to anorexia by lowering appetite and interfering with normal nervous functions, and impairing essential fatty acid metabolism. For these reasons, regular consumption of fish and seafood can be recommended during weight restoration and maintenance.

Precipitating factors

Stress

It is common to find some sort of a stressor before the beginning of anorexia. This could be almost anything: biological, psychological and social factors, such as loss or trauma of some sort.[81] Stress hormones are activated by a wide range of environmental factors, and have profound effects on human physiological and psychological functioning. The increase in stress hormones is well documented in anorexia nervosa. However, it is difficult to know to what extent this is the cause of the illness or a consequence of the resulting starvation.[82]

It is also not unusual for anorexia to be triggered by some kind of physical illness that results in loss of appetite and reduced food intake. This is interesting in itself. Why is it that some people are vulnerable to anorexia in the context of appetite loss due to an illness, whilst others are not? Is there anything special about certain illnesses that can trigger anorexia? It has also been suggested that anorexia may be caused by Streptococcal infection. However, the evidence for this is rather weak at present.[83]

Stress, together with various inflammatory illnesses, may reduce appetite and cause weight loss through the inflammatory hormones (cytokines). Omega-3 fatty acids can reduce these hormones, whilst omega-6 fatty acids increase them. It is therefore possible that dietary and stress-related factors are both important in triggering the illness in people who have a genetic vulnerability.

Dieting

Dietary restriction is a central feature of anorexia nervosa. Without dieting, the illness cannot develop. Sometimes, patients report that their anorexia developed after dieting for reasons other than being worried about weight and shape, such as religious fasting.

There is growing evidence that peer relationships influence dieting behaviour in adolescent girls.[84] It is likely that socio-cultural pressures to diet have a greater negative impact on those who already have low self-esteem, or concerns about their body image. More and more people are dieting and at increasingly younger ages.[85] On the other hand, adult women reduce their dieting with marriage and having children and the rate of anorexia goes down in parallel.[86]

However, it is not clear why only a few people who diet

become trapped in a vicious circle of anorexia, whilst, for the majority, the body's safety mechanisms are effective in preventing dangerous weight loss. It is important to remember that most women in the West diet at some time during their lives, yet only a small proportion develop anorexia.[87, 88] It is likely that there are additional risk factors.[89]

Ultimate causes

The evolutionary approach is a relatively recent development in psychology. This theoretical model tries to understand human behaviour and emotional functioning from an evolutionary perspective. Charles Darwin was the first to reflect on the similarities between humans and animals in his book *The expression of the emotions in man and animals*.[90]

More than 150 years on, this is still a controversial field. Some experts heavily criticise the methods of evolutionary psychology as 'just so' stories, which cannot be tested scientifically. Undeniably, evolutionary psychology theories are speculative to some extent, as it is not possible to observe human behaviours directly through millennia. However, the evolutionary theory has revolutionised the field of biology, as was famously captured by Dobzhansky: 'Nothing in biology makes sense except in the light of evolution.'[91]

Human sciences cannot ignore this forever. Furthermore, like other scientific hypotheses, evolutionary psychology can offer predictions that can be tested.

According to the evolutionary framework, there are *proximate* and *ultimate* causes of biological phenomena. Proximate causes explain the immediate mechanisms, and it is these which are relevant to the present, whilst ultimate causes are concerned with the evolutionary advantage over many generations. The basis of this theory is that any gene combination/behaviour that reduces the reproductive success of individuals in a given environment would be selected out over time. For example, the proximate cause of obesity is overeating, and the ultimate cause would be that evolutionary pressures have favoured reproductive success of individuals (with the coding genes) with a tendency to overeat, as food has been scarce during most of human evolutionary history. Proximate causes of anorexia could be all of the factors discussed so far, such as social pressures, poor self-esteem, negative life events and so on. In this section, I will reflect on the possible ultimate causes.

How can the existence of an *illness* be explained by evolutionary advantage? This is not as improbable as it at first sounds. For example, one of the blood disorders (sickle cell anaemia) has become quite common in some African populations because having one copy of the gene associated with it offers some degree of protection from malaria. If a person carries two copies of the sickle cell gene, the disease is lethal. Therefore, a genetic variation which results in an illness can also carry an advantage in certain environments. In this case, there is a 'trade-off' between the two diseases. In other populations, sickle cell anaemia is extremely rare. This example shows that evolutionary pressures can work in a relatively short time (within a few dozen generations) and they can affect only certain populations that are exposed to that specific environmental factor. This explains the difference in the frequency of some diseases between ethnic groups originating from different environments.

Type-2 diabetes is another example of an illness that carries evolutionary advantage. Women who develop type-2 diabetes later in life tend to have larger babies and this results in improved infant survival rates at times of food shortages. This evolutionary advantage disappears in modern societies where infant mortality is low. On the contrary: the easy availability of foods increases the disease frequency, causing major public health problems, without any of the original benefits.

There are a number of evolutionary theories about the possible ultimate causes of anorexia.[92] I will briefly summarise Abed's theory[93] here, which in my view fits the clinical experience best, adding some of my own thoughts for consideration.

Intra-sexual competition theory

RT Abed's hypothesis is based on the role of intra-sexual competition between females. Competition has been a central feature of evolutionary theory ever since Darwin published the *Origin of Species*.[94] However, there has been much less discussion about competition between females than males. Sarah Blaffer Hrdy drew attention to this oversight in her book, *The woman that never evolved*.[95]

On reflection, if there is any truth in the theory of evolution, females cannot be exempt from competition. This does not necessarily mean that they use the same strategies for attracting mates as males. There is much less emphasis on display of strength and aggression in human females and much more on beauty and caring, as these are advantageous qualities for reproductive success. In contrast with most animal species – in which the males display their physical appearance like plumage or antlers, and females blend into the background for safety – women display themselves visually for mate attraction. This visual display is particularly important during adolescence, when the competition for partners emerges. Women know that men respond to visual signals first and instinctively, and for this reason, they take a lot of time and effort to make sure that they look their best. 'Love at first sight' is dependent on good looks.

The definition of 'good' looks has to carry some advantage from the evolutionary point of view. Why could thinness in a woman be attractive? As we have seen with the sickle cell disease example, certain characteristics may carry an advantage in certain environments only. Despite the recent emergence of sexual liberalism in Western societies, the long-term mate value of females is increased with virginity. This is because males prefer to invest in a long-term relationship if they can be confident that the resulting children are theirs. During human evolution, virginal females have been very young, peri-pubertal. Young brides were almost invariably slender, with a thin waist and a flat stomach publicly demonstrating their virginity. Even today, slenderness is associated with youth, and as we all know, youth is highly valued in modern society. In contrast, the time of marriage and childbearing has been delayed. With this delay, there is a more intense and prolonged competition for high-quality males. In a society with an increased risk of obesity, dieting and weight control are an important, even logical course of action in attempting to maintain a youthful and slender appearance with the hope of being able to attract a high-quality male. The alternative female reproductive strategy is early sexual activity leading to teenage pregnancies. It seems that these two strategies are at opposite extremes.

In the majority of cases, keeping slim but healthy is a successful female mating strategy.[96-99] If you think about it, how many aristocrats or wealthy men have fat brides? In some cases, however, the strategy can get out of control, and results in the tragedy of anorexia. Interestingly, anorexia also suppresses sexuality during the illness. This feature of the illness literally prolongs the virginal state. Maybe men find the ability to suppress sexuality attractive in a long-term relationship: the woman is more likely to be faithful in the long term.

However, the relative value of virginity, thinness and the ability to suppress sexual desires is balanced against the fertility of the woman and the likely survival rate of her children. In environments where food is scarce, a thin body shape does not carry any advantage, and hence a plumper body shape is favoured by men.[100] This sexual selection has resulted in different female body shapes in different ethnic groups, and it may explain the differences in anorexia rates.

At first, it may sound questionable that an evolutionary adaptive strategy (competing to be as attractive as possible) can be potentially dangerous for some individuals. However, we do not question this aspect of male competition. In almost all species, males compete with each other for mates and status using aggression. This strategy can be either very successful, or life threatening for the individual, depending on their ability to use aggression flexibly. In sophisticated human societies, brute aggression often backfires, but more subtle aggression can lead to success. It is well documented that highly aggressive men have a higher rate of mortality, particularly at a young age. However, these men also have higher numbers of offspring.

Why should competition be less dangerous for females? Female reproductive strategy is different from that of males. As producing and nurturing a child require much more investment from a woman than from a man, choosing the right partner is important for the reproductive success of females. Prolonging a virginal state until the highest quality mate comes along can be an advantageous strategy in the long run. However, this dilemma arises only in environments where there is a risk of obesity and the start of childbearing age is significantly delayed. Before the development of modern contraceptive methods, the age of sexual maturity and childbearing were much closer together in women, and the risk of obesity was low, so there was much less pressure for prolonged dietary restriction to maintain a youthful appearance. In many traditional societies, this is still the case. This could explain the increased rate of anorexia since the start of the 20th century in Western countries.

Modern women who are able to succeed with this strategy will have more security for their children. Recent epidemiological research confirms this on a large scale: a study of 12,000 French adults showed that obese women were more likely to have unwanted pregnancies and abortions than normal or underweight women.[101] Maybe those who can keep their bodies slender have a reproductive advantage, but those who can only use the strategy rigidly develop anorexia, which is potentially genetically lethal. This would be similar to male aggression: being able to use aggression flexibly can be a very successful strategy, whilst indiscriminate aggression leads to prison or worse. Too much of a 'good thing' can be dangerous.

Anyone, who has worked with anorexia sufferers, or who knows someone with the illness, realises that competition is a central feature. It can be subtle, or intense. With the rise of the internet, pro-anorexia websites have appeared which, on the surface, are supportive for members. On these sites, young women exchange ideas about how to achieve weight loss, but also compare themselves with each other. 'Who is the slimmest?'[102] This can lead to tragedy at times. Similarly, in hospitals, patients can start competing with each other, prolonging each other's illness. For the sufferer, the competition may not even be conscious all of the time, or it is perceived subjectively very differently: 'Everyone is thinner (or prettier) than me. I must try harder.'[103] This is similar to the subjective perception of competition in males: they are more likely to be conscious of the threat from others, and underestimate their own aggressive responses. Subjectively experienced threat from your rivals can maintain both aggression and dietary restriction.

This psychological perspective on anorexia is radical, and it is not yet widely accepted. However, it captures features of anorexia which are ignored by other psychological theories. It also explains why anorexia appears more frequently in modern cultures with abundant availability of foods. In traditional societies, girls marry at a younger age, and the risk of obesity is low. Furthermore, in societies experiencing regular shortages of food, self-induced starvation does not bring about any benefits. Abed also argues that in a strongly paternalistic society of arranged marriages at a young age, the need for intra-sexual competition between young women is reduced, and this may explain the lower risk of anorexia in these cultures. (However, this does not follow that anorexia may be cured by an arranged marriage.)

This evolutionary hypothesis portrays people with anorexia in an active role rather than just as the victims of circumstances. Clinical experience confirms this view: sufferers are not simply victims; they are actively engaged in maintaining their illness. Anorexia nervosa is hard work.

There are a number of predictions from this hypothesis, which can be tested out:

1.   Anorexia should be more common among single unmarried females. This has been a consistent finding in epidemiological studies. There is also evidence that dieting behaviours reduce after women start having families.

2.   Anorexia should be much less common among males, as they use different intra-sexual competition strategies. There is good epidemiological evidence for this.

3.   The primary motivation for weight loss should be to increase attractiveness and desirability. Whilst other theories state that the weight loss associated with anorexia is an expression of fear of growing up and sexuality, the intra-sexual competition hypothesis assumes that the motivation for weight loss is to increase attractiveness (with this getting out of control in some individuals). The wish to have breast implants amongst women with anorexia confirms this aspect of the hypothesis. Furthermore, most patients state explicitly that they want to be thin because they want to be prettier, or slimmer, than everyone else.

4.   There should be a focus on 'virginal' appearance. In clinical experience, the majority of patients are often concerned about having a flat stomach, and not looking 'pregnant'.

5.   Anorexia should be more common among young females in a group situation, particularly where the main focus is on physical beauty (such as models, dancers etc). Again, this is a consistent finding.

6. In contrast, early marriage/motherhood should protect from the illness, unless the competition for the husband remains intense ('footballers' wives'). This may also explain the cultural differences: in cultures where early marriage/motherhood occurs and divorce is extremely rare, the risk is lower.

7. It would also explain why young females resist reaching a higher weight than their mother or stepmother. Daughters do compete with their mothers during adolescence, as much as sons compete with their fathers. This is part of growing up.

8. Young people who perceive themselves as 'low value' compared to their peers, or who have difficulties with processing complex social information, would be more at risk of developing the illness. This is a similar phenomenon to the increased risk of aggression in males with various developmental and learning difficulties: they cannot use strategies that are more sophisticated.

9. In this theoretical framework, the images of thin women in glossy magazines intensify this competition, rather than cause it. According to the intra-sexual competition hypothesis, the reason why the population has not become bored with these magazines has evolutionary origins: men like to look at the bodies of young women, and women want to compare themselves with the 'competition'.

10. The theory is also compatible with the ethnic differences in anorexia. Sexual selection by men will define female beauty. This is dependent on the trade-off between the woman's perceived youth ('virginity') and the survival success of her children. In harsh environments, thinness does not carry an advantage, and therefore the genes that cause predisposition to the illness have become less common.

11. The theory is compatible with the observation that both genetic and environmental factors are important in the development of anorexia. (Ultimate causes are mediated by the success of certain gene combinations, which offer advantages

in certain environments.)

12. Furthermore, it is compatible with the results of twin studies that show that, apart from genetic factors, the individual's overall environment is more important than their family environment.

13. Some of the associated behaviours seen in anorexia also fit with this theory. For example, feeding others, particularly other females, is common in anorexia. According to the intra-sexual competition theory, this could serve two purposes: firstly, a public demonstration of caring (potential to be a good mother), and secondly, making sure that the 'competition' is fattened-up and so becomes less attractive.

14. It is also compatible with the observation that homosexual men or those with gender identity disorders are more at risk of developing anorexia than heterosexual men.

15. The intra-sexual competition hypothesis also offers predictions about potential treatment approaches. Remaining in a highly competitive group is likely to maintain the problem.

a. For this reason, group therapy is less likely to be helpful, as it may intensify the competition regardless of the therapists' intentions.

b. Similarly, engagement with pro-anorexia websites reinforces the illness by exposure to an abnormal peer group that can amplify the competition.

c. Continuing with an occupation that emphasises the importance of weight and shape in a competitive way, such as performing arts or modelling, is likely to maintain the illness.

d. On the other hand, information about reduced fertility (such as abnormal ovarian ultrasound) could be helpful.

e. Similarly, therapies that directly address the desire to be attractive and have positive relationships are likely to be more helpful. These include some aspects of cognitive therapies, and interpersonal therapy (see chapter 7).

Summary

In this chapter, I have examined the various factors that may predispose people to anorexia nervosa. Intra-sexual competition is the potential ultimate cause of extreme self-induced dieting. The proximate and immediate causes of anorexia are complex and they are likely to vary to some degree from individual to individual.

Apart from the obvious cultural influences, current research evidence suggests that there is a significant genetic vulnerability to the development of the illness. However, it is not known yet how many genes are involved and how the genes and also the environmental factors, including modern diet, interact. In addition to the genes, almost half of the risk is related to factors in the individual's environment, and family factors only minimally contribute to the risk. Certain psychological predisposing factors have been identified, but they tend to be general, such as low self-esteem, perfectionism and anxiety. Negative life events can trigger the illness, possibly due to activation of the stress hormones. There is also a strong possibility that diet itself has a significant role, although this is still a poorly researched area. Omega-3 fatty acids and various other deficiencies related to Western vegetarian diet need further study.

References

1. Berger U, Schilkel C, Strauss B. Weight concerns and dieting among 8 to 12-year-old children. *Psychotherapie Psychosomatik Medizinische Psychologie* 2005; **55(7)**: 331-338.
2. Dohnt HK, Tiggemann M. Body image concerns in young girls: the role of peers and media prior to adolescence. *Journal of Youth and Adolescence* 2006; **35(2)**: 141-151.
3. Taylor JY, Caldwell CH, Baser RE, Faison N, Jackson JS. Prevalence of eating disorders among Blacks in the national

survey of American life. *International Journal of Eating Disorders* 2007; **40**: S10-S14.

4. Sussman NM, Truong N, Lim J. Who experiences 'America the beautiful'?: Ethnicity moderating the effect of acculturation on body image and risks for eating disorders among immigrant women. *International Journal of Intercultural Relations* 2007; **31(1)**: 29-49.

5. Agras S, Hammer L, McNicholas F. A prospective study of the influence of eating-disordered mothers on their children. *International Journal of Eating Disorders* 1999; **25(3)**: 253-262.

6. Stein A, Woolley H, Cooper S, Winterbottom J, Fairburn CG, Cortina-Borja M. Eating habits and attitudes among 10-year-old children of mothers with eating disorders: longitudinal study. *British Journal of Psychiatry* 2006; **189**: 324-329.

7. Cooper PJ, Whelan E, Woolgar M, Morrell J, Murray L. Association between childhood feeding problems and maternal eating disorder: role of the family environment. *British Journal of Psychiatry* 2004; **184**: 210-215.

8. Wilksch SM, Wade TD. Risk factors for clinically significant importance of shape and weight in adolescent girls. *Journal of Abnormal Psychology* 2010; **119(1)**: 206-215.

9. Keery H, Boutelle K, van den Berg P, Thompson JK. The impact of appearance-related teasing by family members. *Journal of Adolescent Health* 2005; **37(2)**: 120-127.

10. Wilksch SM, Wade TD. Risk factors for clinically significant importance of shape and weight in adolescent girls. *Journal of Abnormal Psychology* 2010; **119(1)**: 206-215.

11. Markey CN, Markey PM, Birch LL. Interpersonal predictors of dieting practices among married couples. *Journal of Family Psychology* 2001; **15(3)**: 464-475.

12. Nicholls DE, Viner RM. Childhood risk factors for lifetime

anorexia nervosa by age 30 years in a national birth cohort. *Journal of the American Academy of Child and Adolescent Psychiatry* 2009; **48(8)**: 791-799.

13. Bulik CM, Sullivan PF, Tozzi F, Furberg H, Lichtenstein P, Pedersen NL. Prevalence, heritability, and prospective risk factors for anorexia nervosa. *Archives of General Psychiatry* 2006; **63(3)**: 305-312.

14. Kaye WH, Bulik CM, Thornton L, Barbarich N, Masters K. Comorbidity of anxiety disorders with anorexia and bulimia nervosa. *American Journal of Psychiatry* 2004; **161(12)**: 2215-2221.

15. Wade TD, Tiggemann M, Bulik CM, Fairburn CG, Wray NR, Martin NG. Shared temperament risk factors for anorexia nervosa: A twin study. *Psychosomatic Medicine* 2008; 70(2): 239-244.

16. Southgate L, Tchanturia K, Treasure J. Information processing bias in anorexia nervosa. *Psychiatry Research* 2008; **160(2)**: 221-227.

17. Lopez C, Tchanturia K, Stahl D, Booth R, Holliday J, Treasure J. An examination of the concept of central coherence in women with anorexia nervosa. *International Journal of Eating Disorders* 2008; **41(2)**: 143-152.

18. Wagner A, Wockel L, Bolte S, Radeloff D, Lehmkuhl G, Schmidt MH et al. Mental disorders among relatives of patients with anorexia nervosa and bulimia nervosa. *Zeitschrift fur Kinder-und Jugendpsychiatrie und Psychotherapie* 2008; **36(3)**: 177-184.

19. Strober M, Freeman R, Lampert C, Diamond J, Kaye W. Controlled family study of anorexia nervosa and bulimia nervosa: Evidence of shared liability and transmission of partial syndromes. *American Journal of Psychiatry* 2000; 157(3): 393-401.

20. Fairburn CG, Cowen PJ, Harrison PJ. Twin studies and the etiology of eating disorders. *International Journal of Eating*

Disorders 1999; **26(4)**: 349-358.

21. Klump KL, Burt A, Mcgue M, Iacono WG. Changes in genetic and environmental influences on disordered eating across adolescence – A longitudinal twin study. *Archives of General Psychiatry* 2007; **64(12)**: 1409-1415.

22. Scherag S, Hebebrand J, Hinney A. Eating disorders: the current status of molecular genetic research. *European Child & Adolescent Psychiatry* 2010; **19(3)**: 211-226.

23. Bulik CM, Slof-Op't Landt MC, van Furth EF, Sullivan PF. The genetics of anorexia nervosa. *Annual Review of Nutrition* 2007.

24. Bergen AW, Yeager M, Welch RA, Haque K, Ganjei JK, van den Bree MB et al. Association of multiple DRD2 polymorphisms with anorexia nervosa. *Neuropsychopharmacology* 2005; **30(9)**: 1703-1710.

25. Dardennes RM, Zizzari P, Tolle V, Foulon C, Kipman A, Romo L et al. Family trios analysis of common polymorphisms in the obestatin/ghrelin, BDNF and AGRP genes in patients with anorexia nervosa: Association with subtype, body-mass index, severity and age of onset. *Psychoneuroendocrinology* 2007; **32(2)**: 106-113.

26. Kaye WH, Bulik CM, Plotnicov K, Thornton L, Devlin B, Fichter MM et al. The genetics of anorexia nervosa collaborative study: Methods and sample description. *International Journal of Eating Disorders* 2008; **41(4)**: 289-300.

27. Roddy E, Zhang W, Doherty M. The changing epidemiology of gout. *Nature Clinical Practice Rheumatology* 2007; **3(8)**: 443-449.

28. O'Connor MA, Touyz SW, Dunn SM, Beumont PJ. Vegetarianism in anorexia nervosa? A review of 116 consecutive cases. *Medical Journal of Australia* 1987; **147(11-12)**: 540-542.

29. Bas M, Karabudak E, Kiziltan G. Vegetarianism and eating disorders: association between eating attitudes and other

psychological factors among Turkish adolescents. *Appetite* 2005; **44(3)**: 309-315.

30. Klopp SA, Heiss CJ, Smith HS. Self-reported vegetarianism may be a marker for college women at risk for disordered eating. *Journal of the American Dietetic Association* 2003; **103(6)**: 745-747.

31. Lindeman M. The state of mind of vegetarians: Psychological well-being or distress? *Ecology of Food and Nutrition* 2002; **41(1)**: 75-86.

32. Martins Y, Pliner P, O'Connor R. Restrained eating among vegetarians: Does a vegetarian eating style mask concerns about weight? *Appetite* 1999; **32(1)**: 145-154.

33. Yackobovitch-Gavan M, Golan M, Valevski A, Kreitler S, Bachar E, Lieblich A et al. An integrative quantitative model of factors influencing the course of anorexia nervosa over time. *International Journal of Eating Disorders* 2009; **42(4)**: 306-317.

34. Arneth W. Do vegetarians eat or live more healthy? A critical study of literature. *Fleischwirtschaft* 2005; **85(12)**: 123-128.

35. Baines S, Powers J, Brown WJ. How do the health and well-being of young Australian vegetarian and semi-vegetarian women compare with non-vegetarions? *Public Health Nutrition* 2007; **10(5)**: 436-442.

36. Key TJ, Appleby PN, Rosell MS. Health effects of vegetarian and vegan diets. *Proceedings of the Nutrition Society* 2006; **65(1)**: 35-41.

37. Rosell MS, Lloyd-Wright Z, Appleby PN, Sanders TAB, Allen NE, Key TJ. Long-chain n-3 polyunsaturated fatty acids in plasma in British meat-eating, vegetarian, and vegan men. *American Journal of Clinical Nutrition* 2005; **82(2)**: 327-334.

38. Davey GK, Spencer EA, Appleby PN, Allen NE, Knox KH, Key TJ. EPIC-Oxford: lifestyle characteristics and nutrient intakes in a cohort of 33,883 meat-eaters and 31,546 non

meat-eaters in the UK. *Public Health Nutrition* 2003; **6(3)**: 259-268.

39. Peet M, Glen I, Horrobin DF. *Phospholipid spectrum disorder in psychiatry*. Carnforth, Lancashire: Marius Press; 1999.

40. Bjerve KS, Thoresen L, Mostad IL, Alme K. Alpha-linolenic acid deficiency in man: effect of essential fatty acids on fatty acid composition. *Advances in Prostaglandin, Thromboxane, & Leukotriene Research* 1987; 17B: 862-865.

41. Leaf A. Historical overview of n-3 fatty acids and coronary heart disease. *American Journal of Clinical Nutrition* 2008; **87(6)**: 1978S-1980S.

42. Walker Bynum C. *Holy Feast and Holy Fast: The Religious Significance of Food to Medieval Women*. Berkeley: University of California Press; 1987.

43. Mann N. Dietary lean red meat and human evolution. *European Journal of Nutrition* 2000; **39(2)**: 71-79.

44. Simopoulos AP. Essential fatty acids in health and chronic disease. *American Journal of Clinical Nutrition* 1999; **70(3 Suppl)**: 560S-569S.

45. Hibbeln JR, Nieminen LRG, Blasbalg TL, Riggs JA, Lands WEM. Healthy intakes of n-3 and n-6 fatty acids: estimations considering worldwide diversity. *American Journal of Clinical Nutrition* 2006; **83(6)**: 1483S-1493S.

46. Conklin SM, Harris JI, Manuck SB, Yao JK, Hibbeln JR, Muldoon MF. Serum omega-3 fatty acids are associated with variation in mood, personality and behavior in hyper-cholesterolemic community volunteers. *Psychiatry Research* 2007; 152(1): 1-10.

47. Tanskanen A, Hibbeln JR, Tuomilehto J, Uutela A, Haukkala A, Spacing D et al. Fish consumption and depressive symptoms in the general population in Finland. *Psychiatric Services* 2001; **52(4)**: 529-531.

48. Harper CR, Jacobson TA. Beyond the Mediterranean diet: the role of omega-3 fatty acids in the prevention of coronary

heart disease. *Preventive Cardiology* 2003; **6(3)**: 136-146.

49. Gruppo Italiano per lo Studio della Sopravvivenza nell'Infarto miocardico. Dietary supplementation with n-3 polyunsaturated fatty acids and vitamin E after myocardial infarction: results of the GISSI-Prevenzione trial. *The Lancet* 1999; **354(9177)**: 447-455.

50. Durrington PN, Bhatnagar D, Mackness MI, Morgan J, Julier K, Khan MA et al. An omega-3 polyunsaturated fatty acid concentrate administered for one year decreased triglycerides in simvastatin treated patients with coronary heart disease and persisting hypertriglyceridaemia. *Heart (British Cardiac Society)* 2001; **85(5)**: 544-548.

51. Calder PC. Polyunsaturated fatty acids, inflammation, and immunity. *Lipids* 2001; **36(9)**: 1007-1024.

52. Kelley DS. Modulation of human immune and inflammatory responses by dietary fatty acids. [Review] [51 refs]. *Nutrition* 2001; **17(7-8)**: 669-673.

53. Tisdale MJ, Dhesi JK. Inhibition of weight loss by omega-3 fatty acids in an experimental cachexia model. *Cancer Research* 1990; **50(16)**: 5022-5026.

54. Karmali RA. Historical perspective and potential use of n-3 fatty acids in therapy of cancer cachexia. *Nutrition* 1996; **12(1 Suppl)**: S2-S4.

55. Wigmore SJ, Ross JA, Falconer JS, Plester CE, Tisdale MJ, Carter DC et al. The effect of polyunsaturated fatty acids on the progress of cachexia in patients with pancreatic cancer. *Nutrition* 1996; **12(1 Suppl)**: S27-S30.

56. Ramos EJB, Romanova IV, Suzuki S, Chen C, Ugrumov MV, Sato T et al. Effects of omega-3 fatty acids on orexigenic and anorexigenic modulators at the onset of anorexia. *Brain Research* 2005; **1046(1-2)**: 157-164.

57. Horrobin DF, Bennett CN. Depression and bipolar disorder: relationships to impaired fatty acid and phospholipid metabolism and to diabetes, cardiovascular disease, immu-

nological abnormalities, cancer, ageing and osteoporosis. Possible candidate genes. [Review] [252 refs]. *Prostaglandins Leukotrienes & Essential Fatty Acids* 1999; **60(4)**: 217-234.

58. Puri BK, Counsell SJ, Richardson AJ, Horrobin DF. Eicosapentaenoic acid in treatment-resistant depression. *Archives of General Psychiatry* 2002; **59(1)**: 91-92.

59. Nemets B, Stahl Z, Belmaker RH. Addition of omega-3 fatty acid to maintenance medication treatment for recurrent unipolar depressive disorder. *American Journal of Psychiatry* 2002; **159(3)**: 477-479.

60. Peet M, Horrobin DF. A dose ranging study of the effects of ethyl-eicosapentaenoate in patients with ongoing depression despite apparently adequate treatment with standard drugs. *Archives of General Psychiatry* 2002; **59(10)**: 913-920.

61. Owen C, Rees AM, Parker G. The role of fatty acids in the development and treatment of mood disorders. *Current Opinion in Psychiatry* 2008; **21(1)**: 19-24.

62. Jazayeri S, Tehrani-Doost M, Keshavarz SA, Hosseini M, Djazayery A, Amini H et al. Comparison of therapeutic effects of omega-3 fatty acid eicosapentaenoic acid and fluoxetine, separately and in combination, in major depressive disorder. *Australian and New Zealand Journal of Psychiatry* 2008; **42(3)**: 192-198.

63. Hibbeln JR, Umhau JC, George DT, Salem N, Jr. Do plasma polyunsaturates predict hostility and depression? *World Review of Nutrition & Dietetics* 1997; **82**: 175-186.

64. Hibbeln JR, Umhau JC, Linnoila M, George DT, Ragan PW, Shoaf SE et al. A replication study of violent and nonviolent subjects: cerebrospinal fluid metabolites of serotonin and dopamine are predicted by plasma essential fatty acids. *Biological Psychiatry* 1998; **44(4)**: 243-249.

65. Buydens-Branch L, Branchey M, McMakin DL, Hibbeln JR. Polyunsaturated fatty acid status and aggression in

cocaine addicts. *Drug and Alcohol Dependence* 2003; In Press; Corrected Proof.

66. Hallahan B, Hibbeln JR, Davis JM, Garland MR. Omega-3 fatty acid supplementation in patients with recurrent self-harm – Single-centre double-blind randomised controlled trial. *British Journal of Psychiatry* 2007; **190**: 118-122.

67. Ayton AK. Dietary polyunsaturated fatty acids and anorexia nervosa: Is there a link? *Nutritional Neuroscience* 2004; **7(1)**: 1-12.

68. Langan SM, Farrell PM. Vitamin E, vitamin A and essential fatty acid status of patients hospitalized for anorexia nervosa. *American Journal of Clinical Nutrition* 1985; **41(5)**: 1054-1060.

69. Holman RT, Adams CE, Nelson RA, Grater SJ, Jaskiewicz JA, Johnson SB et al. Patients with anorexia nervosa demonstrate deficiencies of selected essential fatty acids, compensatory changes in nonessential fatty acids and decreased fluidity of plasma lipids. *Journal of Nutrition* 1995; **125(4)**: 901-907.

70. Zak A, Vecka M, Tvrzicka E, Hruby M, Novak F, Papezova H et al. Composition of plasma fatty acids and non-cholesterol sterols in anorexia nervosa. *Physiological Research* 2005; **54(4)**: 443-451.

71. Goncalves CG, Ramos EJB, Suzuki S, Meguid MM. Omega-3 fatty acids and anorexia. *Current Opinion in Clinical Nutrition and Metabolic Care* 2005; **8(4)**: 403-407.

72. Anand RG, Alkadri M, Lavie CJ, Milani RV. The role of fish oil in arrhythmia prevention. *Journal of Cardiopulmonary Rehabilitation and Prevention* 2008; **28(2)**: 92-98.

73. Ayton AK, Azaz A, Horrobin DF. Rapid improvement of severe anorexia nervosa during treatment with ethyl-eicosapentaenoate and micronutrients. *European Psychiatry* 2004; **19(5)**: 317-319.

74. Ayton AK, Azaz A, Horrobin DF. A pilot open case series

of Ethyl-EPA supplementation in the treatment of anorexia nervosa. *Prostaglandins Leukotrienes and Essential Fatty Acids* 2004; 71(4): 205-209.

75. Ball MJ, Ackland ML. Zinc intake and status in Australian vegetarians. *British Journal of Nutrition* 2000; **83(1)**: 27-33.

76. Bakan R, Birmingham CL, Aeberhardt L, Goldner EM. Dietary zinc intake of vegetarian and nonvegetarian patients with anorexia-nervosa. *International Journal of Eating Disorders* 1993; **13(2)**: 229-233.

77. Castro J, Deulofeu R, Gila A, Puig J, Toro J. Persistence of nutritional deficiencies after short-term weight recovery in adolescents with anorexia nervosa. *International Journal of Eating Disorders* 2004; **35(2)**: 169-178.

78. Shay NF, Mangian HF. Neurobiology of zinc-influenced eating behavior. *Journal of Nutrition* 2000; **130 (5S Suppl)**: 1493S-1499S.

79. Horrobin DF, Cunnane SC. Interactions between zinc, essential fatty acids and prostaglandins: relevance to acrodermatitis enteropathica, total parenteral nutrition, the glucagonoma syndrome, diabetes, anorexia nervosa and sickle cell anaemia. *Medical Hypotheses* 1980; **6(3)**: 277-296.

80. Eder K, Kirchgessner M. Zinc deficiency and the desaturation of linoleic acid in rats force-fed fat-free diets. *Biological Trace Element Research* 1996; **54(2)**: 173-183.

81. Klinkowski N, Korte A, Pfeiffer E, Lehmkuhl U, Salbach-Andrae H. Psychopathology in elite rhythmic gymnasts and anorexia nervosa patients. *European Child & Adolescent Psychiatry* 2008; **17(2)**: 108-113.

82. Schmidt UH, Troop NA, Treasure JL. Events and the onset of eating disorders: correcting an 'age old' myth. *International Journal of Eating Disorders* 1999; **25(1)**: 83-88.

83. Puxley F, Midtsund M, Losif A, Lask B. PANDAS anorexia nervosa – Endangered, extinct or nonexistent? *International*

Journal of Eating Disorders 2008; **41(1)**: 15-21.

84. Peterson KA, Paulson SE, Williams KK. Relations of eating disorder symptomology with perceptions of pressures from mother, peers, and media in adolescent girls and boys. *Sex Roles* 2007; **57(9-10)**: 629-639.

85. Dohnt H, Tiggemann M. The contribution of peer and media influences to the development of body satisfaction and self-esteem in young girls: A prospective study. *Developmental Psychology* 2006; **42(5)**: 929-936.

86. Keel PK, Baxter MG, Heatherton TF, Joiner TE. A 20-year longitudinal study of body weight, dieting, and eating disorder symptoms. *Journal of Abnormal Psychology* 2007; **116(2)**: 422-432.

87. Keski-Rahkonen A, Hoek HW, Susser ES, Linna MS, Sihvola E, Raevuori A et al. Epidemiology and course of anorexia nervosa in the community. *American Journal of Psychiatry* 2007; **164(8)**: 1259-1265.

88. Williams L, Germov J, Young A. Preventing weight gain: a population cohort study of the nature and effectiveness of mid-age women's weight control practices. *International Journal of Obesity* 2007; **31(6)**: 978-986.

89. Kim EK, Kleman AM, Ronnett GV. Fatty acid synthase gene regulation in primary hypothalamic neurons. *Neuroscience Letters* 2007; **423(3)**: 200-204.

90. Darwin C. *The expression of the emotions in man and animals.* Great Britain: John Murray; 1872.

91. Dobzhansky T. Nothing in biology makes sense except in light of evolution. *American Biology Teacher* 1973; **35(3)**: 125-129.

92. Gatward N. Anorexia nervosa: an evolutionary puzzle. *European Eating Disorders Review* 2007; **15(1)**: 1-12.

93. Abed RT. The sexual competition hypothesis for eating disorders. *British Journal of Medical Psychology* 1998; **71(Pt 4)**: 525-547.

94. Darwin C. *The Origin of Species*. Great Britain: John Murray; 1859.

95. Hrdy SB. *The woman that never evolved*. Cambridge, Massachusetts and London, England: Harvard University Press; 1981.

96. Lipowicz A. Effect of husbands' education on fatness of wives. *American Journal of Human Biology* 2003; **15(1)**: 1-7.

97. Lipowicz A, Gronkiewicz S, Malina RM. Body mass index, overweight and obesity in married and never married men and women in Poland. *American Journal of Human Biology* 2002; **14(4)**: 468-475.

98. Averett S, Korenman S. The economic reality of the beauty myth. *Journal of Human Resources* 1996; **31(2)**: 304-330.

99. Ball K, Crawford D. Socioeconomic status and weight change in adults: a review. *Social Science & Medicine* 2005; **60(9)**: 1987-2010.

100. Holdsworth M, Gartner A, Landais E, Maire B, Delpeuch F. Perceptions of healthy and desirable body size in urban Senegalese women. *International Journal of Obesity* 2004; **28(12)**: 1561-1568.

101. Bajos N, Wellings K, Laborde C, Moreau C, for the CSF Group. Sexuality and obesity, a gender perspective: results from French national random probability survey of sexual behaviours. *British Medical Journal* 2010; **340**: c2573.

102. Lapinski MK. StarvingforPerfect.com: A theoretically based content analysis of pro-eating disorder web sites. *Health Communication* 2006; **20(3)**: 243-253.

103. Hutchinson DM, Rapee RM. Do friends share similar body image and eating problems? The role of social networks and peer influences in early adolescence. *Behaviour Research and Therapy* 2007; **45(7)**: 1557-1577.

Chapter 4

Maintaining factors: what keeps anorexia nervosa going?

'What keeps anorexia nervosa going?' is probably the most important question to answer if you want to recover from the condition or if you want to help someone who has it. It is useful to think through what might have caused anorexia – mainly because this can reduce the feelings of guilt that often paralyse both sufferers and families. However, there is nothing that you can do about predisposing factors, such as evolutionary mechanisms, your genes or the media around you. Equally, even if you know what might have triggered the illness, you cannot undo the past. However, without the maintaining factors the illness would not continue. If you have a good understanding of what keeps anorexia going, then you have a chance of stopping the vicious circle that is so relentlessly destructive and dangerous.

This is similar to what you would need to think through if you or a member of your family suffered a severe injury, for example, as a result of a car crash. It would be futile to focus your energies on what caused the accident in the first place, as this would not make a difference in terms of your overall outcome. However, you would need to understand the nature of the injury, the time needed for recovery, how to manage the pain, how to build up your strength again, and how to cope with life's demands during recovery. For example, if you broke several bones in your leg or injured your spine, it could take a long time before you could walk again. Life would not be the same for some time, regardless of the original cause of the injury. Your family's life would also have to change, as they would need to adjust to your increased needs. However, without a sustained effort towards recovery, you might end up in a wheelchair. For example if you avoided gradual exercise because of the pain, your muscles and joints could suffer long-term damage and atrophy and thus maintain, or even worsen, the effects of the original injury. This is similar in anorexia: if dietary intake and weight do not change, people end up chronically ill.

The maintaining factors of anorexia are complex: they include various psychological and social factors, which are specific to the individual. However, the biological consequences of starvation that maintain anorexia are common to all.

I will discuss the psychological maintaining factors first. It is important to think through these carefully, as they vary from individual to individual. You need to understand how they maintain anorexia for you or your loved one, as this should help you to draw up a plan of how best to bring about change.

Psychological factors

Denial

The first and most important maintaining factor is probably denial. If you do not have a problem, why would you try to change anything?

There is a difference between conscious denial, when people lie to hide the truth, and unconscious denial, when people cannot see that there is a problem (although the two may be related).[1-3] Denial is ultimately the reason why patients die from anorexia, because nobody realises the danger before it is too late. A recent high-profile case demonstrates this phenomenon clearly: a 49-year-old woman professor of psychology died of anorexia in England weighing just under 4 stone (56 pounds or 24.5 kilograms) in April 2008. What is more, it was reported that her colleagues were surprised! Looking at her picture on the web, it should have been obvious to anyone that she was severely starving herself and had become dangerously ill. Yet somehow, her highly intelligent colleagues missed the obvious.

Denial is a fascinating phenomenon. It can affect anyone: patients, families and professionals. Denial is described as one of the most basic psychological defence mechanisms. It is a normal human response to unexpected losses and tragedies. When something terrible happens to any of us, we respond with disbelief at first. Bad things happen to other people, to other people's children, or friends, but not to us. Families facing problems often hold on strongly to the belief that 'at least the children are doing fine' despite all evidence to the contrary. It is incredibly painful and frightening to face the reality that your child or loved one has a potentially life-threatening illness, such as anorexia. Denial protects people from this pain. Whilst this works as short-term relief, it can make the situation much more dangerous in the long term, because of the delay in taking action.

Many families cannot comprehend the change that occurs with anorexia. Some believe that the weight loss is caused by some mystery disease, and endlessly search for alternative remedies for a cure. We do not expect anyone in the Western world to die of starvation, so we close our minds to this possibility. Alternatively, if the illness is chronic, denial can be a result of getting used to an abnormal and highly anxiety-provoking situation: 'It cannot be that dangerous, as she has always managed to pull through. Maybe she has a different metabolism to everyone else.'

People suffering from anorexia are not superhuman. They need food to function and survive like the rest of us. They pay a terrible price for being chronically underweight and malnourished, both in the short term and in the long term.

Denial by the sufferer is sometimes related to age (most young people believe that they are immortal) or it may be related to problems with body image estimation. While patients are fully aware of their struggle with hunger when restricting their diet, checking the fat tissue under the skin and looking at 'fat-free' adverts in the supermarkets continue to reinforce the belief that they are still fat. If you believe you are fat, you cannot have anorexia, because people with anorexia are thin, right? Severe starvation also numbs the mind, and consequently the patient's judgement can become impaired.

Parents can also fall victim to denial if their child shows particular talent for something. In some of these cases, the parents become very enthused by the potential their child shows, and completely miss the importance of the physical and mental health needed for success. Your child will not become the next Olympic athlete, world-class ballerina or singer if she is unable to eat sufficient amounts to maintain a healthy weight. The chances are that he or she will be in and out of hospital instead (or worse). A healthy body and mind are essential for success.

The problem with denial is that it prevents you from taking action in times of danger, and so it can be detrimental to the outcome of many illnesses. For example, denial can increase the risk of dying of a heart attack because people do not seek treatment in time.[4] Successful approaches to the treatment of anorexia, such as family therapy and cognitive behavioural therapy, address denial early on. As a reader of this book, you must have started tackling denial. Otherwise, you would not have been searching for answers on the bookshelves or the internet. However, you may need to help other members of your family to confront the issue. Understanding anorexia and talking to other people can help to overcome denial, and this is the necessary first step to recovery.

Lack of knowledge

People are not born with knowledge and understanding of

anorexia nervosa. It is a rare disease and, apart from specialists, even the majority of doctors receive minimal training about it. Because of this, it would be unrealistic to expect carers and sufferers to know much to start with. Unfortunately, there are many unhelpful myths and stereotypes about anorexia which can stand in the way of helping people.

Sufferers are often blamed for their illness, for example: 'You brought this upon yourself, so it is up to you to get out of it – just stop being so stupid.' Alternatively, sometimes the family feels that the sufferer deliberately tries to upset people around them by not eating, and responds with anger, which can exacerbate conflict and fear. At other times, anorexia is seen as a harmless phase, and this can prevent the family acting in time.

The more you learn about the illness, the fewer surprises and disappointments you will have to face on the way to recovery, and the more confidence you will gain to help manage any problems that can arise during the journey. It is fundamentally important to understand the physical and emotional consequences of starvation. Without this, you cannot fully understand anorexia.

Fear

As emphasised in the earlier chapters, fear is a central feature of anorexia, and it is also an important maintaining factor. It is of the utmost importance that this is understood, as fear explains many of the difficult behaviours displayed by anorexics. Sufferers are afraid of getting fat and not being attractive and loveable. These fears are particularly overwhelming at mealtimes. Without fear, the normal response to hunger signals would override the desire to lose weight. Patients are afraid that even a small amount of food will 'blow them up' out of all proportion, or they are afraid that if they start eating, they will not be able to stop. Another fear common to sufferers of anorexia is that of being deceived by others, by being offered 'too much' food, or being given 'false' reassurances that they are not fat, and so on. This fear leads to distrust and deceitful behaviours, such as lying about dietary intake, hiding food, and lying about vomiting and purging. Families find it very difficult to tolerate these behaviours, particularly as they are often totally out of character.

Fear can lead to aggression, both verbal and physical. It can help in managing these problems if you understand that these behaviours are driven by anorexic fears, rather than by deliberately wanting to upset others or to cause harm. Acknowledgement of the fear and distress usually helps.

Fear can also paralyse parents and carers. Family members are often afraid of upsetting the fragile sufferer, or losing the relationship by challenging anorexic behaviours. They may be frightened of making things worse, or of not having enough skill to help. It is highly unlikely that other people can make anorexia worse. However, refraining from taking any action, because of a fear of the consequences, can be lethal.

Fear of fear can sometimes result in a vicious circle between family members. This most commonly occurs between parents and their children rather than between partners. For most parents, it is very distressing to see their child afraid. Usually, the parents realise that the fear is irrational, and their calm response can reassure their child. This helps the young person to learn not to be afraid. Indeed, most parents can teach a child not to be afraid of the dark this way. However, seeing your child afraid of food can be very frightening, because of the potentially life-threatening consequences.

Unfortunately, a frightened response can increase the child's fears further, which in turn can make the parent panic even more. More often than not, it is mothers who respond with fear, whilst fathers tend to get frustrated by this high level of anxiety and end up shouting at both mother and child as a masculine attempt to calm the situation. This contrasting response can cause confusion for the already frightened child, and also divide parents at a time when unity and consistency are crucial. Parents arguing with each other will fuel the child's fears further. There is evidence that parental disagreements have a negative impact on the outcome of anorexia.

If this is happening in your family, it is important for the parents to sit down and discuss as calmly as they can how best to help their child to overcome his or her anorexic fears. A calm and joint response, which acknowledges the fear, but does not give in to it, can be tremendously helpful.

Sometimes, if the mother herself has a fear of eating, this is very difficult to achieve. Under these circumstances, the best thing is to seek help for the mother as well so that she can learn to manage her own fears relating to food. To illustrate the importance of this, it is worth considering what the impact of other fears might be in the same family. For example, if a mother had arachnophobia, she would not be able to help her child's fear of spiders; she would need to address her own fears first. Even if the child received therapy to address his or her fear of spiders, the effect would be much less likely to last if at home Mum continued to be frightened of them. Fear of eating is no different: it can be reinforced between family members. On the positive side, the child's difficulties can powerfully motivate the mother to overcome her own problems.

Perfectionism and obsessionality

Trying to do one's best serves most people well. Perfectionism, on the other hand, is a recipe for chronic dissatisfaction. If you have very high standards about most aspects of your life, then you can make yourself very unhappy; regardless of what you achieve, it is never going to be good enough. Similarly, the pursuit of a perfect body is futile. Most healthy people are happy looking 'good', or looking 'their best', but do not even try to achieve perfection, because they realise that this is unattainable.

In anorexia, sufferers often strive for the perfect body, but they are never satisfied with how they look, always finding flaws. This often fuels dietary restriction and exercise. If you look for imperfections in your body, you will find them.

Many anorexia sufferers are described by their families as perfectionists. This characteristic can often get worse during the illness, because starvation increases rigidity of thinking. Perfectionism is often shared by family members, and can maintain the illness in various ways. For example, parents may believe that if they were perfect, they would produce the perfect child, and therefore expect high standards of their children, in terms of both achievement and appearance. Their child, on the other hand, may be very fearful that she cannot meet her parents' expectations. So, she may try very hard to become perfect, whilst feeling increasingly miserable and angry as she fails to achieve 'perfection'. This vicious circle is very sad, as perfectionist parents love their children dearly just like anyone else, and do not want to cause them any harm.

Trying to offer reassurances that the person is 'perfect' can paradoxically fuel the problem even more. The sufferer will interpret these reassurances as an expectation that nothing less will do. Instead, it is better for friends and family to emphasise that nobody is perfect. We all have our frailties, and we need to learn to accept them as we mature. Perfectionism often interferes with social relationships, and can lead to isolation, either as a result of feeling that one is not perfect, therefore expecting rejection; or by rejecting others as not good enough. It can also contribute to chronically low self-esteem and depression.

If you recognise that perfectionism is an issue for you or your loved one, try to reflect on how this has affected your life. People often believe that perfectionism is a very helpful and important quality until they stop and think about the consequences. How much enjoyment do you have in your life? Try not to give yourself such a hard time. You may find that allowing yourself to relax and have fun enriches your life and improves your relationships with people, and surprisingly it may even improve your performance.

Obsessive-compulsive symptoms are often related to perfectionism, but they represent the extreme end of the spectrum. During starvation, people often become obsessional about food, and this can also spread to issues of cleanliness, or rules about eating or exercise. The more malnourished a person is, the worse these problems can get, and they can be very frightening for both the sufferer and the family. Fortunately, in the majority of cases, weight restoration itself can resolve these problems, with only a minority of sufferers needing additional treatment. However, obsessive symptoms are associated with the worst outcomes in anorexia, and there are a number of reasons for this. People with obsessive symptoms tend to suffer from a higher level of anxiety, and they tend to have a higher level of rigidity in their thinking. These features make it more challenging for them to achieve weight restoration, and many of them give up prematurely and end up chronically malnourished, which maintains the anorexic cycle. In these cases, professional help is often necessary.

Depression

There is a complex interaction between depression and anorexia. A large twin study has found that there are common genetic factors that increase the vulnerability to both disorders,[5] and this has also been confirmed by other research finding that the incidence of depression is higher amongst family members of people with eating disorders.[6,7] Unfortunately, this co-occurrence also means that carers who themselves struggle with depression will find it more difficult to support their loved ones through anorexia and remain positive during the difficult journey to recovery. If you are a carer and you suffer from depression, it is important to think how to help yourself, as this will have a positive effect for everybody in the family.

Although the preoccupation with weight and shape is specific to anorexia, depressive symptoms are common in the illness.[8] On the other hand, severe depression itself can be associated with significant loss of appetite and weight, and some atypical eating disorders are difficult to distinguish from it (particularly in children). The majority of patients suffering from anorexia report low mood and poor self-esteem prior to the onset of their illness.[9] The trouble is that starvation itself causes depression, and therefore worsens the problem. When a person is significantly underweight or malnourished, depressed mood is inevitable.

Unfortunately, depression can maintain anorexia in several ways. Depressed people feel hopeless and cannot believe that things can change for the better, therefore they are unable to motivate themselves. Alternatively, they may believe that they do not deserve good things (including food, or help). As a result, they withdraw from normal activities, or become irritable, which alienates people and the vicious circle carries on.

Sufferers often strongly hold the belief that further weight loss will improve their mood. While this may happen on a very short-term basis (a fleeting sense of achievement with further weight loss), in reality the opposite is true. This is similar to what happens in drug and alcohol addiction: people experience a brief relief, but in the long term, their mood and mental health progressively deteriorate.

It is very important to understand that depression does not get better without weight restoration, and it may even get worse in the short term. Antidepressants do not seem to work well in underweight patients,[10] so weight restoration is crucial to improving mood. There is no therapy which is effective in lifting mood in a starved person, other than a nutritionally balanced diet.

If there is still ongoing depression after weight restoration, it will need to be treated separately. However, during weight restoration it is also important to address beliefs and behaviours that contribute to maintaining depression by encouraging social contact and doing things for fun. This, in combination with weight restoration, is sufficient to resolve depressed mood in most cases. The supplementation of omega-3 fatty acids can also be beneficial, improving mood and breaking the vicious circle of anorexia and depression.

Shame and guilt

Both sufferers and carers may feel paralysed by feelings of shame and guilt, even if they are not clinically depressed.[11] Sufferers often feel ashamed of their bodies, seeing themselves as enormous and disgusting. They also can feel ashamed of being weak. This weakness could be related to eating 'too much', losing control, being ill, upsetting other people, or all of the above.

Shame is particularly intense if the person induces vomiting as weight control. Vomiting is unpleasant and it is often associated with intense feelings of shame and guilt, leading to secrecy and lying. You also need to be aware that sexually abusive experiences are more common in people with bulimia and the purging sub-type of anorexia, in both males and females.[12, 13] Shame and guilt can be particularly severe for these sufferers. If this is the case, trauma-specific therapy is important to address these underlying problems as a part of the overall treatment.

Parents, mothers in particular, can be overwhelmed and paralysed by guilt. 'If I was a better parent, this would not have happened. I must be a bad parent, and therefore whatever I try to do is only likely to make things worse.'

Shame also prevents people seeking help, not just from professionals, but also from friends and family. Many patients want to keep their anorexia secret from their classmates or colleagues, or even from their families. This is unlikely to be possible, as anorexia is a highly visible illness. This shame leads to isolation, as people just do not know how to respond to a person who is quite clearly not telling the truth. The polite Western response is to back off, leaving the sufferer even more alone. Shame and guilt also worsen depression. It may be helpful to remind yourself what we have learnt from genetic studies: anorexia is a multi-factorial disorder, and therefore it is nobody's fault.

Carers often find it extremely helpful to get in touch with other families struggling with the same problems. This can provide an opportunity to realise that they are not on their own, and can help to relieve feelings of guilt and shame.

Avoidance

If you are afraid or ashamed of something, it may seem easier to avoid it altogether. The problem is that avoidance makes fear worse. This is how eating certain foods, such as a small chocolate bar, can become an unimaginable task in anorexia. The only remedy to fear is practice. Mental health professionals use the strategy of graded exposure and response prevention to help people with various fears. This means that people are advised to face the object of their fear in a planned way, and to stay with it until the fear goes away. It is usually easier to build this up gradually, such as making a list of things with increasing difficulties, and then tackling them from the easiest to the most difficult, building upon each success. This approach is helpful with all sorts of fears, such as fear of heights, public speaking, social phobia, various obsessive-compulsive problems, and it will also reduce fears related to eating.

Patients with anorexia often avoid certain foods or eating in public. At the same time, they also know that these behaviours are abnormal. Planning ahead and practising will help. Practice can challenge the underlying belief that fuels the fear such as: 'If I eat a piece of cake I won't be able to stop,' or 'I will put on a lot of weight.' Family members can be very helpful in supporting the person through this process. This is what experienced nursing staff will do to help the patient in hospital, and there is no reason why the family could not offer the same at home. It is important that the family does not collude with the patient's avoidance, even if the person becomes very distressed. Remember, all fears subside with time and practice but avoidance will make them worse.

Avoidance can also affect family and friends. Usually, this is also driven by fear, or guilt: 'I might make things worse, so it is better not to say or do anything.' Fathers often respond this way, and they literally remove themselves from the situation, spending increasing amounts of time away from home. Unfortunately, this usually reinforces the patient's poor self-esteem and isolation.

Alternatively, avoidance of conflict could be the result of wanting to be 'nice' or 'not upsetting' the patient.[14] One common example is that the patient avoids eating with the rest of the family, but is not rebuked, as the family wish to be 'nice' about the situation. Unfortunately, the family's avoidance reinforces anorexic behaviours and denial: 'Nobody is saying or doing anything, so I cannot be seriously ill.' Anorexia sometimes can be a cry for help, or an expression of wanting to be looked after. If nobody responds to the obviously starving patient, he or she is likely to 'try harder'.

All sufferers know that it is normal to enjoy a meal together with friends and family. They all can remember times before anorexia. If the family can address and acknowledge the problem, that can be immensely helpful, even if it causes temporary upset. Other times, this short-term upset in itself can lead to avoidance: friends and family members are put off trying to help if the patient repeatedly responds in a hostile or aggressive way.

If this is happening in your family, try to set aside a time to discuss this process when everyone is relatively calm. This will usually help to generate some solutions. Although most patients panic during mealtimes, at other times they can be more constructive and rational. They will be grateful for your recognition of their fears and your perseverance in helping to eliminate the avoidance behaviour that maintains them.

Isolation

Lonely young women tend to be miserable and preoccupied with themselves, as was entertainingly captured in *Bridget Jones's Diary*. Starvation increases introspection and preoccupation with weight and shape, and isolation takes this to the extreme. Patients often isolate themselves deliberately: it is easier to maintain anorexic behaviours on your own. Children insist on 'eating' separately from their parents, or adults break off contact with their friends and families. This can result in a dangerous vicious circle driven by anorexic thoughts: 'If I lose more weight, I will be more attractive. People will like me more, and I will not be alone.' Anorexic logic often ignores the simple truth that in order to be able to maintain a rewarding and reciprocal relationship, it is essential to be interested in the other person and not just in oneself. Self-centred people rarely have loving relationships, so the ongoing pursuit of the 'slimmest body' is futile, as it can never achieve its final goal; you will just become even more preoccupied with yourself. When the much-desired happiness does not happen, further weight loss seems to be the solution. This can be best achieved in isolation, but this will increase unhappiness, and so the vicious circle gets out of control.

Social isolation is probably the main reason why the outcome of anorexia is worse in adulthood. Children and young people are not normally left to their own devices. If they seriously starve themselves, parents and professionals have a duty to intervene. Addressing isolation is much more difficult with adults, due to the strong emphasis on individual freedom and responsibility in Western cultures. Maybe the increase in anorexia in the 20th century is partially related to this cultural shift in attitudes. In the past, families would not have let their children starve themselves to the detriment of their health regardless of their age, and such a situation would still be unimaginable in more family-orientated cultures today. In Western societies it is often professionals who take on this supporting role.

If you are a parent of an adult suffering from anorexia, remember that there is a vicious circle between isolation and anorexia. More often than not, the chances are that the only important relationship your child has is with you, so you are still in the best position to help. Whilst it is not customary for Western families to 'interfere' with their adult children's affairs, this is a time of crisis: your child needs you, as much as if she/he were a helpless baby.

After recovery from anorexia, relationships will gradually return to normal. Even if you do not live in the same household, there are many ways you can be helpful and supportive, perhaps by acknowledging the problem (tackling denial), recognising anxiety, encouraging the need for change, or offering help with avoidance. Parents remain important for their children for a lifetime, regardless of their age.

On the other hand, isolation can affect carers too. This is often related to shame and trying to keep the illness a secret. This is sometimes done with the best intentions; keeping confidentiality, worrying about the consequences of stigma or not putting the burden on others. However, this can also deprive carers of valuable social support at a time of severe anxiety and distress. Joining a carers' group or asking for support from voluntary organisations, such as B-EAT (www.b-eat.co.uk) in the UK, can be very helpful in preventing the isolation of carers.

Competitive peer group/environment

Apart from isolation, being in a competitive environment where there is a focus on weight and shape can also maintain anorexia. These two are not necessarily mutually exclusive; people can feel very isolated in a competitive environment, particularly if they feel that they are not doing as well as others. An environment which places a strong emphasis on being thin can be toxic for a person trying to recover from anorexia. Nobody would expect a recovering alcoholic to do well if he worked in a pub, or in the brewing industry. This also applies to anorexia. In an environment where there is a strong focus on the importance of being thin or having the 'perfect' body, it is unlikely that people will get better. Sadly, many beautiful and talented young people compare themselves negatively to others, and drive themselves to destruction because they want to get on top of the competition.

If you develop anorexia in such an environment, you need to ask yourself: 'Is this worth it? Am I cut out for this? Can I cope with this without sacrificing my health and happiness?' In some ways, anorexia is a warning sign that the high-pressure environment is making you ill. You cannot be successful and have anorexia at the same time. Anorexia takes over and comes above everything. If you have a child who develops anorexia doing ballet, modelling, acting or sports, you need to ask the same question yourself, and help him/her to find safer alternatives.

As discussed before, adolescent girls compete within their own familes, most commonly with their mothers, step-mothers, or sisters. If this is happening in your family, try to think long and hard about how best to help. In my clinical experience, it is next to impossible for a young person to achieve his or her minimum healthy weight (for someone who is 158 cm/5 feet 2 inches it is around 50 kg/110 lb) if his/her mother or a sister is underweight (for example, just 45 kg with the same height). This scenario is usually a recipe for prolonged anorexia in the child.

The best thing to do in this situation is to be honest even if it is hard at first. As we have seen, genetic factors are important in anorexia, as much as in heart disease, so it should not be surprising that several members of the same family can be affected to varying degrees. The comparison with heart disease can be helpful. Most people would not keep the family history of heart disease a secret. People may ignore the risk for a long time, but if somebody becomes ill within the family, that can focus minds on addressing the problem in everyone. If someone suffered a heart attack in your family, everyone else would start thinking about the implications for themselves and seeking to reduce the risk by introducing lifestyle changes. They would be much more motivated to start making positive changes, such as stopping smoking or taking more exercise than previously.

If, as in the previous example, you are a mother or a sister and unable to reach a body mass index (BMI) within the range of 20-25, you probably need to consider treatment for yourself. Your child's illness could act as a motivating factor. As a parent, you will be keen to help your child as much as possible, so it is important for you to be aware that your own behaviour and weight will have a significant effect on your child's chance of recovery.

With sisters, this can be even more difficult, as they often do not have the same desire to help each other, and the competition between them can be intense. It is important for other family members to be aware of the problem, so that they can support both siblings and not expect that two people with eating disorders can rely on just each other. This would be similar to expecting two people with drink problems to help each other. Without encouragement from others, they would be more likely to end up sharing the habit. On the other hand, if only one of them tried to give up in the same household, the chances of success would be very poor. This is the same for eating disorders. It is impossible to achieve lasting changes if there is another person in the house who restricts his/her diet, or uses various compensatory strategies, such as excessive exercise or vomiting. Families find different solutions to this scenario: sometimes a third person can help both sufferers (husband or grandmother), but other times, only separation of the two people can work in the short term.

Communication problems

If you do not believe that you have a problem, then you will not even consider asking for help. However, communicating that you want help is very difficult if you feel afraid, ashamed and guilty. Secrecy and isolation seem less stressful in the short term, and that explains why it can take so long for people to start addressing their eating disorder and to seek help. This reluctance maintains denial, avoidance and isolation, and the anorexic vicious circle.

A small but significant proportion of patients may have underlying autistic traits, which means that they have pre-existing social communication problems. Unfortunately, anorexia tends to make these problems even worse; thinking may become even more rigid and inaccessible to rational arguments with starvation.

Family and friends often do not know what to say to the patient. Sometimes, they do not say anything, because they hope the problem will go away, or because they are afraid of making things worse. Alternatively, people lose their temper and say things that are hurtful or even plain nasty, and push the sufferer into even deeper isolation. Other times, there are endless discussions about weight and shape or food, in an attempt to try and help the patient to see things rationally. These conversations often just reinforce anorexic preoccupations.

So, to put it simply: there are two main types of communication problem: not saying enough, or saying too much and too harshly. Not surprisingly, neither of them is helpful; it is important to find a way somewhere in the middle.

The only way you *can* help someone with anorexia is by talking to him or her, so open and effective communication is very important. Mind your language though, and try not to be rude, even if you are frustrated. It is surprising how often people who are perfectly able to communicate in their professional roles in a polite and respectful manner believe that it is fine to shout abuse at each other at home. Try to let off steam in a different way. Your family members deserve the same respect as your boss or customers!

Anorexia can also be maintained by unhelpful compromises, driven by well-meaning but misplaced kindness. Many friends and family members fall into this trap. It happens like this: the sufferer gets very upset about eating a normal amount and variety of foods, but is willing to accept two salad leaves, or a carrot, or a cup of slimmer soup and the like. Desperate relatives think if the patient is upset, she is less likely to eat, and it is better to eat something than nothing at all, so they agree with the patient in the hope that things will change gradually but do not make this expectation explicit. Unfortunately, the patient will interpret their response as either that it is fine to eat just two salad leaves, or worse, that she is being too greedy despite eating so little, because nobody is asking her to eat more. Alternatively, if this situation ends up in a shouting match, carers may stop trying to help the patient next time because the arguments are too unpleasant.

It is much easier to communicate if you trust someone, if you have a good relationship, and if you are reasonably calm. However, trust is often difficult to achieve if someone has anorexia. This is because the illness makes sufferers see themselves differently from everyone else, as if they were wearing image-distorting glasses. Patients are convinced that they need to lose weight, and when family members disagree, the sufferers often resort to lying.

If you are a carer, do not take this personally: this is part of the illness, and it will pass after recovery. It is helpful to know that patients do not like lying to their loved ones. If you are a sufferer, try to reflect on the effect lying has on your relationships. Rebuilding trust with others is crucial for your recovery. Acknowledging the fear of weight gain, which causes the lying, can be a helpful way to start the communication.

It is usually easier for the family than for the patient to raise the problem first. It is also important that all family members talk to each other, so that they can come to a common understanding and agree on how best to help, and work as a team. Differing views and approaches are likely to cause confusion and even hostility, and consequently can worsen anorexia.

If the biological parents are separated, but the child has regular contact with both sides, it is vital that the parents develop a style of communication which is direct, respectful and practical, rather than use the patient as a go-between, or even worse force him or her to choose or take sides. Respectful and practical communication is usually very difficult to achieve for parents who divorced under acrimonious circumstances.

Although about 40% of marriages end in divorce, most couples who split up have no idea nor receive any guidance on how to function well as parents after the separation, despite loving their children dearly. Many do not communicate at all, or they do so only through lawyers. This is usually very painful for their children, for whom both parents remain important, and who did not choose the divorce in the first place. I often ask divorced parents who do not wish to communicate with each other to consider what they would do if their child was ill with cancer. Most people would be able to put their differences aside in a crisis if they realised that their child could die. Anorexia is no less of a crisis. It can kill, and it can cause suffering and disability for a long time. Parents who are able to work as a team despite their separation are more likely to be able to help their child.

On a very practical level, how would you know whether your child had eaten before visiting you without ever asking your ex-partner? Not communicating with the other natural parent of your child can also increase the child's feelings of shame, guilt and isolation, which all contribute to the vicious maintaining circle of anorexia.

Impatience

Helping someone recovering from anorexia requires the patience of a saint, and dogged perseverance. It is common for families and friends to expect a miracle, pursue quick fixes and become angry and frustrated when these do not work. The resulting disappointment can make communication problems worse, push the sufferer into further isolation, and generate feelings of hopelessness, thus maintaining anorexia.

Similarly, if you are a sufferer, give yourself time to recover. If you do not feel better immediately, that does not mean that it will never happen. It just means it will not happen overnight. Recovering from anorexia is a long and bumpy ride for everybody. You are more likely to be successful if you prepare yourself for a long process, which can take many months, or even years.[15]

Using the example of time and adjustment needed to recover after a serious injury can be helpful. Recovery from anorexia takes months at the very minimum. This is due to the effects of starvation, which cause biological damage to the body and the brain. You need to take a long-term perspective if you want to achieve recovery. It is important to think about the consequences for family life when taking this into consideration. Life cannot be the same as it was before the illness for a long time. The family needs to adjust to the patient's requirements during recovery, even if it means significant changes in routines, communication and diet. If you prepare yourself for a long haul, you are more likely to succeed, and less likely to be disheartened.

Biological factors

While psychological factors are important, biological maintaining factors are fundamental. This is often forgotten. Ignore biology at your peril. In contrast to the psychological maintaining factors, which tend to vary between people, biological factors affect everyone in much the same way.

The most important biological factor that keeps anorexia going is starvation itself. This cannot be emphasised enough. Anyone who promises to help you without addressing the starvation is either ignorant or deceitful (or both). Starvation has a profound effect on the human body and mind, as was beautifully demonstrated over 60 years ago by the Minnesota study. This was one of the seminal research projects in the history of medicine. Although it was carried out in 1945, the lessons learnt in this study have continued to stand the test of time. They also have important implications for understanding what happens biologically and psychologically in anorexia, and for this reason, it is helpful to describe the study here in more detail.

The effects of starvation: the Minnesota study

The Minnesota study[16] is often quoted in psycho-educational materials for anorexia sufferers and carers, but the details of this work are rarely discussed. This is probably because the original publication is not easily accessible for the general public. Although it was carried out more than 60 years ago, the study is unique in the history of medicine and it is still highly relevant to the understanding of the physical and psychological consequences of starvation, and thus helps us to understand the biological maintaining factors in anorexia.

Given the atrocities of concentration and labour camps during World War II, there was grave concern about the effects of human starvation, both for armies and for the civilian population. At the University of Minnesota, Ancel Keys and his research team were asked to examine the physical and psychological effects of experimental starvation and its consequences. They worked with conscientious objectors who would not fight but still wanted to contribute to the war effort. These individuals did so by taking part in research that involved six months of controlled dietary restriction and subsequent weight restoration.

In addition to the authors' own scientific observations, the final report of the Minnesota study also included a detailed review of the historical literature on human starvation, such as information about autopsies of people who died of starvation in the Warsaw ghetto and other concentration camps during World War II, and written records of various historical famines. This made the final publication the most comprehensive research to date on the consequences of starvation in humans.

Although the project did not set out to examine anorexia nervosa, it remains the only systematic study of the consequences of chronic dietary restriction and controlled weight restoration on human health; both of these are relevant to understanding the illness. The study has remained unique, not just because current ethical regulations would not allow its replication, but because no one since has undertaken a systematic study of the consequences of self-induced starvation in healthy men.

As discussed in the previous chapters, there is much less research on the consequences of anorexia nervosa in males, but the Minnesota study fills this gap. Many of the study's findings have been confirmed by subsequent research in anorexia, so we now know that the findings are also applicable to women. While the physical consequences of famines had been well documented before this experiment, the evaluation of psychological and behavioural changes associated with starvation and weight restoration were new and groundbreaking. The unexpected finding of the study was that many of the behavioural and psychological features of eating disorders emerged in healthy volunteers purely because of starvation. Furthermore, these symptoms lasted well beyond weight restoration. This finding provides powerful evidence that starvation itself contributes to the symptoms and maintenance of a vicious circle that sustains anorexia nervosa.

Participants in the Minnesota study

To understand fully the similarities and differences between anorexia and the Minnesota study, it is important to consider the participants in the original study. They were all healthy young men who volunteered for religious reasons, fully understanding the purpose of the experiment. In effect, the participants agreed to lose weight deliberately for altruistic reasons. Their motives were similar to those of the starving saints of the past, rather than those of anorexia sufferers, who are focused on physical appearance.

Women were not included in the study.

Before accepting applicants, the research team screened hundreds of volunteers for any physical and mental health problems, to ensure that all participants would be perfectly healthy and free of any pre-existing psychological problems. The final selected group was slightly slimmer than average (BMI: 22) and their IQ was higher. Many of them were university students. These are important differences in comparison with the sufferers of anorexia, who tend to be female, and usually have some degree of pre-existing psychological problem such as anxiety, obsessive-compulsive symptoms or depressed mood. Anorexia sufferers as a group also have average intelligence. On the whole, these differences make them more vulnerable than the Minnesota participants were.

Altogether 36 young men started the experiment, but four had to be excluded due to psychological breakdown during the semi-starvation. This was a crucial observation: about 12% of these perfectly healthy young people experienced major psychological disturbance simply as a result of self-induced dietary restriction, to such an extent that some of them had to be admitted to the local psychiatric hospital. This cannot be emphasised enough for patients and carers: starvation itself can seriously damage a person's mental health. The psychological abnormalities were wide ranging from psychosis to an intense sense of guilt and shame, self-harm and bulimia. Presumably, the different responses to starvation reflected individual (possibly genetic) vulnerabilities.

Methodology

The 36 young men spent 12 preliminary ('control') weeks together preparing for the experiment, during which time the researchers got to know them well, and they performed various baseline medical and psychological tests. They were expected to maintain an active lifestyle throughout the experiment, which included 48 hours per week of work (either paid or voluntary), in addition to three miles per day walking relevant to daily activities, 22 miles per week outdoor walks, and 30 minutes of aerobic exercise on a treadmill per week. The average daily food intake was 3500 kcal/day, which was necessary for weight maintenance because of the high activity levels.

This was followed by 24 weeks of restricted diet ('semi-starvation'), and after that, 12 weeks of controlled rehabilitation and 33-56 weeks of follow-up observation. The average daily food intake during the semi-starvation phase was 1570 kcal, including 50 g protein and 30 g fat. This was a low fat diet, providing 17% of calories in the form of fats (as opposed to the current guidelines recommending 30% of calories from fats). The average BMI by the 24th week was 16.4, and the rate of weight loss was 0.7 kg per week. The estimated ratio of omega-6 to omega-3 was 6:4 during the semi-starvation, and 8:1 during weight restoration (in contrast to 15-20:1 using the modern Western diet).

This is sobering information: these young people on a 1500 kcal diet lost about one quarter of their body weight within six months, and developed various physical and psychological problems. Many anorexia sufferers consume far fewer calories and much less dietary fat than this for much longer periods of time, and develop a worse BMI. No wonder that they change beyond recognition during their illness.

For the first 12 weeks of re-feeding, participants were divided into four groups receiving between 2400 and 3400 kcal per day to assess the effects of various weight restoration regimes. Participants in the top group gained more weight (0.73 kg per week) than people in the lower calorie groups (0.28 kg per week in the lowest group), but nobody returned to their normal weight within three months.

After this phase of the experiment, participants could eat as much as they wanted. During this time, they chose to consume between 3200 and 4500 kcal per day, resulting on average in a weight gain of 1.5 kg per week. Even with this high level of intake, full weight restoration took about 20 weeks.

During the 'free' phase of rehabilitation, participants had a tendency to overeat. (This had also been observed in historical research after famines.) Some participants reported an 'odd sensation of being full, but still hungry'. This is something that patients recovering from anorexia also report. Although some became slightly heavier than their original weight by 33 weeks, they all returned to their normal slim BMI of 21.8 by 56 weeks. This finding should give reassurance to anorexia sufferers, who often fear that eating what their appetite dictates will result in 'getting out of control' and becoming overweight. The results showed that the body's feedback systems prevent this happening in the long run.

The lesson from the Minnesota experiment is that rebuilding your body and your mind after severe weight loss takes a long time. The time to recovery was about 8-12 months after participants lost 24% of their body weight. If the weight loss is more severe, the time to recovery will be longer. Furthermore, if people remain underweight, they cannot recover.

Main findings

The authors of the Minnesota study considered the physical consequences of starvation first. By the end of the six-month period, all organs in the body had been affected by starvation (although the body tried to protect the vital organs, such as the heart and the brain as much as possible). These findings were indistinguishable from physical findings in anorexia, and therefore I shall discuss them in more detail when talking about the negative physical consequences of the illness (see page 142).

Psychological and behavioural consequences of self-induced starvation

Ancel Keys' reseearch team used various rating scales and detailed individual case descriptions to document psychological changes. During the first 12 weeks, when participants received 3500 kcal daily, the group was described by the researchers as enthusiastic and gregarious.

After 12 weeks of semi-starvation (on average 12 kg weight loss, BMI 17.8) there were profound psychological and behavioural changes: the young men had become depressed and withdrawn, and had slowed down. This gradually worsened by the end of the experiment. All of them lost their sexual interest and their relationships with their girlfriends suffered to the extent that some engagements broke off. Sexual dreams were replaced by dreams relating to food. The participants became much more self-centred and irritable, and some of them became verbally and even physically aggressive – traits which were totally out of character.

All of these symptoms appear in anorexia: patients become increasingly self-centred, and this can harm relationships with loved ones, resulting in isolation and deepening despair. It is important to know that these are the consequences of starvation rather than some mystery psychological problem.

Participants also developed a preoccupation with food, and various strange eating habits, such as eating very slowly (or sometimes very fast), cutting food up into small pieces, using various strange concoctions, drinking too much water, or wanting their food very hot. All of these behaviours can emerge in anorexia, and these symptoms are also the result of starvation.

Some participants developed bulimic type behaviours: these people could not keep to the diet, binged secretly, felt intensely guilty about eating, and tried to compensate by either doing too much exercise, or fasting. These behaviours were the result of the same conflict between mind and body as in anorexia: although participants were committed to losing weight as part of the experiment, their bodies' urges for food became overwhelming for some of them. This struggle is often seen in eating disorders, particularly in the bingeing, purging sub-type of anorexia.

The lesson for patients with anorexia and their carers is that abnormal eating habits are symptoms of starvation, and they will not get better while starvation continues. On the contrary, in the Minnesota experiment, the normalisation of eating behaviour took several months after weight restoration. Recognising this can be helpful for patients: they know that their eating behaviour is abnormal, but do not necessarily understand why. This finding is also helpful for carers: eating behaviours will only normalise several months after weight restoration, and this is not because the sufferer wants to be deliberately difficult. It takes time to recover from anorexia. Recovery in the Minnesota study took about 8-12 months. It is sobering to consider that these were all healthy young people who wanted to lose weight only as part of the experiment and were highly motivated to get better. Recovery from anorexia is likely to take longer.

Hunger did not cease during weight loss, and this was also confirmed by the authors' historical review of the literature: only people in the terminal phase of starvation reported loss of hunger in famines and concentration camps. This should be a serious warning-sign in anorexia too. However, loss of appetite may be difficult to recognise, as most patients do not admit to feeling hungry: they may feel greedy or guilty when experiencing hunger. Patients with anorexia often learn to ignore hunger, and they are very rarely prepared to discuss it. They often regard hunger as the enemy that will make them fat. Acknowledging and normalising hunger can be helpful. Dietary restriction will inevitably result in an increase in hunger, and chronic starvation will make this worse. Constant hunger will increase preoccupation with food and eating.

The other most important finding was that participants did not return to their normal emotional functioning immediately after starting weight restoration. Before the Minnesota study, most medical observations were based on natural famines or the consequences of war, and they stopped when food became available. As a result, there was a common myth, which still persists today, that the emotional problems magically disappear when food arrives. The Minnesota study showed that this is not so simple. The preoccupation with food continued for many months. The depression and anxiety that developed during starvation turned into increased irritability and verbal aggression during weight restoration. Interestingly, during this stage of the experiment participants turned against the scientists and started questioning their knowledge and motives.

This phenomenon is so commonly observed in clinical practice that Bryant-Waugh and Lask described it in their book, *Eating Disorders – a parents' guide*, as the second 'assertive phase' of recovery from anorexia.[17] According to the observations in the Minnesota study, the reason for this behaviour has a biological origin relating to starvation. However, this irritability can become a maintaining factor if carers do not understand what is going on. It can be very off-putting if, after months of trying to help someone with anorexia, he or she becomes hostile to you. Parents or friends often withdraw and give up trying to help because of this. However, it is important to remember that this is part of the recovery process, and it will improve over time. It may be difficult to see at this stage, but things are getting better. Do not give up now!

By 20 weeks of rehabilitation, most participants had regained their original weight (some even higher), but their psychological symptoms did not return to normal until 32 weeks. Depressive symptoms were particularly slow to change. One participant severely self-harmed during controlled weight restoration: he chopped three of his fingers off. Although he later claimed that this had been an 'accident', the researchers believed that it was more likely to have been deliberate injury, as he had referred to self-harm urges prior to this incident. Patients with anorexia often self-harm, and this is usually understood as a co-morbid problem. Because of the emergence of this behaviour during the Minnesota experiment in a person who did not have pre-morbid psychological problems, it seems possible that self-harm is also a result of starvation. It is theoretically interesting that this occurred during weight restoration.

Deliberate self-harm is often a challenging problem during hospital treatment of eating disorders. It is important for patients to understand the self-harm urges (which often cause much distress) could also be the result of starvation, and it is not a sign of 'going mad'.

Participants in the highest calorie group, consuming a higher protein diet, did better psychologically during the first 12 weeks of weight restoration. This finding has not received much attention in pertinent scientific literature since, yet it suggests that having a faster weight restoration programme may reduce the duration of the psychological problems, even if it is anxiety-provoking in the short term. It is important this be investigated further.

Sexual interest and functioning were slow to return. Again, this is crucial information for anorexia sufferers. Many patients start dieting because they are desperately lonely and hope that, by achieving a 'perfect' figure, they will find much desired love and affection. In reality, starvation suppresses sexual feelings, and the hope of finding a loving relationship fades further and further away with weight loss.

The most important implication of the Minnesota study for patients and carers with anorexia nervosa is that after severe malnutrition, the mind takes longer to recover than the body. In some ways, this should not be surprising: a healthy mind is dependent on a healthy body. If you are weak, and your organs do not function normally, you will feel miserable and unwell. Furthermore, rebuilding lost lipids and essential nutrients into the brain takes longer than simply replacing the body's energy stores.

This is why it is important to think about a realistic time scale for recovery: if a person needs to regain about 20 kg in weight, weight restoration in itself can take between 20 and 40 weeks. After that, even in perfectly healthy people, emotional and behavioural recovery can take at least another 12 weeks according to the Minnesota experiment. The ongoing depression, irritability and loss of sexual drive all can contribute to isolation and lack of motivation to change. This is why it is so important to use support from family and friends who are more able to take the long-term perspective and help the patient through the phase of recovery when it is difficult for him/her to see any positive changes. Remind yourself of the example of having to learn to walk again after a serious injury: initially, it will be painful and slow, but persistence and practice will bring results with time. In the long term, it will be worth it.

Depletion of essential nutrients

We have already discussed certain dietary habits that may predispose vulnerable people to anorexia. The depletion of essential nutrients can also contribute to the maintenance of the illness. In theory, all essential nutrients can be depleted in anorexia, depending on the diet of the sufferer.[18, 19] Many patients exclude animal products from their diet (even if they are not vegetarian to start with), leading to the depletion of essential amino acids, vitamins and essential fatty acids. Some of these deficiencies are more researched than others. It is known, for example, that in anorexia people can suffer brain damage due to thiamine deficiency. This is particularly dangerous if the person has an alcohol problem in addition to the eating disorder.

Often, nutritional deficiencies are related to fat-phobia and avoidance of dietary fats, such as depletion of essential fatty acids and fat-soluble vitamins. Out of these, possibly the most important factors for mood and mental wellbeing are omega-3 fatty acids and vitamin D. We have already discussed the role of omega-3 PUFAs among the predisposing factors, but ongoing low intake can also contribute to the maintenance of the illness by contributing to low mood. Vitamin D deficiency can also develop, mainly in anorexia sufferers who do not expose their skin to the sun and consume a purely vegetarian diet.[20] Vitamin D has many important roles in the body; it is essential for bone health, but also has an important protective role in the nervous system. Its deficiency contributes to the development of osteoporosis.

Alcohol and drugs

Fortunately, only a small proportion of sufferers will develop alcohol or drug problems during their illness. As I mentioned earlier, the development of alcohol abuse is often related to anxiety, particularly as an attempt to manage social anxiety. The problem is that patients with anorexia take into consideration only that alcohol is high in calories and ignore the fact that it is also a cell poison. Moderate consumption of alcohol (1-2 units per day) may be beneficial in the context of a Mediterranean diet, which is high in vitamins and antioxidants, but if alcohol becomes a main source of energy intake at the expense of a mixed, balanced diet, the risk of liver and brain damage is high. Alcohol is also a depressant of the nervous system, so it will contribute to ongoing depression. Taking all these issues into consideration, it should not be surprising that alcohol abuse is related to a poor outcome and increased risk of mortality in anorexia.[21, 22]

Drug abuse is equally dangerous. People with eating disorders may use amphetamines, heroin or cocaine for suppressing appetite; or laxatives, diuretics or thyroid hormones for short-term weight loss; or steroids for muscle building. All of these carry their own risks, and maintain a dangerous, vicious circle. Laxatives and diuretics can cause electrolyte disturbances, and can damage bowel and kidney functions respectively. Amphetamines and cocaine are highly addictive. They damage the brain and sexual functioning, and cause depression. Steroids also cause damage to sexual functioning as well as leading to osteoporosis and depression. People with anorexia are more sensitive to these side effects because their bodies are already deprived of many protective essential nutrients, and their hearts are weakened. Most of these drugs can cause depression, and as we have seen, depression is an important maintaining factor in anorexia. They also increase feelings of shame, guilt and isolation.

It is important to understand that abuse of alcohol and/or drugs increases the risk of death in anorexia. One famous example was the singer, Karen Carpenter, who abused laxatives and emetics and thyroid tablets, which resulted in heart failure. To prevent such a tragic waste of life and talent, compulsory treatment is sometimes the only option, although attitudes towards compulsory treatment vary a great deal between different countries.

Exercise

A significant proportion of patients keep their weight low by excessive exercise in addition to dietary restriction. Excessive exercise has a biological effect on the brain: it suppresses appetite and increases endorphins. These effects maintain the illness, not just because of using excessive energy, but also because of reduced appetite, short-term improvement in mood and reinforcement of preoccupation with the body. Exercise in underweight patients also can cause injury and damage the heart.

In pre-pubertal children, excessive exercise can lead to the stunting of growth, particularly if their diet is reduced. This can happen with child gymnasts and ballerinas. Parents and sports schools should monitor the physical development of children in their care.

Summary

Anorexia is maintained by a complex interaction of psychological, social and biological factors. It is very important to understand and tackle these factors when you are trying to recover from the illness, or trying to help your loved one. The psychological and social factors tend to vary from person to person, but the biological effects of starvation are the same for everybody.

The Minnesota study demonstrated the profound effect of starvation on the human body, mind and functioning. Starvation itself can produce some of the symptoms and problems experienced in anorexia. Given that in anorexia the length of starvation is generally longer and more severe than during the Minnesota experiment, the consequences are also more severe. However, this study showed that these symptoms are reversible with weight restoration, but that physical recovery is necessary before the mind can return to normal. Furthermore, some of the psychological symptoms, such as depression and irritability, and even self-harm, can get worse during the process of weight restoration. It is important to be aware of this, so that you do not give up prematurely.

References

1. Vandereycken W, Van Humbeeck I. Denial and concealment of eating disorders: A retrospective survey. *European Eating Disorders Review* 2008; **16(2)**: 109-114.
2. Vandereycken W. Denial of illness in anorexia nervosa – A conceptual review: Part 1 Diagnostic significance and assessment. *European Eating Disorders Review* 2006; **14(5)**: 341-351.
3. Vandereycken W. Denial of illness in anorexia nervosa – A conceptual review: Part 2. Different forms and meanings. *European Eating Disorders Review* 2006; **14(5)**: 352-368.
4. Stenstrom U, Nilsson AK, Stridh C, Nijm J, Nyrinder I, Jonsson A et al. Denial in patients with a first-time myocardial infarction: relations to pre-hospital delay and attendance to a cardiac rehabilitation programme. *European Journal of Cardiovascular Prevention & Rehabilitation* 2005; **12(6)**: 568-571.
5. Wade TD, Bulik CM, Neale M, Kendler KS. Anorexia nervosa and major depression: Shared genetic and environmental risk factors. *American Journal of Psychiatry* 2000; **157(3)**: 469-471.
6. Wagner A, Wockel L, Bolte S, Radeloff D, Lehmkuhl G, Schmidt MH et al. Mental disorders among relatives of patients with anorexia nervosa and bulimia nervosa. *Zeitschrift fur Kinder-und Jugendpsychiatrie und Psychotherapie* 2008; **36(3)**: 177-184.
7. Nicholls DE, Viner RM. Childhood risk factors for lifetime anorexia nervosa by age 30 years in a national birth cohort. *Journal of the American Academy of Child and Adolescent Psychiatry* 2009; **48(8)**: 791-799.
8. O'Brien KM, Vincent NK. Psychiatric comorbidity in anorexia and bulimia nervosa: nature, prevalence, and causal relationships. *Clinical Psychology Review* 2003; **23(1)**: 57-74.

9. Karwautz A, Rabe-Hesketh S, Collier DA, Treasure JL. Premorbid psychiatric morbidity, comorbidity and personality in patients with anorexia nervosa compared to their healthy sisters. *European Eating Disorders Review* 2002; **10(4)**: 255-270.
10. Claudino AM, Hay P, Lima MS, Bacaltchuk J, Schmidt U, Treasure J. Antidepressants for anorexia nervosa. *Cochrane Database of Systematic Reviews* 2006; **(1)**.
11. Troop NA, Allan S, Serpell L, Treasure JL. Shame in women with a history of eating disorders. *European Eating Disorders Review* 2008; **16(6)**: 480-488.
12. Sanci L, Coffey C, Epi GD, Olsson C, Reid S, Carlin JB et al. Childhood sexual abuse and eating disorders in females. *Archives of Pediatrics & Adolescent Medicine* 2008; **162(3)**: 261-267.
13. Feldman MB, Meyer IH. Childhood abuse and eating disorders in gay and bisexual men. *International Journal of Eating Disorders* 2007; **40(5)**: 418-423.
14. Latzer Y, Gaber LB. Pathological conflict avoidance in anorexia nervosa: Family perspectives. *Contemporary Family Therapy* 1998; **20(4)**: 539-551.
15. Keski-Rahkonen A, Hoek HW, Susser ES, Linna MS, Sihvola E, Raevuori A et al. Epidemiology and course of anorexia nervosa in the community. *American Journal of Psychiatry* 2007; **164(8)**: 1259-1265.
16. Keys A, Brozek J, Henschel A, Mickelsen O, Taylor HL. *The biology of human starvation*. Minneapolis: University of Minnesota Press; 1950.
17. Bryant-Waugh R, Lask B. *Eating disorders: a parents' guide* (Revised Edition). Hove, New York: Brunner-Routledge; 2004.
18. Christopher K, Tammaro D, Wing EJ. Early scurvy complicating anorexia nervosa. *Southern Medical Journal* 2002; **95(9)**: 1065-1066.
19. Castro J, Deulofeu R, Gila A, Puig J, Toro J. Persistence of

nutritional deficiencies after short-term weight recovery in adolescents with anorexia nervosa. *International Journal of Eating Disorders* 2004; **35(2)**: 169-178.

20. Calvo MS, Whiting SJ, Barton CN. Vitamin D intake: A global perspective of current status. *Journal of Nutrition* 2005; **135(2)**: 310-316.

21. Bulik CM, Klump KL, Thornton L, Kaplan AS, Devlin B, Fichter MM et al. Alcohol use disorder comorbidity in eating disorders: A multicenter study. *Journal of Clinical Psychiatry* 2004; **65(7)**: 1000-1006.

22. Keel PK, Dorer DJ, Eddy KT, Franko D, Charatan DL, Herzog DB. Predictors of mortality in eating disorders. *Archives of General Psychiatry* 2003; **60(2)**: 179-183.

Chapter 5

The pros and cons of anorexia nervosa

Even when anorexia sufferers have a good understanding of the illness, it does not necessarily follow that they want to get better. Why is that?

During the last 20 years there has been increasing interest in the motivational treatment model of anorexia nervosa.[1] The idea was borrowed from drug and alcohol addiction, and it is based on the recognition that people often go through a similar psychological journey before deciding to change a behaviour that is harmful. In alcoholism, for example, there is often a key event which is very important for the individual in question in providing the motivation to stop drinking. More often than not, this is about experiencing severe negative consequences of heavy drinking; it may be the threat of losing a job, a marriage, or getting ill that makes the person realise that continuing the behaviour is not worth it any more. Up to that point, denial and the short-term positive effects of the habit overrule any warning signs of the need to change. Interestingly, these short-term positive effects in both alcohol addiction and anorexia are usually related to im-provement in mood and reduction in anxiety. In this sense, there are similarities between addiction and anorexia: there is a short-term relief of anxiety (by intoxication or not eating), at a cost of long-term damage to physical and mental health, and general happiness and fulfilment in life. In addition, when the person tries to stop the behaviour he or she will experience unpleasant short-term consequences, making the change difficult. However, biologically, the two problems are not the same; alcohol and various other drugs can cause physical dependence, whilst starvation cannot. Therefore, on the basic biological level it should be easier to overcome anorexia than addiction.

The good things about anorexia nervosa

Looking at it from the outside, it is very difficult to understand that there is anything good about anorexia. What can possibly be good about self-induced starvation? Surely it is unpleasant and dangerous? However, sufferers see things differently; otherwise, they would not persist with keeping their weight low. Anorexia is hard work, so there must be a reason why people keep it going.

In chapter 3 I discussed the evolutionary hypothesis. Initial weight loss can be useful in increasing attractiveness when competition for high-quality mates is intense, particularly if the sufferer feels inferior to others for any reason. At the beginning of the illness, most patients receive positive comments from friends and family about their weight loss. I remember the father of one of my patients, who commented with a proud glint in his eyes that his daughter looked 'stunning' after her first stone of weight loss. At age 16 and very thin, she probably did look like a model on the cover of a magazine. For the daughter, who was desperate for affection and praise from her father at a time when her family was disintegrating, his throw-away remark became 'proof' that important men in her life would like her more if she was thin.

Fathers' comments are very significant for their developing daughters.[2, 3] The father's approval is an important factor for a young woman's self-esteem, as he is the first male to accept her as a developing female. We have already discussed the importance of wanting to be prettier than other female members of the family. There is no intra-sexual competition with the father, but his approval is very important as he provides a model for future male response (signalling male sexual selection strategies). The father leaving the family for a thinner woman can also be a very powerful message for an adolescent girl. Unfortunately, many fathers are unaware of this, and inadvertently make insensitive comments, which can fuel their daughters' body image distortion and ongoing desire to lose weight.

This patient was also proud of herself: she was successful at losing weight, while other people usually failed. The sense of achievement is often very important, particularly if succeeding in other aspects of life is difficult.

Sometimes, in these situations, further weight loss can also be helpful in blocking out emotional pain. In starvation, as we have seen, people cannot think about anything else apart from food (and in anorexia, weight and shape), so the person does not have to think about other potentially more painful issues. This can happen after loss events, such as parental divorce, or break-up of a relationship. 'I must be an unlovable person, and regardless of how hard I try, nobody will ever love me.' These are intensely painful thoughts to contemplate. It may be easier to worry about food and shape instead, even though this will only add to the original problem and not solve anything.

Being significantly underweight can have other positive consequences: the person becomes special, and the centre of attention.[4] For example, parents are more likely to focus on their anorexic child than her healthy siblings' needs, and this can be a positive consequence for the anorexia sufferer, even if the original trigger of the illness was something else. Middle children usually feel that they are not getting as much parental attention as the younger or older sibling in the family: anorexia can change all that. Or, if there is a step-parent and a half-sibling in the family, having anorexia refocuses attention on the sufferer, who has probably been feeling left out.[5] When you are frail, people treat you differently: they are gentler, more careful not to upset you.

Having anorexia can also provide a way out of an intolerable situation. Another patient of mine was an international student at a prestigious ballet school many thousands of miles away from home. She was desperately unhappy, torn between her ambitions and missing her home and family. Her anorexia started originally as an attempt to compete with her peers but it also became an 'honourable' way out, allowing her to return home without being regarded a failure by people in her community, or risking rejection by her ambitious parents.

Anorexia can also be helpful in communicating what is too difficult to say. What you are not able to change by using verbal reasoning may be 'easier' to achieve by not eating. Wasting away is a very powerful way of communicating to the family and the wider world that you are unhappy without having to spell it out in words. It also presents a context in which people are more likely to be willing to change and review their views and attitudes. Perhaps this is the reason why many people with anorexia feel in control, even when they are quite clearly out of control from the point of view of their physical health.

Even infertility and loss of sexual desire can be advantageous for some anorexia sufferers. These can be protective against unwelcome sexual advances, or unwanted pregnancy. It may even be a successful long-term strategy in modern societies. One could argue that many Hollywood actresses pursue extreme thinness to maintain a youthful figure in the hope of long-term social and financial success, even if it means giving up their fertility in the short term.

Alternatively, there may be a very good reason why the sufferer wants to block out any sexual feelings. This could be related to sexually abusive experiences, or ambivalence about sexual orientation. At other times, when parental relationships break down due to extramarital affairs, their child may conclude that sexual feelings are destructive and dangerous, and anorexia provides the perfect escape.

These examples show that there could be many 'good' things about anorexia for the sufferer in the early stages. The problem is that when weight loss continues, patients start feeling increasingly miserable, but because of their initial positive experiences they believe that further weight loss will bring the elusive satisfaction and happiness. This never happens. The further weight loss just becomes an out-of-control strategy that seems to be successful only at the beginning of the illness, but later leads to destruction.

Physical health

Surprisingly, there are even some positive physical consequences to anorexia (though not many). It has been known since the Minnesota study that in starvation various allergic conditions such as hay fever and eczema, and some skin conditions such as acne, can get better. Acne is particularly important for young people, as when it re-appears during weight restoration it can cause significant distress, and provide 'evidence' for the sufferer that weight gain is unhelpful. Fortunately, acne can be treated nowadays, and it is important to remember this during anorexia treatment. I have often seen patients taken off their antibiotic treatment after admission to hospital in a severely malnourished state. This is unnecessary and unhelpful. If this happens to you, ask the doctor politely to restart the medication. (In the UK, prescriptions in hospitals are often done by junior doctors, who do not necessarily receive training about acne and anorexia.)

Type-2 diabetes can also improve with starvation. However, in type-1 (insulin dependent) diabetes, starvation is highly dangerous, as there is a risk of hypoglycaemic coma and sudden death.

Tooth decay is less common in chronic starvation, but if people use self-induced vomiting as a part of their weight control, that can ruin their teeth.

Long-term studies have also shown that those who recover from anorexia have a much lower risk of obesity, greater physical activity, and better health satisfaction than those who have never had anorexia nervosa.[6] This should be reassuring for patients, who often worry that if they started eating they would get out of control. The research evidence shows the opposite.

The bad things about anorexia nervosa

The bad things about anorexia are often minimised by sufferers. As we have seen, not facing the reality of the negative consequences of anorexia helps to maintain the illness. This is similar to smokers who ignore the long-term risk of heart disease and lung cancer when lighting up a cigarette. The difference between these two conditions is that anorexia can damage your health and can kill much sooner. In smoking, or in alcoholism, the physical consequences take years or decades to develop, whilst in anorexia, people can become dangerously ill within just a few weeks or months of starvation. If people remain chronically malnourished, there are many disabling consequences for their physical and psychological health, and also for their social functioning.

In the description of the Minnesota study, I have already discussed the emotional consequences of self-induced starvation, so I will not repeat them here. (Please refer back to the previous chapter if you need to reflect on the emotional and behavioural consequences.) Here I shall focus on the physical and social consequences.

Think through the next sections carefully. You need to understand what is happening to you or your loved one, and you need to be aware of the risks and warning signs. Think about what is relevant to you, and this should help you to become more motivated to change, and put anorexia behind you.

Physical health

The negative physical consequences of anorexia are the result of starvation, and were documented in detail in the Minnesota study. As previously mentioned, in addition to carefully monitoring physical and psychological changes in the participants, the researchers evaluated all previous research on starvation victims. There has been very little change in our knowledge since, and despite the ongoing famines in the developing world, there is little research on the effects of human starvation in the modern scientific literature. The two main exceptions are modern neuro-imaging studies in anorexia, and the long-term follow-up studies of the consequences of famines during World War II.

Patients and carers are sometimes surprised that the physical and psychological consequences of anorexia are indistinguishable from starvation. Some of them regard dieting as 'healthy' and therefore different from starvation. On a biological level, there is no difference: if you are significantly underweight, your body is starved regardless of whether the weight loss is self-induced or not.

Body weight

It is important to make a distinction between body weight and body fat mass. Anorexia sufferers often regard these two things as the same. When people start dieting, they initially lose their body fat mass, as one of the functions of the fat tissue is to provide quickly accessible energy during hard times. However, when this starts running out, the body will start using up as fuel all the other tissues and other lipids that support important functions in different organs. Some say anorexia is self-cannibalism, because the body eats itself up in an attempt to survive.

Records of famines indicate that most human beings can tolerate a weight loss of 5-10% with relatively few functional problems. At the other extreme, most human beings do not survive weight losses greater than 35-40%. This cannot be emphasised enough: patients' lives can be at risk if they are around or below BMI 13 (for adults), or if they lose a large amount of their body weight quickly. Severe famines commonly result in 15-35% weight loss. This percentage is common in anorexia nervosa, and it is helpful to reflect on this by putting the severity of the weight loss into context. It is paradoxical that the amount of weight loss that would create an international outrage at a population level (in Africa, for example) is often regarded as a personal choice on an individual level (and therefore not to be interfered with) by the well-meaning public and some professionals in the West. This is particularly incongruent when young people are affected by anorexia nervosa and suffer irreversible consequences.

Historical studies have demonstrated that males are more vulnerable to the effects of starvation than females. For example, in the Dutch famine in 1944-45, males were more likely to die than females. The increase in mortality was 269% in men and 179% in women. There are several reasons for this. Men have lower body fat mass than women and tend to be more physically active, and therefore they exhaust their energy reserves quicker. This also holds true if they suffer from anorexia nervosa. Male sufferers usually have a higher urge to exercise, as many of them would like to build up a muscular and fat-free body. This is biologically unachievable. If total body fat is used up, the person dies, and this has been documented by autopsies of starvation victims throughout history (such as in the Warsaw ghetto). The normal fat around the heart and kidneys had been replaced by a jelly-like substance. This provided clear evidence that being fat-free is incompatible with human life.

For children, even less weight loss can be dangerous. This information may surprise you, as sufferers of anorexia, and sometimes even their family members, do not realise how dangerous the weight loss can be. Patients in the UK often first ask their doctor to help when they have a BMI of 13 or even less, which is equivalent to a weight for height ratio of 60% for people over 16 years of age. By this stage, the body is probably in the final stages of starvation, and often hospital admission is essential to manage the risks safely. This is also the reason why some patients can be dangerously unwell even at a higher weight, if they have lost 30-40% of their body weight quickly. In the Warsaw ghetto, obese people who lost weight very rapidly died earlier.

The Minnesota study also demonstrated that during weight restoration body fat mass increases first. This is because lipid reserves can be restored more quickly than any other tissues. It takes longer for the body to build up bones, muscle and various internal organs, including the brain (up to one year). This is very important to understand: weight restoration is impossible without increasing the body's fat stores first.[7] This is a short-term response from the body, which is desperate to store energy as quickly as possible. Anorexia sufferers often struggle to understand this, believing that families or professionals are trying to make them 'fat'. The family can be helpful in reducing the patient's anxiety during weight restoration by taking a long-term perspective.

Body height
It may surprise you to learn that even adults can lose some of their height because of starvation and this can continue after weight restoration. This was observed among the participants of the Minnesota study. The authors hypothesised that this could have been due to loss of muscle tone, and the thinning of the inter-vertebral discs.

Malnourished children often become stunted. If their weight is not restored within a few months, the stunting can become permanent. This effect has been repeatedly shown in famines, or in young people with chronic anorexia who have not finished their growth. (In girls, the majority of growth is finished before their first period; in boys, it is in the late teens.)[8] The final stunting can be as much as 10-15 cm reduction in height.[9] The stunting of height in children is only reversible if the weight restoration is as quick as possible.[10, 11]

Weight for height charts are very helpful in picking up stunting before it becomes visible, by which time it is usually too late. Unlike loss of weight, slowing of growth may not be noticeable, so most parents are not aware of this happening to their child. It helps if you have information about your child's growth before the illness, because this will give you an accurate prediction of what would have been expected. This may be available from the general practitioner, the health visitor or the school nurse. Children usually follow a certain 'centile' during their development, and this is normally determined by their genes. For example, if the parents are of average height, the chances are that their child's growth will also be average (around the 50th centile on the chart). If the child is significantly malnourished, the growth will start dropping on the height chart from the 50th to the lower centiles. It is often helpful to explain to children what is happening to their bodies. Unless they are very tall, they usually do not want to end up stunted, and this information can help them to make positive changes before it is too late to reverse the damage. Weight restoration before the completion of growth can reverse the process.[10, 12]

Basal metabolic rate

'Basal metabolic rate' means the amount of energy needed to sustain life without any additional activity. It is related to maintaining basic functions necessary for life, such as keeping our hearts beating, our bodies warm, our minds conscious, breathing, and so on. Dietary restriction results in reduced basal metabolic rate. This means that the body uses up less energy to maintain life in an attempt to preserve energy, almost as if the person was hibernating. Energy saving can happen only if some life functions are reduced. These include lower body temperature, lower heart rate, less physical activity, reduction in sexual functions and so on. The reduced basal metabolic rate explains why some chronic anorexia sufferers get by with very small amounts of food; they use up less energy when severely malnourished.

In the Minnesota experiment, the reduction in basal metabolic rate was 40% by the end of the 24th week, resulting in about a 600 kcal reduction in daily requirement just to maintain weight. This is the same in anorexia. When the dietary intake is increased, basal metabolic rate improves within a few weeks. The patient starts feeling warmer and more energetic, and the energy requirement increases in parallel. This is one of the reasons why gradual increase of daily intake is necessary during weight restoration. If there is a regular energy supply, the body starts burning off more to keep warm, so further additional energy intake is necessary for rebuilding lost tissues.

Skin, hair and nails

Starvation has a significant effect on the quality of skin, hair and nails. In the Minnesota experiment, participants developed dry, scaly skin, dry, thin hair, and fragile nails by 23 weeks. Brownish, patchy pigmentation of the skin was also observed, making the participants look prematurely aged. As a result of malnutrition, some patients with anorexia can also look like little old ladies even if they are young. The participants' skin was also cold to the touch, and fingers and toes were blue because of poor circulation (cyanosis). In chronic starvation and anorexia, fine downy hair (lanugo) can also develop. Experts believe that this may be an attempt by the body to prevent heat loss.

Dry skin is usually related to essential nutrient deficiencies, such as zinc and polyunsaturated fatty acid (PUFA) deficiency. If the sufferer's diet mainly consists of yellow vegetables, a yellow discoloration of the skin can occur. If this happens, it is important to seek medical advice, as the yellowish colour could also be related to liver damage. Rarely, patients may also develop vitamin deficiencies, such as scurvy, which results in easy bruising and bleeding gums, or pellagra due to vitamin B deficiency, which manifests as discoloration of sun-exposed areas. Self-induced vomiting can result in a callus on the base of the middle finger.

In severe starvation, sufferers can develop pressure sores, as the normal fat tissue that protects the skin from pressure from the bones is lost.

Most sufferers are troubled by these changes, as they quite clearly do not help to improve their attractiveness, and they want to reduce them. The recognition that poor skin and hair are the result of self-induced starvation can help the sufferer realise that the strategy has gone too far and has become harmful. It can be very helpful to show your child that anorexia damages the body including the skin, causes abnormal hair growth, and so on.

Skin abnormalities can be detected by experienced doctors during physical examination. This is why a full physical examination is important. If you have a child with anorexia, it is important to examine his or her body in a sensitive way. As a parent, you will be able to recognise any abnormalities, and alert the doctor if necessary.

Digestive system
Autopsy studies of famine victims have demonstrated reduction in the size of the stomach, the liver and the intestines. By the end of semi-starvation in the Minnesota experiment, stomach emptying into the small intestine after the digestion of a meal occurred after more than four hours (compared with three hours normally). This explains why at the beginning of weight restoration, anorexia sufferers often feel full or sick. The reason for this delay is the slowing down and shrinkage of the digestive system,[13] and because of this, it is important to start weight restoration with small and frequent meals. Otherwise – in extreme

cases – there is a risk of serious complications such as stomach dilation and rupture. Omega-3 fatty acids can help to speed up gastric emptying, so they can be helpful during weight restoration.[14]

Constipation is also an inevitable consequence of starvation. This is partially because of the slowing down of the bowels, and partially due to the small amount of food consumed. If not much is going in, not much can come out. Using laxatives can damage the normal movements of the bowels, and people build up a tolerance towards them which means they need increasing quantities, and are not then able to come off them easily. Some patients use large amount of laxatives to achieve short-term weight loss. This is a dangerous practice as it can cause significant loss of fluids and electrolytes, and can result in life-threatening heart arrhythmias. Needless to say, laxative use is an ineffective method of weight control as it results only in short-term fluid loss. In severe chronic cases, incontinence can develop, due to the weakness of the muscles of the pelvic floor.

Apart from the atrophy (shrinkage), fatty degeneration of the liver occurs in more than 50% of people in severe starvation.[15, 16] This is partially due to the lack of essential nutrients, and the liver's attempts to manufacture alternative fatty acids, to substitute for the loss of poly-unsaturated fatty acids (PUFAs) in various cell membranes in the body. In severe malnutrition, the liver's sugar reserves are also depleted. This can result in hypoglycaemia (low blood sugar level), which can kill. Frequent but small meals help to prevent this during initial re-feeding. Late night snacks that are high in complex carbohydrates (such as a banana) can be helpful in preventing early morning hypoglycaemia.

In purging-type anorexia, there are other complications that may affect the digestive tract. Self-induced vomiting damages the teeth, particularly if sufferers use acid-containing foods, such as fizzy drinks or acidic mouthwash. The damage to the teeth can be irreversible. To prevent lasting damage, it is important to rinse the mouth with water, and to avoid brushing the teeth for about 30 minutes after vomiting. Regular dental check-ups are also important.

Purging can also cause the salivary glands to swell, and as a result, the sufferer can develop a hamster-like face. Sufferers often misinterpret this sign as evidence of 'fatness' and having a chubby face. It is important to help them understand that this change is the result of vomiting.

Forced vomiting can also damage the oesophagus (the pipe between the mouth and the stomach). One of the life-threatening consequences of purging is bleeding from the oesophagus. This can be recognised as fresh blood in vomit. If it happens, you need urgent medical help.

Very rarely, other severe abdominal complications can occur.

Kidney

The kidneys are relatively preserved during starvation. However, problems can arise if the sufferer restricts fluid intake as part of their attempt to lose weight. Kidney damage can also develop as a result of vomiting or laxative abuse.[17] On rare occasions, kidney stones can also occur.

Endocrine system

The endocrine system produces hormones, which are essential for growth in children and for maintaining and regulating body functioning in everyone. It includes many different organs, which are all important for life and normal functioning. Hormones also have powerful effects on the brain and on general well-being. Autopsy studies of starvation victims have shown widespread atrophy (shrinkage) of the endocrine organs, such as the pituitary gland in the brain, and the thyroid gland in the neck. The adrenal glands initially enlarge, but at the final stages they too become atrophied.

The sexual organs also atrophy: the breasts and ovaries in females and the testes in males. It is well documented that fertility drops during famines in both men and women. The most obvious sign of this is the disappearance of periods (amenor-rhoea) in women. The lack of periods simply signals the severity of malnutrition, and it is not specific to self-induced starvation. It means that there is insufficient energy in the system. Modern pelvic ultrasound can monitor ovarian changes during weight restoration, so minimal healthy weight can be identified ob-jectively at an individual level. However, the return of regular periods also gives the same information. On the other hand, it is important to be aware that in rare cases, periods can continue even in severe malnutrition, therefore the return of periods needs to be interpreted as one of many signs of physical health and not the only one.

There has been much less research about male sexual impair-ment and fertility issues in anorexia. However, the Minnesota study demonstrated significant impairment of male sexual organs and functioning. These effects included the loss of sexual desire and libido, and the loss of interest in the opposite sex and relationships. There was a parallel reduction in size of the testes, and a reduction in sperm volume and count of 75%. These hormonal changes also had a significant impact on the partici-pants' relationships with their loved ones, and as discusseded in chapter 4, some of the participants broke off engagements during the experiment.

It can be assumed that information about the sexual con-sequences of starvation is at least as powerful a motivator for male sufferers as pelvic ultrasound findings can be for females. The measurement of testicular size has not become common in clinical practice, although it could be equally useful.

In children, there may be a delay in the development of secondary sexual features, such as hair growth characteristic to gender, the growth of external genitals in boys, and the growth of breasts and the starting of periods in girls. The timing of the first period is genetically and nutritionally regulated. Under normal circumstances, the age of first period of the daughter will be similar to her mother's. However, if there is significant malnutrition, sexual development will be arrested. One of my patients was still pre-pubertal at the age of 19 years as a result of chronic anorexia from the age of 12. This had a devastating effect on the quality of her life and personality development.

Muscle

In starvation, there is a significant loss of muscle mass.[18, 19] Most patients with anorexia do not realise this and hope that, by losing weight, they will achieve a much leaner, but trim, muscular body. In reality, the body uses up muscle as fuel to maintain life if there is insufficient food. In males, the loss of muscle is even more severe, due to the loss of male hormones, which are necessary for the higher muscle mass in men. This is in stark contrast with the sufferers' desire to achieve an idealised muscular body. Muscle loss is highly visible; sometimes it can even be seen through clothes. The shocking pictures of concentration camp victims (and of the Minnesota study participants) demonstrate this well: arms and legs get thinner; the ribs, the hipbones and the shoulder blades stick out.

Despite the muscle loss, patients do not necessarily feel weak until the very last stages of starvation. The main reason for this is that, although there is less muscle, there is also a lighter body to move. One of my patients remarked that she was able to swim for longer when she was severely underweight. This relative preservation of strength can be misleading. Families can be falsely reassured that nothing is wrong, as the patient appears to be as strong as ever.

However, at the final stages, people become weak and tired. If you care for someone with anorexia, you need to know that muscular weakness is a severe danger signal. If sufferers cannot stand up from a squatting position, or walk upstairs easily, this usually means that they are seriously unwell, and they need to go to hospital before it is too late. By this stage, muscle is starting to break down, and patients are usually unable to recognise the danger themselves. You may have to take action to save your loved one's life.

Restoring muscle (and any other) tissue takes much longer than restoring weight, so initially the weight gain will be fat tissue. Quite often, the initial weight gain appears on the tummy, causing much distress to the patient trying to recover from anorexia. This is inevitable, as shown by the Minnesota study. It is important to remember that this is a temporary phenomenon, which usually resolves itself within a few months, as the body can rebuild the muscles as a result of normal activity. Exercise too early during weight restoration does not help, and it causes unnecessary stress on the starving body, including the heart.[20] You have to be patient and give your body time to restore itself: it will do so just as a result of normal activity.

People who yo-yo diet with normal eating are likely to end up with less muscle tissue and more fat tissue overall because there is not enough time for the body to restore muscle tissue between the dieting phases. So, instead of having a leaner body, yo-yo dieters end up with a relatively fatter one, which is the opposite of what they are trying to achieve.

The secret of a lean body is simple: stay within the healthy weight range, and do physical activity that you enjoy. The type of exercise does not matter. Any exercise needs to be built up gradually, and it needs to be weight bearing, but low impact, as the risk of injury is high in anorexia. When people are mal-nourished, their joints, bones and muscles are weak. Walking outdoors or swimming are the best starting points. Try to avoid anything that can cause falls (ice skating, horse riding, various team games) until your weight has stabilised at a healthy level, and you have regained your fitness levels.

Heart

The heart is essentially a special muscle, which is normally surrounded by a small amount of fatty tissue. In starvation, the body is trying to protect the heart as much as possible, as it is essential for survival. As a result, the loss of heart muscle is not quite proportional to the overall weight loss. Among the Minnesota participants, heart volume was reduced by 17% by the end of the semi-starvation phase (as compared with the 24% total weight loss). In anorexia, if the weight loss is more severe, the heart can shrink by as much as 30-35%. This also explains why it is potentially dangerous to start exercise too early: the heart is not strong enough to cope with intensive exercise.

The heart also slows down. The lowest resting pulse rate in the Minnesota study was 27 beats per minute in a lying down position, while normal resting pulse rate should be around 60 to 70. In my own clinical practice, the worst heart rate in a starved patient was around 28 at night. However, this is very unusual, and risk assessment guidelines recommend that all patients who have a heart rate below 40 should be admitted to hospital urgently.

If starvation continues, people often die of heart complications.[21] They start feeling weak and lethargic, and one day they do not wake up. In the purging sub-type of anorexia this can happen much earlier, as the heart is sensitive to the electrolyte imbalances purging can cause, resulting in fatal rhythm abnormalities. If you or your loved one is significantly underweight, it is important to know whether there is any risk to the heart. Any chest pain, pulse irregularity or shortness of breath needs to be taken very seriously. Ask your doctor to perform an ECG (electrocardiogram), which can show danger signs. Sometimes doctors arrange 24-hour heart monitoring to check for rhythm abnormalities. A weakened heart also can suffer if weight restoration is too fast. This is another reason why the diet during weight restoration needs to be built up gradually.

People with chronic anorexia can also develop arteriosclerosis, which is the hardening of blood vessels. This is probably due to lipid abnormalities, high levels of stress, and the high rate of smoking among chronic anorexic patients, who may smoke to suppress appetite. Omega-3 PUFA supplementation can correct some of these lipid abnormalities, and it would be important to research further whether this would also reduce the risk of death.

Although you cannot measure the size of your heart, it is easy to check at home if there is a problem by counting the pulse on your neck or on your wrist. Normal resting pulse is around 72 beats per minutes during the daytime, and it goes down to around 50-60 at night. If your daytime pulse is below 60, that means that your heart has significantly slowed down to conserve energy to keep your life going despite starvation. Usually, by this stage, there are other symptoms of poor circulation, such as bluish discolouration of the feet and hands (cyanosis), or feeling cold and faint at times. You can also measure your blood pressure and pulse at home, although you need to be aware that not all commercially available machines are reliable. By checking your pulse, you can also detect any heart rate abnormalities. If your heart rate is irregular, or if you feel faint or weak, you are in significant danger, and you need to seek medical help urgently.

Bones

Osteoporosis, often known as 'brittle bones', is a common consequence of chronic anorexia.[22] The bones lose mineral content in prolonged malnutrition, becoming lighter and more fragile. There are multiple reasons for this bone loss, including the lack of necessary nutrients such as calcium and vitamin D (a fat-soluble vitamin), and hormonal abnormalities, such as low testosterone and oestrogen. For example, osteoporosis is a common problem in elderly women who have stopped having their periods and do not get much sunshine or oily fish or do much weight-bearing exercise. With chronic starvation, the body stops producing sexual hormones, so in effect, the person becomes prematurely aged.

The risk of fractures, even because of minor injuries such as those which may be sustained while playing a ball game, is much higher if people have osteoporosis. This needs to be taken into consideration during weight restoration. It is not a good idea to start high impact sports for at least 12 months after full weight restoration. Most specialists will check the level of osteoporosis by arranging bone scans, and this can give an assessment of the risk of fractures. However, you need to be aware that bone scans are not very sensitive to change, in that bones are slow to respond to both starvation and weight restoration.

There was no evidence of osteoporosis in the Minnesota study's participants, presumably because the length of semi-starvation was only six months. This finding has important implications; it shows that if weight restoration is completed within a year of the onset of the illness, the risk of osteoporosis can be greatly reduced. It also means that it is unlikely that an anorexia sufferer will have an abnormal bone scan if the length of illness is just six months. Later studies have confirmed that osteoporosis usually develops after 12 months of starvation. Normalisation of sexual hormones (return of periods in women and testosterone in men) is essential for rebuilding bones, as is sufficient calcium, omega-3 and vitamin D intake.[22] Sardines and herrings are rich in these nutrients. All of these benefits are dependent on normalisation of weight (BMI should be between 20 and 25 for adults) and having a mixed balanced diet. If the malnutrition is prolonged, the risk of fractures can last for a long time, and the full restoration of bone loss may not be possible.[8, 23] In chronic anorexia, it is advisable to arrange to have a bone scan on a yearly basis, including one year after full weight restoration has been achieved.

Blood and bone marrow

In starvation, paleness and anaemia are common. In autopsy

studies of starvation victims marrow in the bones has been found to be depleted. This has also been confirmed in anorexia in modern scanning studies.[24, 25] The Minnesota experiment documented anaemia due to insufficient intake of vitamin B12 and folic acid, and low white blood cell counts among the participants after 24 weeks of starvation, but red blood cell production was relatively normal. Total blood volume was reduced by 500 ml (about 1 pint) on average. The loss of spleen weight was relatively more than the overall proportion of weight loss.

In anorexia, it is also common to find a low white blood cell count. These are the cells that protect us from various infections. Paradoxically, the risk of infection is lower than usual when people are underweight, but at the final stages of starvation, a significant proportion of patients die of 'silent' infections. This means that although there is an infection, there are no symptoms, because the body cannot produce an effective immune response.[26]

Some patients with anorexia cut themselves (self-harm), and this can also result in iron-deficiency anaemia. In these cases, it is important to monitor the full blood count on a regular basis, as malnourished patients cannot easily replace the blood loss caused by cutting. Iron deficiency anaemia can also develop in purging-type anorexia, if there is bleeding as a result of vomiting or diarrhoea.

Brain and nervous system

The review of the historical autopsy studies by the Minnesota scientists found consistent evidence of loss of brain tissue in famine victims. This reached between 4% and 10%. Modern imaging techniques confirm that there is shrinkage and a loss of lipids from the brain during starvation caused by anorexia.[27-29] To put it simply, a proportion of the brain is used up as fuel during starvation, regardless of whether the starvation is self-induced or not.

Two studies have shown that phospholipids in the brain are broken down during anorexia and used as energy.[27, 30] Some authors suggest that this loss of brain tissue may not be fully reversible with weight restoration, but this research has not proved conclusive as yet.[31–33] This inconsistency between studies may be due to different timescales between full weight restoration and the final scans, and not taking into consideration the time needed for the brain to recover from starvation. It is clear that the loss of brain tissue does not improve if the person remains underweight,[33] but it is not known how much time is needed for the brain to recover from starvation.

It has long been known that certain essential nutrient deficiencies can damage important parts of the brain, sometimes permanently. For example, thiamine deficiency can cause memory problems and even permanent brain damage.[34] The risk of this is particularly high if there is an additional alcohol problem.[35]

Starved patients usually develop a set of characteristic changes indicating impaired brain functions. These include depression and irritability initially. Later on, rigid thinking appears, and after that, apathy, and concentration and memory problems can develop. People often recognise that they feel unwell, but do not know why. Seriously starved patients can have trouble retaining and processing information. If this is the case, they are usually unable to make treatment decisions for themselves.

Sleep is disturbed and people often report dreams about food. While the loss of sleep is unpleasant, it is an adaptive mechanism to keep the body alive and to prevent dangerous slowing of the heart. At the final stages of starvation, people become sleepy and eventually they do not wake up.

Patients often find this information decisive when making a commitment to weight restoration. Most people with anorexia tend to be ambitious, and it is frightening to realise that your brain can shrink and can be damaged because of self-induced starvation. This should not be so surprising. The brain is part of the body, and it cannot be fully protected from malnutrition. In fact, the brain is a high-energy maintenance organ: it makes up only 2% of the body's mass, but it needs about 20% of the energy consumed. When people restrict their calorie intake by 30-40%, their brain will suffer, despite all the body's efforts to protect it. Most people with anorexia (those who still can think rationally) do not want to damage their brains.

This information should also help family members to understand why the person they love seems to have changed so much with the illness. It is because starvation has a profound effect on the brain. Full recovery from this damage takes a long time. The brain is the last organ to recover after starvation, as was demonstrated in the Minnesota study.

Other parts of the nervous system can also be damaged. These are often related to various essential nutrient deficiencies. For example, vitamin B12 deficiency can cause pernicious anaemia, and damage to the spinal cord. Vitamin B group deficit can cause neuropathy, which involves impaired reflexes, loss of sensation in the lower arms and legs, and sometimes problems with coordination.

The course of the illness

One of the worst things about anorexia is that it can last a long time with devastating impact on the patient's physical and psychological health, and preventing any chance of personal happiness. This is one of the tragic paradoxes of the illness: most sufferers relentlessly pursue thinness as a way of finding happiness and admiration, whilst prolonged starvation leads to misery and deterioration of health. The illness does not just affect the sufferers, but their families also pay a heavy price over the years, both emotionally and financially.[36]

The medical literature relating to the outcome and the cost of anorexia nervosa provide grim reading. Research suggests that about two thirds of patients get better within five years, and only the minority become symptom free.[37-39]

Reviewing the international medical literature of the 20th century, Steinhausen[40] found significant variations across long-term follow-up studies. On average, less than one half of patients suffering from anorexia recovered, one third improved, and 20% remained chronically ill. About 30-60% developed bulimic symptoms at some point. The risk of other psychiatric disorders at long-term follow-up was high, even decades after the eating disorder had subsided. These included anxiety disorders and depression, but alcoholism was also common.[41]

It is worth mentioning that clinic-based studies usually find poorer long-term outcomes than studies within the general population. This may be because those people who do not present themselves to services are less severely ill, or have more support and resilience than those who seek professional help. Similarly, those who cannot avoid hospital admission tend to do worse in the long run.[42]

It is difficult to predict the outcome for an individual person. Most studies find vomiting, bulimia, purgative abuse, prolonged length of illness and obsessive-compulsive symptoms are associated with poor outcomes, such as prolonged illness or even death.[40] These may be frightening facts to read. However, to achieve recovery, or at least a good quality of life, it is crucial to be realistic and well informed about the nature of the illness you are facing. This is widely recognised in other chronic medical conditions, such as diabetes, asthma, or even cancer. Without knowing how the illness can affect your health, quality of life, and life expectancy, why would you want to make changes in your lifestyle? Recovering from anorexia requires sustained effort, and dogged persistence not just from the sufferer, but also from loved ones. If you believe that this is just a passing phase or a personal choice, why would you want to persist through a difficult period of change?

If the illness starts in adolescence, the outcome tends to be better. This is mainly because a starving adolescent is more likely to accept encouragement from parents, and the vicious circle of dieting and starvation can be stopped by using the family's resources.[43-45] With adult patients this is much more difficult to achieve, particularly in Western societies, where there is so much emphasis on individual freedom and choice. However, most long-term research studies have found that patients can recover from anorexia even after decades, and therefore it is important never to give up hope of recovery.

Long-term consequences

The longer the illness lasts, the worse the consequences. If people fully recover from malnutrition within a few months of the start of anorexia, the long-term harm is minimal. The Minnesota study participants returned to their normal functioning a few months after finishing weight restoration, and went on to live healthy lives.

However, if sufferers remain chronically underweight, long-term damage to the body and the mind is inevitable. As described above, the most common physical problems are osteoporosis and the reduction in sex hormones, which result in a prematurely aged biological state. Young people who are chronically malnourished are at risk of stunting and developmental delay, and as adults they are more likely to develop early menopause and have an increased risk of breast cancer and heart disease. [46, 47] Furthermore, people who are chronically underweight are at a high risk of depression and various anxiety symptoms.[41] In addition, anorexic preoccupations will be maintained by starvation itself, making recovery increasingly difficult.

Fertility

One of the saddest consequences of anorexia is impaired fertility. Although the most severely underweight people are usually sexually inactive due to loss of libido, those women who are near to normal weight can become pregnant (even if they do not menstruate regularly). In these cases, because of their chronic malnutrition, there are risks to both the mother and the baby. There is an increased risk of miscarriage, pre-term birth, and impaired intra-uterine growth resulting in low weight babies with smaller heads and brains.[48] Furthermore, the risk of post-partum depression is higher, and this can have a negative effect on the developing baby as well as the family's happiness and well-being.

Long-term studies of famines have shown that children born to malnourished mothers have an increased risk of physical problems, such as obesity, coronary heart disease and hypertension later in life. In addition, there is an increased risk of mental health problems, such as schizophrenia, antisocial personality and affective disorders when the child grows up.[46, 47, 49]

These are tragic consequences, particularly in that they affect the unborn child. Anorexia sufferers do not want to harm their children any more than any other mother, and being aware of these consequences of maternal malnutrition can motivate them to work towards recovery. The implications of paternal starvation for the offspring are unknown.

Mortality

The worst thing of all about anorexia is that it can kill. It is often said to have the highest mortality rate among mental disorders. However, this varies significantly between studies: some quote between six and 18 times that of the general population.[50] About 50% of these deaths are due to suicide, confirming that weight loss leads to deterioration in mood, and increasing despair leading to tragedy. Anorexia sufferers often believe that weight loss will make them happy: the evidence is the total opposite. Other causes of death include severe malnutrition, complications of drug or alcohol addiction, and sometimes cancer. This is a stark reminder of how self-induced starvation can destroy people's lives. It is important to bear this in mind before it is too late.

Social consequences

Apart from the physical risks, chronic anorexia also has devastating social consequences. Many young people cannot achieve their educational potential, and adults are often unable to work, and therefore have to rely on state benefits.[51] Most adult sufferers live on their own, or rely heavily on their ageing parents, who struggle to help them.[52] These research findings show that the reality of anorexia has nothing to do with glamour and success. Even when people are managing to cope with their professional lives and remain in employment, anorexia takes away the chance of personal happiness.

Summary

Although anorexia can be life threatening and has severe negative consequences for the sufferer's life in the long term, sufferers often find the illness to be helpful in some ways. For example, it may protect a person from having to deal with an emotionally painful situation, it may help the sufferer to re-negotiate relationships, it may offer a feeling of achievement, or it may give a false promise of happiness if further weight loss can be achieved. These are the reasons why many sufferers are reluctant to change.

Understanding the good and bad things about anorexia is

essential for motivation to change. Read through this chapter again and reflect on what is happening to your health and to your life. Severe weight loss does not just use up fat tissue, but also all other tissues in the body, and it also affects the mind, sometimes with tragic consequences. Long-term anorexia is a debilitating illness, which affects all systems in the body and has a devastating effect on the lives of sufferers and their families in all respects.

References

1. Blake W, Turnbull S, Treasure J. Stages and processes of change in eating disorders: Implications for therapy. *Clinical Psychology & Psychotherapy* 1997; **4(3)**: 186-191.

2. Keery H, Boutelle K, van den Berg P, Thompson JK. The impact of appearance-related teasing by family members. *Journal of Adolescent Health* 2005; **37(2)**: 120-127.

3. Jones CJ, Leung N, Harris G. Father-daughter relationship and eating psychopathology: The mediating role of core beliefs. *British Journal of Clinical Psychology* 2006; **45**: 319-330.

4. Serpell L, Treasure J, Teasdale J, Sullivan V. Anorexia nervosa: Friend or foe? *International Journal of Eating Disorders* 1999; **25(2)**: 177-186.

5. Eagles JM, Johnston MI, Millar HR. A case-control study of family composition in anorexia nervosa. *International Journal of Eating Disorders* 2005; **38(1)**: 49-54.

6. Bulik CM, Sullivan PF, Tozzi F, Furberg H, Lichtenstein P, Pedersen NL. Prevalence, heritability, and prospective risk factors for anorexia nervosa. *Archives of General Psychiatry* 2006; **63(3)**: 305-312.

7. Orphanidou CI, McCargar LJ, Birmingham CL, Belzberg AS. Changes in body composition and fat distribution after short-term weight gain in patients with anorexia nervosa. *American Journal of Clinical Nutrition* 1997; **65(4)**: 1034-1041.

8. Misra M. Long-term skeletal effects of eating disorders with onset in adolescence. *Menstrual Cycle and Adolescent Health* 2008; **1135**: 212-218.

9. Roze C, Doyen C, Le Heuzey MF, Armoogum P, Mouren MC, Leger J. Predictors of late menarche and adult height in children with anorexia nervosa. *Clinical Endocrinology (Oxf)* 2007; **67(3)**: 462-467.

10. Modan-Moses D, Yaroslavsky A, Novikov I, Segev S, Toledano A, Miterany E et al. Stunting of growth as a major feature of anorexia nervosa in male adolescents. *Pediatrics* 2003; **111(2)**: 270-276.

11. Lantzouni E, Frank GR, Golden NH, Shenker RI. Reversibility of growth stunting in early onset anorexia nervosa: a prospective study. *Journal of Adolescent Health* 2002; **31(2)**: 162-165.

12. Swenne I. Weight requirements for catch-up growth in girls with eating disorders and onset of weight loss before menarche. *International Journal of Eating Disorders* 2005; **38(4)**: 340-345.

13. Holt S, Ford MJ, Grant S, Heading RC. Abnormal gastric-emptying in primary anorexia-nervosa. *British Journal of Psychiatry* 1981; **139(Dec)**: 550-552.

14. Robertson MD, Jackson KG, Fielding BA, Morgan LM, Williams CM, Frayn KN. Acute ingestion of a meal rich in n-3 polyunsaturated fatty acids results in rapid gastric emptying in humans. *American Journal of Clinical Nutrition* 2002; **76(1)**: 232-238.

15. Tsukamoto M, Tanaka A, Arai M, Ishii N, Ohta D, Horiki N et al. Hepatocellular injuries observed in patients with an eating disorder prior to nutritional treatment. *Internal Medicine* 2008; **47(16)**: 1447-1450.

16. Gan SK, Watts GF. Is adipose tissue lipolysis always an adaptive response to starvation?: implications for non-alcoholic fatty liver disease. *Clinical Science* 2008; **114(7-8)**: 543-545.

17. Yasuhara D, Naruo T, Taguchi S, Umekita Y, Yoshida H, Nozoe S. 'End-stage kidney' in longstanding bulimia nervosa. *International Journal of Eating Disorders* 2005; **38(4)**: 383-385.

18. Altun G, Akansu B, Altun BU, Azmak D, Yilmaz A. Deaths due to hunger strike: post-mortem findings. *Forensic Science International* 2004; **146(1)**: 35-38.

19. Weiss EP, Racette SB, Villareal DT, Fontana L, Steger-May K, Schechtman KB et al. Lower extremity muscle size and strength and aerobic capacity decrease with caloric restriction but not with exercise-induced weight loss. *Journal of Applied Physiology* 2007; **102(2)**: 634-640.

20. Birmingham CL, Tan AO. Respiratory muscle weakness and anorexia nervosa. *International Journal of Eating Disorders* 2003; **33(2)**: 230-233.

21. Millar HR, Wardell F, Vyvyan JP, Naji SA, Prescott GJ, Eagles JM. Anorexia nervosa mortality in Northeast Scotland, 1965-1999. *American Journal of Psychiatry* 2005; **162(4)**: 753-757.

22. Miller KK, Lee EE, Lawson EA, Misra M, Minihan J, Grinspoon SK et al. Determinants of skeletal loss and recovery in anorexia nervosa. *Journal of Clinical Endocrinology and Metabolism* 2006; **91(8)**: 2931-2937.

23. Lucas AR, Melton LJ, Crowson CS, O'Fallon WM. Long-term fracture risk among women with anorexia nervosa: A population-based cohort study. *Mayo Clinic Proceedings* 1999; **74(10)**: 972-977.

24. Geiser F, Murtz P, Lutterbey G, Traber F, Block W, Imbierowicz K et al. Magnetic resonance spectroscopic and relaxometric determination of bone marrow changes in anorexia nervosa. *Psychosomatic Medicine* 2001; **63(4)**: 631-637.

25. Hutter G, Ganepola S, Hofmann WK. The Hematology of Anorexia Nervosa. *International Journal of Eating Disorders* 2009; **42(4)**: 293-300.

26. Brown RF, Bartrop R, Birmingham CL. Immunological disturbance and infectious disease in anorexia nervosa: a review. *Acta Neuropsychiatrica* 2008; **20(3)**: 117-128.

27. Rzanny R, Freesmeyer D, Reichenbach JR, Mentzel HJ, Pfleiderer SOR, Klemm S et al. P-31-MR spectroscopy of the brain in patients with anorexia nervosa: Characteristic differences in the spectra between patients and healthy control subjects. *Rofo-Fortschritte Auf dem Gebiet der Rontgenstrahlen und der Bildgebenden Verfahren* 2003; **175(1)**: 75-82.

28. Kingston K, Szmukler G, Andrewes D, Tress B, Desmond P. Neuropsychological and structural brain changes in anorexia nervosa before and after refeeding. *Psychological Medicine* 1996; **26(1)**: 15-28.

29. Roser W, Bubl R, Buergin D, Seelig J, Radue EW, Rost B. Metabolic changes in the brain of patients with anorexia and bulimia nervosa as detected by proton magnetic resonance spectroscopy. *International Journal of Eating Disorders* 1999; **26(2)**: 119-136.

30. Kato T, Shioiri T, Murashita J, Inubushi T. Phosphorus-31 magnetic resonance spectroscopic observations in 4 cases with anorexia nervosa. *Progress in Neuro-Psychopharmacology & Biological Psychiatry* 1997; **21(4)**: 719-724.

31. Wagner A, Greer P, Bailer UF, Frank GK, Henry SE, Putnam K et al. Normal brain tissue volumes after long-term recovery in anorexia and bulimia nervosa. *Biological Psychiatry* 2006; **59(3)**:291-293.

32. Lambe EK, Katzman DK, Mikulis DJ, Kennedy SH, Zipursky RB. Cerebral gray matter volume deficits after weight recovery from anorexia nervosa. *Archives of General Psychiatry* 1997; **54(6)**: 537-542.

33. Chui HT, Christensen BK, Zipursky RB, Richards BA, Hanratty MK, Kabani NJ et al. Cognitive function and brain structure in females with a history of adolescent-onset

anorexia nervosa. *Pediatrics* 2008; **122(2)**: E426-E437.

34. Peters TE, Parvin M, Petersen C, Faircloth VC, Levine RL. A case report of Wernicke's encephalopathy in a pediatric patient with anorexia nervosa – restricting type. *Journal of Adolescent Health* 2007; **40(4)**: 376-383.

35. Butterworth RF. Thiamin deficiency and brain disorders. *Nutrition Research Reviews* 2003; **16(2)**: 277-283.

36. Simon J, Schmidt U, Pilling S. The health service use and cost of eating disorders. *Psychological Medicine* 2005; **35(11)**: 1543-1551.

37. von Holle A, Pinheiro AP, Thornton LM, Klump KL, Berrettini WH, Brandt H et al. Temporal patterns of recovery across eating disorder subtypes. *Australian and New Zealand Journal of Psychiatry* 2008; **42(2)**: 108-117.

38. Keski-Rahkonen A, Hoek HW, Susser ES, Linna MS, Sihvola E, Raevuori A et al. Epidemiology and course of anorexia nervosa in the community. *American Journal of Psychiatry* 2007; **164(8)**: 1259-1265.

39. Wade TD, Bergin JL, Tiggemann M, Bulik CM, Fairburn CG. Prevalence and long-term course of lifetime eating disorders in an adult Australian twin cohort. *Australian and New Zealand Journal of Psychiatry* 2006; **40(2)**: 121-128.

40. Steinhausen HC. The outcome of anorexia nervosa in the 20th century. *American Journal of Psychiatry* 2002; **159(8)**: 1284-1293.

41. Berkman ND, Lohr KN, Bulik CM. Outcomes of eating disorders: A systematic review of the literature. *International Journal of Eating Disorders* 2007; **40(4)**: 293-309.

42. Gowers SG, Clark A, Roberts C, Griffiths A, Edwards V, Bryan C et al. Clinical effectiveness of treatments for anorexia nervosa in adolescents – Randomised controlled trial. *British Journal of Psychiatry* 2007; **191**: 427-435.

43. Eisler I, Dare C, Russell GFM, Szmukler G, leGrange D, Dodge E. Family and individual therapy in anorexia nervosa

– a 5-year follow-up. *Archives of General Psychiatry* 1997; **54(11)**: 1025-1030.

44. Eisler I, Simic M, Russell GFM, Dare C. A randomised controlled treatment trial of two forms of family therapy in adolescent anorexia nervosa: a five-year follow-up. *Journal of Child Psychology and Psychiatry* 2007; **48(6)**: 552-560.

45. Anonymous. Anorexia, Maudsley and an impressive recovery: one family's story. *Journal of Paediatric Child Health* 2008; **44(1-2)**: 70-73.

46. Kyle UG, Pichard C. The Dutch Famine of 1944-1945: a pathophysiological model of long-term consequences of wasting disease. *Current Opinion in Clinical Nutrition and Metabolic Care* 2006; **9(4)**: 388-394.

47, Sparen P, Vagero D, Shestov DB, Plavinskaja S, Parfenova N, Hoptiar V et al. Long-term mortality after severe starvation during the siege of Leningrad: prospective cohort study. *British Medical Journal* 2004; **328(7430)**: 11-14A.

48. Kirchengast S, Hartmann S. Maternal prepregnancy weight status and pregnancy weight gain as major determinants for newborn weight and size. *Annals of Human Biology* 1998; **25(1)**: 17-28.

49. Brown AS, Susser ES, Lin SP, Neugebauer R, Gorman JM. Increased risk of affective-disorders in males after 2nd-trimester prenatal exposure to the Dutch-Hunger-Winter of 1944-45. *British Journal of Psychiatry* 1995; **166**: 601-606.

50, Steinhausen HC. Outcome of eating disorders. *Child and Adolescent Psychiatric Clinics of North America* 2009; **18(1)**: 225-230.

51. Hjern A, Lindberg L, Lindblad F. Outcome and prognostic factors for adolescent female in-patients with anorexia nervosa: 9- to 14-year follow-up. *British Journal of Psychiatry* 2006; **189**: 428-432.

52. Arkell J, Robinson P. A pilot case series using qualitative and quantitative methods: biological, psychological and social

outcome in severe and enduring eating disorder (anorexia nervosa). *International Journal of Eating Disorders* 2008; **41(7)**: 650-656.

Chapter 6

Achieving change

Population-based studies have repeatedly shown that a significant proportion of anorexia sufferers can get better without professional help.[1-4] However, apart from some studies using reputable self-help groups or websites,[5] there is very limited research on people who do not engage with health services, so it is not clear why some individuals can overcome anorexia without medical help, whilst others cannot. Despite the limited research, one can make the assumption that recognising the problem, and having support from family and friends, can make a difference in achieving change without professional services.[3]

Clinical experience suggests that there are very few anorexia sufferers who want to get better just by themselves alone. There is almost always somebody in their lives who helps them to realise that there is a problem, and encourages them to make the necessary steps towards change. If you are a carer reading this book and searching for answers about what to do, probably the most important thing you can do is to help your loved one overcome the denial, by considering the consequences anorexia is having on his or her life. Unless the person is very unwell, he or she will be grateful for your acknowledgment of the problem (if not immediately, then later on). Having anorexia is not fun, and most sufferers recognise this. Anorexia is maintained by fears, and not by 'highs', which are responsible for maintaining drug addiction.

Chapter 6

If you understand what the important factors are that maintain the anorexia in you or in your loved one's life, you can achieve change by tackling them. Although some maintaining factors may vary from person to person, others are universal. Professor Fairburn likened the recovery from anorexia to collapsing a house of cards: if you remove the ones at the very bottom, the rest will follow.[6] The 'cards' that are at the bottom of everybody's maintenance cycle are starvation and dietary restriction. The other important factors are fear and isolation. In some people the presence of poor self-esteem, perfectionism or depression may also be important.

It is not possible to recover from anorexia without changing dietary intake and restoring weight to a healthy normal level. It is unlikely that the sufferer can, or will want to, achieve these without help from others. This may be the reason why severe anorexia is less common in traditional societies. If somebody starves himself or herself, it is more likely that the family will intervene sooner than in societies where the emphasis is on individual responsibility. By making sure that the sufferer eats sufficient amounts of food again, they remove the most important maintaining factor, starvation itself, and the person has a much better chance of recovery. Clinical studies have confirmed this, providing consistent evidence that the level of malnutrition, and successful weight restoration, can both influence treatment outcomes and the person's chances of improvement without hospital treatment.[7]

This means that – unless the illness is at a life-threatening stage – you can make some choices as to how best you can achieve change. As a general principle, the younger the sufferers are, the more they need their parents' support. Adults can choose whether they prefer to use the support of their family or talk to professionals instead. There are pros and cons for both. Seeking expert advice can help to confront denial, and can be a first step to recovery. However, engaging with psychiatric services inevitably has some stigma attached to it, and in some countries it can be costly. In the US, many insurance companies offer limited or no cover for anorexia treatment. Even in the UK, where treatment is free, there are hidden costs, such as travelling expenses and higher insurance premiums. On the other hand, family members may be too close to the problem, or may be too afraid, or too preoccupied with other things, to be able to help effectively.

Self-help

As discussed above, research about treatment outcomes is mainly limited to people who engage with professional services. In these studies, it is commonly found that patients on waiting lists for treatment do not get better just by themselves. However, this is in contrast to large population-based studies, which show that some people with a lifetime history of anorexia can get better even if they do not receive help from professional services.[4, 8] The discrepancy between these findings may be due to the differences in attitudes to change, which depend on the person's individual circumstances. It is likely that people seek professional help only as a last resort, and by that stage they cannot change on their own. Alternatively, it may be that after making the decision to engage with services, people do not want to attempt any change by themselves, in case they do something wrong, or because they expect some kind of a miracle from the professionals.

The longer anorexia lasts, the less likely it is that you will succeed just by yourself. Most eating disorder specialists in the UK would recommend that people with a body mass index (BMI) below 15 are likely to need hospital admission (in the case of children, this is approximately 75% average body weight for height ratio). However, even when the weight loss is less severe than this, weight restoration usually requires joint effort and single-minded determination from the sufferer and family members. Keeping the period of malnutrition as short as possible can help to prevent the long-term consequences of the illness. This also means that the sooner you act, the more likely it is that you can get better without professional help.

What conclusions can you draw from this? Perhaps the simplest is that you should rely on self-help only if you can achieve sufficient change to show that this is going to work for you. Think of other people who can give up smoking without using professional help. They manage to change their behaviour, even if it is difficult. Some people can give up smoking by changing their habits and resisting temptation. Their success is often dependent on the environment where they work and live, and the support of their friends and family. People working or living in a smoke-filled environment will be less likely to succeed. The same applies to anorexia: friends and family can help to create the right environment and emotional support to facilitate change.

It can help to focus your mind on recovery if you imagine that, by some miracle, the anorexia disappeared from your life. Imagine waking up one morning and not worrying about weight and shape, or food and eating. How would your life be different in that future? What would you be doing then? How can you achieve more of what you would like in your dreams? Are there any signs of this happening already? Most people want to achieve happiness. Has restricting your diet made you happy? What has been the impact of the illness on your life? And on your family? Write down for yourself how life would be if a miracle happened, and look back at it from time to time when things get tough, to remind yourself why you want to change.

If you want to recover from anorexia, the first step is to get back to a healthy weight, and then give sufficient time for your body and mind to get better. Whilst it may be difficult, if you are able to make this commitment, you can get there. Using a diary to record weight gain and dietary intake can be helpful in this process. Alternatively, you may prefer to use one of the nutritional software products on the market. These are available for computers or smart phones, making them very easy to use. The main flaw is that the majority of these products focus on weight loss rather than weight restoration, so you need to learn to ignore the language when you are using them. Despite this weakness, they can be very helpful for recording your dietary intake, and monitoring your weight restoration and maintenance. Some of them also have a feature which enables you to monitor your thoughts and feelings, which may be helpful in challenging anorexic thinking – for example, 'If I eat more than 2000 kcal a day I shall blow up out of all proportion.'

In addition to restoring your weight, you also need to think about the other maintaining factors that keep the anorexia going in your life. These are likely to be related to feeling bad about yourself, avoiding social contacts, and believing that weight loss will make you happy and provide the opportunity to develop new and fulfilling relationships. Tackling isolation is often the key. Even if it is not easy, persevere. You also need to think about who there is amongst your friends and family that can support you best through recovery. It will *not* be someone with an eating disorder. Contacting reputable self-help groups and websites can also be helpful. Most countries have established charities to help sufferers of eating disorders, and they can guide you in the right direction (see Appendix). In the UK, B-EAT provides an excellent resource for patients and families (http://www.b-eat.co.uk/Home).

Assess the risks

Before you can make an informed decision about the best treatment options for yourself or your loved one, it is crucial to understand the risks that are relevant to you. This is what specialists do first when they assess a new patient. The risks can be divided into short-, medium- and long-term consequences.

Chapter 6

Short-term risks

Short-term risk means an *immediate risk to life*. Always bear in mind that anorexia can kill. As I explained in the previous chapters, 30-40% weight loss can be lethal (this is around a BMI of 13 or less in adult women, but children or men can be dangerously ill at a higher weight than this). The most serious problems include heart problems, low blood sugar, electrolyte imbalances, and muscular breakdown.[9-12] Some sufferers also restrict fluids, which can become life threatening much quicker than food restriction on its own. People need at least 1500 ml of fluid per day (depending on perspiration, this could be significantly higher in the summer), otherwise they become dehydrated within days. This damages the functions of various organs, including the heart and the brain.

If somebody with anorexia faints, feels weak or complains of shortness of breath, it is important to seek medical help immediately. These problems usually develop after significant and/or rapid weight loss, and often the sufferer is too poorly to recognise the danger by this stage. If any of these problems occurs, the starvation is likely to be severe, and the person may need to go to hospital without delay. If someone with anorexia becomes unconscious, make sure that you turn him or her to the recovery position (lying on his/her side), try to give him or her a sugary drink, or a spoonful of honey, check the pulse, and dial for an ambulance. Put a blanket on the person to preserve energy whilst waiting for the emergency services.

Before these life-threatening consequences happen, there are usually warning signs. If the dietary restriction results in weight loss of over 1 kg per week in an underweight person, physical health is likely to deteriorate rapidly within a few weeks. If people purge when underweight, electrolyte imbalances and heart rhythm abnormalities are much more likely to happen. Severely underweight people also exhaust their carbohydrate stores and can develop dangerously low blood sugar levels. In my own clinical practice, this has happened to young people with a BMI of 16 or below, depending on the degree and rate of weight loss. It is important to bear in mind that the actual weight or BMI is not always the best indicator of risk, and if you are in any doubt, seek an expert opinion.

All of these risks to health can be reversed by increasing dietary intake gradually, and by stopping vomiting. If the person is severely unwell and cannot think clearly, it may be necessary to supervise him or her at all times. This is often best done in hospital, as it can be exhausting and very difficult to sustain this at home for a sufficient amount of time (which will be, at the very minimum, for several weeks).

Unfortunately, it is unusual for the sufferer to realise that he or she is in immediate danger. By the time people with anorexia become seriously unwell, they have often lost touch with reality. This is because of the effects of severe starvation on the brain. If this is the case, the family or the professionals have to act to save the sufferer's life. This is not the time to seek compromises; safety needs to be paramount. I will discuss the ethical dilemmas regarding this later (see page 254).

Needless to say, if any of these problems were present, then trying to get better without medical help at home would be highly dangerous.

Medium-term risks

Medium-term risks are related to the chronic course of the illness. Anorexia can last a long time and thus can have a devastating effect on a sufferer's personal life, and educational or career progression. Many are unable to reach their personal potential, so hopes and dreams end up being sacrificed at the altar of anorexia. It also prevents people having any normal relation-ships, and their struggle with the illness has a terrible impact on the people around them.

Long-term risks

Long-term risks include osteoporosis, with increased risk of fractures, infertility, disability, loneliness and suicide. People with chronic anorexia waste their entire lives restricting their dietary intake, and this is an all-consuming activity, at the expense of being able to have a family, a career and any chance of happiness. Many end up living alone in isolation, some on social benefits, and die prematurely.

Young people often find it very difficult to grasp the long-term consequences of anorexia. They commonly believe that losing weight will magically bring about happiness, and solve all their problems. Healthy family members are more able to recognise that this is false logic. If they understand and convey the risk of long-term consequences, they can be very helpful in bringing about change. Usually, they are in the best position to help the sufferer realise that the price of anorexia is just too high.

A note on blood tests

Patients who are severely starved often come to see me believing that they are not ill because their blood test results are normal. The Minnesota study showed that in 'uncomplicated starvation' (without purging), blood tests remain more or less normal for a long time. This is because the body regulates blood levels of various essential electrolytes, proteins and lipids very carefully. It will try to maintain, for example, a normal blood calcium level, even at the cost of using it up from the bones. Therefore, normal blood tests can be very misleading when judging the severity of malnutrition. Professor Birmingham explained this phenomenon by using the analogy of student finances: just because you have money in your pocket, does not mean that you are not broke and you have not exhausted all of your reserves.[13] This analogy helps us to understand why patients, who seem stable, can decompensate very rapidly in the final stages of their illness: there are no further reserves to draw on. It is like the credit crunch. You cannot see that there is a problem until all your reserves have been exhausted.

In patients who purge, the most commonly found abnormality in blood tests is a low potassium level. This can be corrected by potassium supplements, or foods containing high levels of this mineral, such as bananas or potatoes. Stopping vomiting is the only effective long-term solution.

As discussed above, low blood sugar can also be dangerous. This usually happens when people are so severely emaciated that there are insufficient carbohydrate reserves in the body. If this happens, it is very important that the person introduces regular meals, including a late night snack consisting of complex carbohydrates (a banana is a good option for this). Most specialists would recommend three main meals and three snacks, so the body has a continuous energy supply.

Blood sugar can also be checked at home, so if you are worried before you can see a doctor, you can buy a testing kit at your local pharmacy. The best time to see whether there is a significant problem is first thing in the morning on an empty stomach. If you find abnormally low blood sugar levels, this should be a serious warning sign that your body is running out of energy stores. This is not something that people should try to resolve on their own: it is important to involve a health professional, such as a dietician, or a family doctor, to make sure that you are safe. Patients with anorexia who have insulin-dependent diabetes are at high risk of medical consequences, as they tend to disregard medical advice about healthy eating patterns, resulting in poor blood sugar control and the risk of hypoglycaemia and sudden death.

In severe starvation, there could be other abnormalities in blood tests, such as impaired liver function, or signs of dehydration if the person also restricts drinking. All of these signs need to be taken seriously, but it must be understood that a normal blood test does not mean that all is well. If you are uncertain about the risk, it is best to seek specialist advice.

Plan ahead

If there is no immediate risk, you and your family may wish to try to get better at home. It is helpful to make a plan when you start making changes in anorexia. Think about how to manage mealtimes and the temptation to compensate afterwards. If at all possible, it is better to do this jointly with your family members, otherwise it might be too tempting to give up prematurely when things get emotionally too tough.

The first step to recovery is full weight restoration; the second is weight maintenance. By doing so, you are challenging anorexic eating and compensatory behaviours, and allowing your body and brain to rebuild themselves. We have seen in the earlier chapters that starvation itself keeps the vicious circle of anorexia going by having a negative effect on mood and the brain. Furthermore, by definition one cannot recover from anorexia nervosa and remain clinically underweight.

Weight restoration takes a long time. For example, if you need to put back on 10 kg in weight, this alone can take between 10 and 20 weeks of consistent weight gain, and the normalisation of psychological functioning may take an additional 6-9 months. Without planning ahead, people can easily lose their commitment to change because it is difficult to see any progress from one day to the next. Again, comparing the task to giving up smoking can help in understanding this; even if you do not feel any better in the short term, the health benefits will develop over time.

In addition to thinking about the longer-term picture, short-term planning can also be very helpful in managing the anxiety associated with an increased diet. It is easier to reverse the dietary restriction if a clear weekly plan is agreed in advance. This usually fits with most family's food shopping habits.

Alternatively, before you go to the supermarket, sit down and plan the meals for the next few days ahead. This approach can reduce the arguments at mealtimes and in the supermarket.

Most sufferers can recognise that being able to increase the amounts and the variety of food is important for recovery, but that it will take time to achieve this. Usually it is more successful if the diet and the variety of food is built up gradually over a few weeks. We shall come back to the details of weight restoration later (see page 195).

If you do not manage to achieve consistent weight gain within a few weeks at home, it is better to seek professional help rather than risk prolonging the illness.

Family and friends

If you love someone who develops anorexia nervosa, you can either walk away or you can become a carer. Very few family members walk away, but at the same time, most people are un-prepared for the role of carer. When you think about your future, you dream about being able to achieve good things in life, but you do not anticipate having to become a carer for your child or partner with anorexia. When this challenge arises, people face turbulent and confusing times.

The transition to the caring role can be a similar process to grief. People experience denial first: 'This cannot be happening to me/us.' After this they often feel anger: 'I don't deserve this – it is your/his/her fault'; followed by searching for answers: 'Why me/her/him?'; struggling with depression: 'This is the end of the world'; and finally accepting the caring role: 'OK, this is our problem. We need to try to overcome this somehow.' It is helpful to be aware of this process, and reflect on where you are.

Many parents say that anorexia changes their child beyond recognition. It takes time to accept that your hopes for your child may never be realised; on the contrary, his or her life may be at risk. Even when the risks are not life-threatening, the course and the nature of the illness are devastating and very hard to take in. The more you learn about anorexia, and the maintaining factors, the better equipped you can become to cope with this challenge in your life. Eventually you will find a way to be helpful.

Motivation to change

As discussed before, over the last 10 to 20 years, there has been much interest in helping anorexia sufferers to improve their motivation to change.[14] The observation behind this is that giving advice alone can be insufficient and ineffective if the person is not motivated to change. For example, smokers may be aware of the harm they are causing to themselves, but they may not be interested in changing, because the short-term benefits (the relaxing effect of a cigarette) are more important to them than the increased risk of lung cancer decades later. Often change can be achieved only when they experience some significant negative consequence which forces them to review the pros and cons of their smoking habit. Therapists have been working on trying to find ways of helping people reach this stage before the serious consequences occur.[15]

According to Prochaska, changing harmful health-related behaviours can be seen as a cycle, as the diagram on the next page shows.[16]

Stages of change according to Prochaska and Diclemente (Prochaska, 1983)

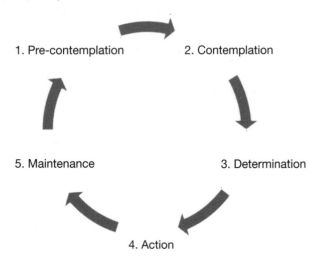

1. Pre-contemplation   2. Contemplation

5. Maintenance   3. Determination

4. Action

The first stage in this cycle is *pre-contemplation*. During this time, the person does not think that there is a need for change; they are still in denial. The second stage is *contemplation*. By this time, it is impossible for the person to deny that there is a problem, but there is still a high level of ambivalence about needing to change because of the perceived benefits as opposed to the harm the habit causes. The benefits tend to be short term, such as feeling more relaxed or happy for a few hours, whilst the harm is usually long term. Human beings are not so good at acting to prevent long-term harm if there are short-term benefits. This is the basis of most harmful behaviours, such as drinking and smoking. The *determination* stage is when people finally decide to make changes. In anorexia, this means when people decide that they need to increase their diet, otherwise the longer-term consequences would be too severe (for example, having to go to hospital, or not being able to carry on with certain activities, not being able to have healthy children, and so on). Stage four, *action*, means working actively on recovery. This is no easy task, and often means a very stormy phase in the anorexia sufferer's life. *Maintenance* means consolidating progress – that is, keeping within a healthy weight range in anorexia. This can also be difficult, as it is easy to slip back into old habits. This is the reason why people are at risk of relapse. Generally, the longer you maintain, the less likely you are to relapse.

People often fluctuate between these stages, just like when trying to give up smoking. The maintaining factors of the condition are important to bear in mind, as it is these that may pull the person back into the vicious circle. Having too many opportunities to slip back makes recovery more difficult to achieve. For an anorexia sufferer, it may be easier not to eat a meal than having to cope with the anxiety during or afterwards. If there is an opportunity to skip a meal, the temptation may be too hard to resist.

Family and friends can be very helpful in increasing the motivation of sufferers. This can be achieved by gentle but clear and consistent communication, explaining why you are concerned about your loved one. For example: 'I have noticed that you have been losing weight for some time. Initially, it seemed fine, but more recently, I have become concerned that you have become unwell, because…' Or, if the problem is more chronic, you can say something like this: 'I know that it is difficult for you to talk about this, but I am really worried about how your eating disorder is affecting your life/health. In particular, I have noticed that…' It is important to be specific to the person's real problems, as this helps to build common ground and to break down their denial.

Sufferers may be aware of the negative consequences but try to ignore them, either because they believe that weight loss will lead to happiness, or because the anxiety is overwhelming, or both. Having someone gently pointing out the obvious can help a person move from pre-contemplation to contemplation, even if it is received with initial resistance. It is crucial not to blame the sufferer. The initial dieting might have been voluntary, but by the time someone has developed anorexia nervosa he/she is not in control any more. It is also important to acknowledge that the person is suffering, and to give hope that things can change for the better. Recent research has shown that for the majority of patients it is important to regain the sense of vitality that is usually lost through the illness.[18]

Even when the person has reached the decision to start making changes, family and friends can offer important support to maintain motivation when things get too hard. This can be a long process, but it will be worth it in the end. Most people go through a bumpy ride, so do not despair if there are setbacks. Use the opportunity to learn something new. As Professor Treasure's recent book emphasises (with a hint of self-mockery): 'every mistake is a treasure'.[19] You can learn from them.

Providing an environment which reduces anorexic pre–occupations is very helpful. This includes banning all diet foods at home, having regular family meals and not talking about diet, weight, or shape. Environmental cues can greatly influence people's behaviours. For example, since the banning of smoking in enclosed places, many people have chosen to give up. This is because they were already contemplating doing so, and a non-smoking environment made the change easier to achieve. The same can be achieved in anorexia, if the family can provide an environment which normalises eating behaviours and where there is a positive commitment to healthy eating – that is, having a mixed balanced diet as opposed to slimming foods.

The family also needs to be mindful about exercise levels. Whilst building up healthy levels of activity is important, try to avoid repetitive and compulsive exercise as this can prolong the illness. Exercise can be covert: walking up and down the stairs all the time, cleaning for hours, getting off the bus early to add miles to the daily routine, or exercising in secret can significantly increase energy requirements.

Helping children and young people

The good news is that there is high quality research to show that parents can help their children recover from anorexia. This research was started by Ivan Eisler's team at the Maudsley Hospital in London more than 20 years ago, and it has yielded several randomised controlled trials with positive results.[20, 21] The emphasis of this approach is on placing the parents in charge of their child's weight restoration.[22] This is usually a very challenging task for parents who have to take firm, but nurturing, control of a child, who may be very fragile but often responds to attempts to help with hostility and aggression. However, this intervention targets two of the most important maintaining factors; starvation and isolation. The child is not allowed to isolate himself or herself, and the parents ensure that he or she eats sufficient amounts to complete weight restoration and maintain a healthy weight. By doing this long enough, the child has a chance to recover from the physical and emotional consequences of starvation, and to overcome his or her anxieties about food, weight and shape. The parents' commitment to weight restoration also addresses denial, giving a clear message that being underweight is harmful and therefore neither desirable nor acceptable.

There was a heartfelt personal story recently reported by parents in one of the medical journals, providing a testament that even a severely ill young person can recover with this approach given sufficient time.[23] In this particular case, it took six months to achieve weight restoration, and it took another five before the child recovered emotionally. The experience of these parents fits in perfectly with the timescales observed in the Minnesota study.

More recently, Professor Eisler's team have been working with multiple families together, and again, the results are very encouraging. The multi-family therapy has the added advantage of reducing the isolation and the related shame and guilt of the parents. When parents are able to share their experiences with each other they realise that they are not on their own, and that most young people with eating disorders have the same difficulties. They can also learn from each other, rather than feeling as if they are being put under a microscope by professionals. Seeing other people struggling with the same problems as you powerfully tackles denial. Young people also learn to accept help from their parents by watching each other.

Multi-family therapy may not be available where you live. However, you can learn something very useful from this research: that young people may recover from anorexia if their parents can ensure the completion of weight restoration, by providing consistent expectations and warm, but firm, support. Being realistic about the timescale necessary is also crucial.

Achieving weight restoration at home is no easy task. It requires a major change to family routines. Most parents expect their teenage children to be able to eat independently, and usually give them freedom to choose what they want. Many families have busy working lives, and people often eat at different times, so the number of joint meals is limited for practical reasons. However, if you have a child with anorexia nervosa, this needs to change until you are absolutely certain that the child has recovered. You have to make sure that you can supervise the child at every meal, for months or even years if necessary. This requires tremendous effort, patience and commitment, but it will be worth it in the end. If you think about it, parents whose children develop other illnesses, such as diabetes, also need to make significant life-style changes to ensure that their child's health is preserved as much as possible. A diabetic child may not understand that having sweet things is dangerous for him or her, but the parents have to make sure that he or she can learn this safely over time, even if it takes years. With anorexia, the principles are the same: the child needs to re-learn that having regular meals and maintaining a healthy weight is fine. The difference between the two illnesses is that children with type-1 diabetes have no chance of full recovery. They have to learn to manage the illness, without ever having the hope of a life without it. So, in this sense, parents of young people with anorexia have much more to hope for. It may feel sometimes that change takes forever, but at least it can happen.

Parallel to the weight restoration, it is important to help sufferers reclaim their lives from the clutches of anorexia. Having fun with friends and family outside of mealtimes can show them that there are worthwhile things in life as opposed to weight loss. Fun and enjoyment also improve self-esteem, and reduce isolation and perfectionism. However, it is important to consider the type of activity depending on the degree of malnutrition, the energy intake and the energy expenditure. For this reason, parents need to be creative with building up fun again in their child's life. Initially, these activities will need to be sedentary to keep the energy expenditure low. But there are many things you can do together such as read stories, play board games or cards, make crafts, play or listen to music, go to the cinema, and so on. Later on, you can introduce more physical activity, such as shopping, walks in the fresh air, going to the zoo or to the seaside. When the child's weight is within a healthy range, low impact sports can be re-introduced, such as swimming, walking, dancing and some team games. High impact sports are better delayed for 12 months after weight restoration, to allow bones to rebuild, and to reduce the risk of fractures.

Sometimes parents desperately want to please their child in the hope that they can cheer him or her up, and end up giving into anorexic demands, such as excessive exercise, a fat-free diet and so on. Always try to think about the long-term consequences: the longer your child remains malnourished and underweight, the more likely it is that he or she will remain miserable and chronically ill. That would be a tragic outcome. Do not panic if your child gets upset when his/her diet is increased. It is important to respond in a calm and reassuring way. You should acknowledge the distress, but should not give into it. If you had a toddler who was ill, but refused a medicine, you would find a way of ensuring that he or she accepted it because otherwise the problem would get worse. Food is medicine for a person with anorexia. Without increased food intake, there is no chance of recovery. It does not matter if it is not enjoyable to start with; it will improve a few months later.

There are other ways of cheering up a child rather than by agreeing with demands driven by anorexia. If you can identify certain psychological maintaining factors, such as perfectionism, low self-esteem or a highly competitive environment, it is important to address these in parallel to the weight restoration. It is surprising how many parents feel powerless to help their children with these psychological problems, simply because of being afraid of doing something 'wrong'. Try to trust your common sense. Siblings can often be very helpful in generating ideas on how to help a struggling youngster start to feel better.

Helping adults

Helping adults can be even more challenging for family members. One of the main reasons for this is that adult sufferers tend to live alone, so you may not realise early enough how serious the problem is, and even when you do, you are not with them for a sufficient amount of time to intervene. If you are worried about a grown-up child, or a partner, the first and most important thing you can do is to explain to him or her as calmly as possible that you are worried that he or she might have a serious eating disorder, such as anorexia nervosa. The chances are that the sufferer already knows this, so open acknowledgment of the problem can be a relief. It helps to motivate them to change if you can be specific and can identify the negative consequences of the illness with them instead of focusing on weight and shape only. Most sufferers believe that they are fat, so arguing about weight is futile, and it can even worsen anorexic preoccupations. However, they can recognise that something is wrong. It is likely that they have some symptoms, such as irritability, feeling cold, having dry skin, experiencing hair loss, being unable to think about anything else apart from food or weight and shape, or losing interest in love and sex. It is important to choose a time when everybody is relatively calm (outside of mealtimes). Sharing information about anorexia, such as reading this book, can help to address denial, and it can be the first step towards recovery.

When people become ill, they often regard anorexia as a glamorous problem. It is important to help them understand that this could not be further from the truth.

It is useful to check the person's weight and height and do the calculations together, rather than just relying on some figure from the past. The level of weight loss can inform both of you of the risks, and this information is important for treatment decisions. You can also encourage the person to think about the consequences of the illness as discussed above.

As previously emphasised, family members can be very influential in motivating the sufferer to change. However, when you try to help someone with anorexia, it is important to think about the relationship between the two of you. You need to have a strong and trusting relationship in order to be able to help effectively. Without this, perhaps the best thing you can do is to encourage the sufferer to take the plunge and seek professional help. At the same time, do not underestimate the strength of family bonds. Parents remain important for people even when they are grown up. Furthermore, people with anorexia often lose their relationships with everyone else. For this reason, parents often remain the only people close enough to help an adult with anorexia.

If you are a partner, offering help may be even more challenging. Perhaps you could start talking about the impact the eating disorder is having on your relationship. The chances are that you are both unhappy, but the eating disorder is making things worse instead of helping. This is similar to living with a partner with an alcohol problem. In both conditions, the unaffected partner can initiate change for the better, but success often depends on the quality of the relationship. If the sufferer feels that the only way to keep the relationship alive is by self-starvation, the motivation to change will be low.

At present, research evidence regarding helping an adult is very limited, but Professor Treasure's team at the Maudsley Hospital has started working on this issue with carers. In some ways, this work is revolutionary as it goes against the orthodoxy of traditional adult psychiatric practices, which emphasise individual responsibilities. Many years ago, Professor Russell's team carried out a small randomised controlled trial comparing individual and family therapy for anorexia nervosa. In that study, family therapy was helpful for adolescents, and individual therapy was more beneficial for adults.[24] After this trial, research with families of adult anorexia sufferers stopped for decades. In fact, some adult mental health services still advocate that it is helpful to exclude the family from the treatment. Apart from some exceptional cases, this does not make any sense. If talking therapies with professionals can be helpful, then surely, talking to loved ones can be too. There is no 'magic' that professionals may deliver which cannot be learnt by anyone. This does not mean that you should become the therapist, but you can learn new perspectives and pick up ideas about how best to help. Professor Treasure's new approach is based on this principle.[25]

Most psychological interventions with adults focus on the motivation to change and therefore address the maintaining factors of the illness. This is the same with adolescents, but the emphasis of treatment is more on the individual. As emphasised before, improving motivation to change has always been a task for the family and friends.

Addressing denial and fear gently complement each other when helping someone with anorexia. Denial is often maintained by fear as it is easier to deny the problem than face the reality that you have developed a severe mental illness. Overcoming anorexia is difficult because the fear is related to food, and the resulting starvation impairs the normal functioning of the brain. However, people with anorexia nervosa know that it is not normal to be afraid of eating. The problem is that when someone is ill with anorexia they believe themselves to be fat, and although they are hungry, they are terrified of eating. Encouragement from the family can be very helpful in overcoming these fears. Professor Treasure's team compare this approach of caring to the behaviour of a dolphin, which nudges you in the right direction until you are safe.[19]

Discuss with the sufferer how best you might help. This may require as little as accompanying the person to appointments with the doctor, or as much as monitoring his/her diet and ensuring he/she can finish all meals. Think about maintaining factors, because they can give you the key to achieving change. Talk to other people openly about potential maintaining factors to get an outside perspective. Sometimes it is difficult to see the obvious if you are too close to a problem.

If the person is ready to change, you can offer support regarding his/her dietary intake and energy expenditure, and decide on how to achieve a positive energy balance. If at all possible, it helps to eat together, rather than leaving the person on his or her own. Eating is a social activity, and joint meals can promote normalisation of eating behaviours. If this is not possible, it may be better to encourage the sufferer to seek professional help, but you can still remain in a supportive role.

It is also important to prepare yourself for a long haul. It takes a long time to recover from starvation, and even longer from anorexia. Do not expect miracles, but keep the hope alive. People with anorexia can get better, even if it sometimes takes years. In chronic cases, it may be more realistic to try improving the person's quality of life. By doing so, you may also be able to increase his/her motivation to change over time.[26]

What is a healthy diet?

Anorexia distorts people's views about healthy eating, and family members are often sucked into this logic. In modern times, people often associate a healthy diet with eating mainly fruit, vegetables and low fat foods, but they ignore the importance of healthy fats and portion sizes. Whilst the majority of the population in the West eat too much, anorexia sufferers eat too little over time. This may be stating the obvious, but patients and carers often miss this simple truth. Having five portions of fruit and vegetables is healthy as a part of a mixed diet, but desperately unhealthy without anything else. The quantity needed to maintain healthy weight is dependent on the age, gender, individual metabolic rate and the level of physical activity of the person in question. People can eat too much or too little of the same foods, resulting in weight gain or loss accordingly. There are very good public information websites that can help you to understand the balance between healthy diet and activity for different age groups. These include the US Department of Agriculture (USDA)   http://www.cnpp.usda.gov/MyPyramid-breakout.html and the Food Standard Agency's website in the UK, http://www.eatwell.gov.uk. Many other countries have similar resources, which can be very helpful if you need to check things.

Historical information from famines suggests that if the average daily intake is below 2000 kcal per day for several months, a semi-starvation state develops in the population. If the average intake is less than 1500 kcal, mortality increases. Diets below 1000 kcal have been described in only a few extreme situations in wars, such as in the Warsaw ghetto and during the Dutch and Stalingrad famines.[27] These were associated with high levels of mortality and other consequences decades after recovery, such as heart disease. These studies provide evidence that a diet of around 2000 kcal per day is necessary for maintaining normal weight for most adult women who are not particularly active. On average, men need about 500 kcal per day more than this. The energy requirements of adolescents are usually higher than those of adults, because they tend to be more active and because they need extra energy for growth and development. For weight restoration, there needs to be an excess energy intake on top of this, approximately 500 kcal per day extra depending on the level of activity.

A healthy diet needs to be mixed and sufficient in quantity (depending on whether you are at the stage of trying to return to a healthy weight or to maintain it). Many patients follow a special diet because of their illness, vegetarianism being one of the most common, mainly for its lower calorie content. The over-representation of vegetarianism in anorexia is interesting. Biologically, human beings are not herbivores like sheep or cows. There are essential nutrients we can obtain only from animals. Western vegetarians, and in particular teenagers, often have an insufficient intake of various essential nutrients, such as vitamin B12, zinc, calcium, omega-3 fatty acids, and vitamin D in Northern countries if there is insufficient exposure to the sun.[28] Certain proteins, particularly essential amino-acids, can be mainly found in protein of animal origin. For example, turkey and chicken meat both have high tryptophan content. This amino-acid is an important building block of serotonin, a neurotransmitter which has a role in sleep and positive mood.

Deficiencies in various essential nutrients can contribute to the stunting of children and to various mental health problems, such as low mood. These are the reasons why strict vegetarian diets are unlikely to be healthy. Fortunately, many 'vegetarians' eat eggs, cheese or even fish. This semi-vegetarian diet is nutritionally much better than a strict vegan diet.

If people insist on remaining vegetarian whilst trying to recover from anorexia, it is important to consult a dietician, so that no essential nutrients are missed out. There is also good quality information available from reputable websites, such as http://www.dietitians.ca/news/downloads/Vegetarian_Food_Guide_for_NA.pdf.

It is also essential to bear in mind that a healthy diet includes around 25% to 35% of calories in the form of dietary fats, and not 0%. Until recently, experts encouraged people to eat less fat. However, new research suggests that dietary fat intake is important. This changed understanding was supported in 2006 by a study of about 49,000 women, which showed that a low-fat diet did not significantly reduce the women's risk of heart disease or cancer.[29]

Apart from providing energy and helping to keep portion sizes at a manageable level, dietary fats also provide various essential nutrients, like fat-soluble vitamins, and essential fatty acids. Trans-fatty acids (hydrogenated oils) are best excluded from the diet, and hopefully they will be banned in most countries in the next decade or so. In contrast, cold-pressed natural oils, nuts and dairy products are all beneficial.

The inclusion of omega-3 fatty acids in the diet can help to improve mood during weight restoration, and hence facilitate recovery. The American Heart Association recommends four 3 oz (85 g) servings of oily fish weekly, or fish oil capsules, as part of a healthy diet.[30] Including sushi, Mediterranean or Caribbean foods in your weekly menu can help you to achieve this.

Of course, too much of a good thing can also be harmful. Excessive meat or fat intake, such as in the Atkins diet, is equally unhealthy. As a general principle, a healthy diet needs to be varied and mixed, and include sufficient amounts of proteins and fats, not just carbohydrates and plant-based foods. Large population-based studies have repeatedly shown the health benefits of the Mediterranean diet. This research was also led by

Ancel Keys after he finished the Minnesota study. He practised what he preached by personally following a Mediterranean diet and he went on to live to the age of 100 years. The Mediterranean diet is high in fruit and vegetables, but, in contrast to popular myths, it is not low in fats or carbohydrates. The consumption of olive oil and various nuts is high in the countries concerned. The consumption of red meat is about once or twice a week, which is less than in the current Western diet.

It is important to find a way of re-introducing a healthy diet as soon as possible when you are trying to recover from anorexia, or help someone else with the illness. Research has shown that the outcome of the illness is worse if the diet range remains limited.[31] There are a number of reasons for this, including the avoidance of certain foods thus maintaining the fears associated with eating, but there is also a possibility that the resulting chronic nutritional deficiencies are harmful to the brain and nervous system.

Weight restoration

Patients and carers are often uncertain what weight to aim for. If you reflect on the Minnesota study, the answer is clearly full weight (BMI 20-25 in adults). Without full weight restoration, people remain preoccupied with food and weight as the body continues to send messages to the brain that it needs more nourishment. The return of normal thinking and emotional functioning takes even longer, until the body can feel relaxed that the starvation has passed. The healthy body weight range in adults is between a BMI of 20 and 25 in most populations, and this is approximately equivalent to 90-110% weight-for-height ratio for children.

There is good evidence from epidemiological studies that this range is associated with the most health benefits, BMI 22-22.5 being ideal for health.[32-34]

Some regard an 'ideal weight' as a subjective view: whatever the person feels happy with. The trouble is that anorexia is often associated with body-image distortion, which means that sufferers see themselves as being much bigger than they actually are. So, when overwhelmed by anorexia, people want an 'ideal weight' that is incompatible with normal functioning and thus maintains the illness. Sometimes family members go along with the sufferer's wishes and accept an unhealthily low weight because they cannot cope with his or her emotional distress.

If this is happening in your family, remember to compare the situation to one where you are trying to help somebody who has just been diagnosed with diabetes. Would it be helpful to agree for her to have cakes because she wants them? If you agreed, you would only hasten disability and premature death. So, it is much more helpful for the family to take the long-term perspective and help the person to make the necessary adjustments to the illness. The principles are the same when helping people with anorexia. If you make unhelpful compromises, which contribute to your loved one remaining underweight, you unwittingly reinforce the maintenance cycle of the illness. It is important to remind each other that a person remains in a state of chronic starvation for as long as he or she is still clinically underweight, and this maintains anorexic preoccupations. The brain is part of the body, so the body needs to change before there is any chance of positive changes in mental functioning. You cannot let anorexia dictate what is a healthy weight because it will give you a distorted view and a dangerous answer.

It is helpful to find objective measures of health rather than relying on what anorexia is telling you. Apart from aiming for a BMI between 20 and 25, regular periods are good objective signs of healthy weight for women after puberty. The equivalent for men is the return of sexual feelings and functions. Physical health is important for most sufferers; they very rarely want to damage their brain, heart or fertility, and they are troubled by other problems such as dry skin or hair loss.

In my clinical experience, for the majority of young people a minimum of 95% weight for height ratio is necessary for the restoration of normal physical functioning, including the return of periods or being able to catch up with growth and development. In adults, this is approximately equivalent to a BMI of 20. Often when patients first hear this information they are horrified, because they believe this would be 'too big'. In fact, this is a slim but healthy body with a lovely 'hourglass' figure in young women (as a result of normal hormonal levels). It is important to bear in mind though that rebuilding muscles and bones will take longer than weight restoration. As explained before, the body initially stores energy as fat tissue, and this can be anxiety-provoking for the sufferer. Give yourself time; this is a temporary phenomenon. The body will rebuild itself with time just as a result of normal activity.

How to do it

As emphasised before, weight restoration is easier and quicker to achieve if it starts as early as possible. The longer people are starved, the more overwhelmed they become with anorexic thoughts, and the more frightened they become of food and any weight gain. Starvation in anorexia is like going down in quicksand. You are unlikely to be able to come out of it without help; you need someone to pull you out. You will be more likely to accept help from a person you can trust. Therapists emphasise the importance of the quality of the therapeutic relationship, motivation and engagement. However, good and helpful relationships are not exclusive to professionals. Family therapists emphasise the importance of families pulling together in a crisis to help the person with anorexia. It is extremely rare for family members not to want to help, and they usually have good enough relationships with the sufferer to be able to do so. Close relatives also have the advantage of knowing the person best, and can remember good times before the illness took hold. They are also around much more than any professional can be, and they are part of the sufferer's life in the long term. Your relationship with your family is much more important than with any mental health professional, regardless of how good or experienced they are.

The main advantage of talking to professionals is that they are neutral and they should not get angry or upset if things do not go well. Eating disorder specialists also have the knowledge and experience to monitor risks, and to explore options for progress with you if things get stuck. They can also be helpful if family relationships are strained for whatever reason. However, most of these skills can be learnt.

Knowing yourself and your family relationships, you can make a judgement whether it is best to involve professionals or not. Over the remainder of this chapter I will discuss how to achieve weight restoration at home. I will explain the professional treatment options in the next chapter. However, the principles of weight restoration are the same regardless of treatment setting.

If someone is severely underweight, or if he or she has been losing weight rapidly at a rate of more than 1 kg per week, it is safer to build up the diet in a gradual way, perhaps over 2-4 weeks, to prevent any complications. For example, one could start with a diet in the first week of about 500 kcal per day more than the diet the patient has been on before starting treatment. In the worst cases, if the sufferer has been allowing herself only about 500-600 calories per day, weight restoration in the first week should start with about 1000-1200 kcal per day. This can be recommended only for a few days, as having a diet at this level would be dangerously low. During the second week, the diet could be increased to 1500-1800 kcal per day, and later (depending on the rate of weight restoration) the diet could be increased further. Although having 1500-1800 kcal per day is a weight loss diet for a normal adult, severely malnourished people, particularly children, may be able to put weight on with this for a few weeks, until their metabolic rate returns to normal.

After a few weeks, most people require a minimum of 2500-3000 kcal per day for weight restoration, depending on their gender and activity levels. Men require more energy than women. As mentioned before, about 500 kcal extra calories a day are needed for weight gain of 0.5 kg per week. This is almost impossible to achieve without the introduction of higher energy density foods (that is, foods which include sufficient dietary fats), such as olive oil, nuts or ice cream in the diet. Some experts suggest the temporary use of high-energy drinks, such as Fortisip, Ensure and so on. In my experience, this can reinforce anorexic behaviours and identity. For example, it is much more normal to have a piece of cake, a smoothie or a small bag of nuts or a cereal bar at break-time in school or at work with your friends than having to disappear somewhere on your own to drink a medically prescribed supplement.

It is important to find a way of achieving weight restoration that fits in with your social life and can be maintained in the long run. Nobody wants to exist on artificial supplements forever. Dietary intake can be adjusted according to weight gain, so you can learn from experience what your body needs to achieve between 0.5 and 1 kg per week.

It is beneficial to introduce meals every few hours, because this helps to provide regular energy supply for the body, and for a starving person it is easier to digest smaller, but frequent meals. This is particularly important after severe weight loss, as by this time the body's reserves are exhausted. Having three main meals and three snacks (including one before bedtime) is the best way of managing this. This also helps to prevent bingeing, and is a helpful way of breaking the vicious circle of bingeing and vomiting.

Most people without an eating disorder snack regularly, without necessarily being consciously aware of it. Just a couple of biscuits with tea, or just one small chocolate bar here and there between meals goes unnoticed, but they add up to the daily dietary intake. People with anorexia do not do this spontaneously, so the snacks need to be planned as part of the diet. Specialists usually recommend three snacks (morning, afternoon and night) in addition to the three main meals. During the first week or two it is sufficient if the snack is just a piece of fruit like an apple or an orange, or a glass of fruit juice, but later on it needs to change to something more substantial, such as a small chocolate bar, a muffin, a smoothie, a small packet of nuts, a couple of biscuits, or a packet of low-salt crisps. The choice is down to individual preference, but having real food is usually nicer, and it is more normal.

In the UK it is difficult to access dieticians through the NHS. As an alternative, you could consider using one of the nutritional software products on the market. Ideally, it is better if carers use these as an aid, as there is a risk that the patient will become obsessively dependent on them, and will become worried about minute differences in calories. However, this decision needs to be taken jointly with the patient. Many sufferers obsessively count calories but have no idea about anything else, so learning the nutritional value of foods including vitamins and other essential nutrients may be helpful for them to start seeing the bigger picture. It is also important to understand that normal eating does not mean that people have to eat exactly the same calories every day. In fact, it is helpful to introduce variation as early as possible to help normalise eating. We all eat different things day by day. It is the average energy balance over time that is important.

Using dietary supplements during weight restoration can be helpful if the person is severely underweight. In my own clinical practice, I often use zinc, multivitamin, thiamine and omega-3 supplements (depending on the patient's dietary intake before treatment). However, these can only help in addition to and not instead of a balanced mixed diet.

There are a few examples of sample menu plans in the appendix. These are just for guidance. It is important to include a variety of foods that fit in with your family's traditions and lifestyle. People with anorexia are often afraid of certain foods and exclude them from their diet, but this avoidance makes their fears of normal foods worse. For this reason, it is also essential to exclude 'diet foods' from the very beginning. Many of these are nutritionally quite poor anyhow. Fat-free foods, for example, are usually high in sugars. It is much better to use fresh foods, cooked at home if at all possible. There are plenty of good cookbooks for busy families, catering for all tastes.

It is useful to chart weight restoration regularly, with clear expectation of a consistent weight gain week by week. Current UK guidelines recommend about 0.5-1 kg of weight gain per week if treatment is at home. The Minnesota study showed that if people can eat as much as they want during weight restoration, they put on about 1.5 kg per week without any problems. Although most anorexia sufferers would prefer a slower rate because they can become very anxious about any weight gain, the longer the weight restoration takes, the longer the time is to recovery. So, there is a trade-off: quicker weight restoration may be more anxiety-provoking in the short term, but it also shortens the time to recovery.

Keeping a weight chart can also help to challenge some of the anorexic fears, such as putting on a large amount of weight by eating certain foods (chocolate, etc). Nutritional software packages and smart-phone applications provide this automatically. It is also helpful to agree on how to monitor weight restoration. Most specialists recommend 1-2 weighing days per week depending on progress. This can be done at home, preferably with someone else, or at the doctor's surgery. Obsessive weighing every day is unhelpful as it is can reinforce anorexic preoccupations. You need to be aware that there are significant fluctuations during the day (as much as 2 kg) and that there is about 2-5% variation between scales. So it is helpful to use the same scales, and the same time of the day.

Usually the first few weeks of weight restoration are very difficult for the sufferer, and it is useful to prepare everyone for this and agree in advance how best to support the person during this time. It cannot be emphasised enough that during weight restoration, depression and irritability often get worse initially. Furthermore, it takes more than six months for mental symptoms to normalise even after full weight restoration and maintenance. This is important to know in advance if you start feeling worse initially; this is not a sign that you are doing anything wrong. You will get better with time as your physical health improves. Think of it as similar to giving up smoking. When people stop smoking, they may become more irritable than before, and they do not necessarily feel better straight away. It is important to persist.

It may also be helpful to compare recovering from anorexia to training an unfit person for a marathon. Both require motivation, determination and dogged perseverance. If you were training for a marathon, you would expect it to be difficult, sometimes painful, and you would need to remind yourself of the long-term goal when things get tough. Otherwise, you would not succeed. You would also need your friends and family to support you, to keep up your spirits and motivation.

Having meals with the family can help to prevent anorexic temptations. People's eating behaviour is very much influenced by social clues, and by others around them. It is important to have an agreement on this in advance, so there are no surprises at mealtimes. Supporting someone with an eating disorder through mealtimes can be a challenging task. Family members are more likely to succeed, if they can agree with the sufferer what approach is the most helpful. It is important that the person feels listened to and can make positive choices. It is also essential to recognise anorexic traps and not to fall into them.

Anorexic traps

'I am not hungry.'
'I do not like this.'
It is perfectly fine for people without an eating disorder not to eat when they are not hungry, or only to eat things they like. However, when people are ill with anorexia, their appetite regulation and their enjoyment of food are impaired, and these take a long time to return to normal. Furthermore, weight restoration is possible only if people achieve a positive energy balance, meaning that the person needs to eat more than others who do not need to regain weight. It is important to acknowledge that this is neither easy, nor pleasurable for the sufferer, but it is absolutely essential for recovery.

It is important for carers not to give in, nor to put a meal off when these arguments are used. Do not try to make a different meal as a desperate attempt to please, as this will not be liked either, and it will just waste everyone's time and escalate conflict. Whatever else you offer will trigger further anxiety, prolonging the amount of time spent trying to eat, instead of finishing a meal and being able to move on to something else less stressful and not food related.

It can help to say things that you might say to a sick child:
'I know that you are not hungry, my darling, but it is really important that you finish all your meals, and we stick to the plan.'
Or:
'I am sorry that you do not like this right now. Try to think of food as the medicine that will help you get better. There was a time when you used to be able to enjoy your food like anyone else. It is important that you will get there again.'

Or:

'I understand that this is very difficult for you now, but it will get better over time if you keep on persevering.'

Most people with anorexia find this approach helpful.

'This is too much.'

Patients with anorexia are terrified of weight gain, so any amount of food will be seen as 'too much'. Even when the person agrees to weight restoration, learning to deal with an increased diet can be very difficult because of this fear. You and your family need to find a way that works best to manage this anxiety. It will get better with time and practice. Usually, planning the meals ahead jointly and reviewing the amounts regularly according to weight gain helps. Anorexic fears of portions sizes can be overcome only by testing it out, as if you were doing an experiment. If you do not have the option to access regular dietetic advice, you can use cookbooks to check portion sizes and calorie content of foods, or try nutritional/diet software. In my experience, diabetic cookbooks tend to be quite useful in anorexia. This is because most people with anorexia are terrified about having too much sugar or fats. Using a cookbook written for people with diabetes can be helpful in alleviating these anxieties, and they usually have sensible advice about portion sizes and tend to emphasise healthy eating. They also often include meal plans for the week, but you need to adjust the portion sizes required to achieve weight restoration. As described before, during weight restoration the diet needs to be built up gradually, week by week (usually by an extra 500 kcal per day), until a consistent weight gain of around 0. 5 kg or 1 lb per week is achieved. So, you can agree to check weight changes if the diet is increased by 500 kcal a day, and then use the information as evidence for future plans to complete weight restoration.

Writing down the meal plan in a diary for the week ahead can be a practical aid for everybody to manage fears relating to portion sizes, and helps to prevent conflict at mealtimes. This requires significant commitment and changes to the family's routines. Families often complain about losing the flexibility around mealtimes when somebody develops anorexia. This is certainly the case during weight restoration, but joint planning and routines can be helpful in taming the anxiety that maintains anorexia. Think of it as somebody needing crutches after breaking a leg. It will not be necessary forever (in the case of anorexia, probably about a year or so – if the weight restoration goes well).

'This is too fatty.'
'I don't want any oil or butter in my food; they are unhealthy.'
Most anorexia sufferers have fat-phobia, so they will be worried about the fat content of foods. Some insist on making sure that foods are prepared without any oils or fats, causing arguments before mealtimes. It can be helpful to check healthy eating guidelines together from reputable websites, such as the US Department of Health (http://www.health.gov/dietaryguide-lines/dga2005/document/pdf/DGA2005.pdf) or the Food Standards Agency in the UK (http://www.eatwell.gov.uk/). As explained before, a healthy diet includes 25-35% of calories from fats (including about 20 g of saturated fat for adult women and 30 g for men). Although these guidelines are aimed at overweight or obese people, they can be helpful for patients with anorexia, as they make it clear that we all need significant amounts of fats in our diet, even when people are trying to lose weight. Most patients understand that there are healthy fats. These include poly-unsaturated and mono-unsaturated fats, such as olive and almond oil, nuts and oily fish. Butter, cream and chocolate in moderation can also be part of a healthy diet. In contrast with popular beliefs, these do not contain 100% saturated fats, and can be a good source of fat-soluble vitamins and various other essential nutrients. However, it is important to avoid hydrogen-ated fatty acids (or trans-fatty acids). In some countries, these are

already banned, but not in the UK or in the US. Hydrogenated fats are mainly found in processed foods, spreads, and various shop-bought cakes and biscuits. These days, most supermarkets offer alternatives, but you need to keep your eyes open to find them. It is also beneficial to keep the omega-3 and -6 consumption balanced, so try not to use too much corn, soy or sunflower seed oil. More information is available from Dr Simopolous's book, *The Omega Diet*.[35]

'I cannot eat in front of other people.'
Eating alone is highly likely to maintain abnormal eating habits (food restriction, bingeing and vomiting). However, it is important to acknowledge that eating in front of others can provoke intense anxiety for anorexia sufferers. They often worry that other people will judge them in a negative way, such as being too greedy or fussy, or that they will have to eat more than they want (this is particularly the case with children). To avoid having to eat with others, sufferers can find numerous excuses. Parents with busy jobs and a relaxed attitude to food often do not notice for quite some time that their adolescent child has stopped eating with the family. It may start with the child skipping breakfast, and saying that he or she has had dinner before the parents come home in the evening, or taking food into the bedroom because of wanting to watch telly.

Remember, one of the maintaining factors of anorexia is isolation. Although it may be anxiety-provoking to eat in front of other people, eating alone is much more likely to result in insufficient dietary intake. It is much more difficult to block out anorexic thoughts on your own. Eating with others also can help to normalise eating behaviours, including the portion sizes, the variation of foods, and the time needed to finish the meal. Anorexia sufferers know that eating with others should be a joyous, social occasion, and if they cannot do this, they are losing out on an everyday social pleasure. Special days of the year can be a stark reminder of this when the sufferer is unable to have a Christmas meal, or a slice of birthday cake to share the celebration. Whilst these situations may be upsetting, they can also challenge the anorexic belief that dietary restriction will bring happiness.

Furthermore, it is impossible to function in life if you are unable to eat with others in school or at work. Because of this, it is important to introduce social meals as early and as often as it is possible. As a first step, this may require significant reorganisation of family routines. You may need to ask everyone in the family to make the commitment to start the day half an hour earlier in order to have breakfast together, or to make sure that everybody sits down at the table in the evenings. It is important to plan for this, so there are no surprises at the table, and the atmosphere can be as pleasant and relaxed as possible.

It is also helpful to remember that it is acceptable for different family members to have different portion sizes. During weight restoration, a person with anorexia needs to eat more than other people who are not underweight. This needs to be managed sensitively in discussion with the sufferer, as they usually struggle to accept this. Different approaches work for different people. Some might choose having the same meal as everyone else, and have additional high calorie nutritional supplements. Others might prefer to have additional snacks, and so on. An open discussion can help you to find a solution that works in your house.

In addition to having family meals in the home, it is also important to help the sufferer overcome his or her fears of eating in public, such as eating in coffee shops and restaurants, or having picnics on trips out. Most sufferers recognise the importance of these tasks as necessary for reclaiming normality in their lives. These may be frightening at first, but with preparation, they can be done. For example, many fast-food chains and restaurants have their menus on the web, so you can plan the meal ahead as part of the daily dietary intake. Start with a relatively easy task such as a snack, and then build it up gradually to help to manage the anxiety of eating in a public place. Success with these challenges can be morale boosting for both the sufferer and the family, and can increase motivation to change.

Compensatory behaviours

Even when the person agrees to an increased diet, anorexia will cause urges to 'compensate'. This means trying to get rid of the extra energy in various forms, such as not quite finishing the meal or subsequent meals, or even refusing to eat altogether for a while, secret (or not so secret) exercise, vomiting or laxative use. These compensatory behaviours are usually driven by a high level of anxiety.

Laxative use

Laxative use is a totally ineffective method of weight control, because it leads only to fluid loss. Large amount of laxatives can also disturb electrolytes in the blood, and this can cause danger-ous heart problems. Most people understand this after an initial explanation, and this usually helps them to stop. If sufferers use large amounts of laxatives, they may need to come off them gradually, because the body can develop a tolerance to these drugs, and severe constipation can develop if they are stopped too suddenly. However, this can be achieved within a few weeks or so.

Excessive exercise

Tackling vomiting and excessive exercise can be more challeng-ing. Let us start with exercise first. Many anorexia sufferers use exercise as a form of weight control, and exercise obsessively, often in secret. When people are severely underweight, strenu-ous activity puts extra strain on the body, resulting in injuries or heart problems. Some patients find any opportunity to exercise, such as fidgeting all the time, cleaning, walking long distances instead of using other forms of transport, or doing exercise at night. This tends to happen when people are seriously unwell, and have little motivation to change. Excessive exercise can maintain anorexia.

Overcoming exercise is very difficult in isolation, so the family have a significant role in helping the sufferer achieve this. One way to do this is to express your concern about the level of exercise and the consequences on the physical health of the person. People who are a healthy weight, or overweight, are advised to walk at least 10,000 steps per day (equivalent to 2-3 miles), or to do at least half an hour of aerobic exercise every day. When people are severely underweight, this level would be too much, as the body desperately needs rest to save energy.

Underweight children should stop doing PE lessons and attending sport groups until their weight is within the normal range. This does not mean that they should not move around at all, but the level of exercise should be kept within normal day-to-day activities, and it should be built up in a gradual way. Gentle walks and swimming can be a good way to start. Swimming can also help to overcome anxieties regarding shape. In public swimming pools you will meet people of all shapes and sizes, and this may help to reduce anxieties around not being perfect. When weight restoration is near completion (above 85% weight for height ratio in children), plan a sensible exercise routine that fits in with the person's, and the rest of the family's, interests. So, if you enjoy badminton or tennis, you can build it up to having two or three lessons per week, but be careful not to introduce high-impact sports early.

Sometimes patients become very anxious when as a result of weight restoration they no longer have a 'fat-free' body. However, it is important not to start exercise too early, as it can become obsessive and maintain the illness. People who develop anorexia whilst engaged in competitive sports usually have a very strong urge to continue exercising. This, on the surface, may appear to be just pursuit of the previous interest, and families often go along with this wish. You need to stop and think before you do. How many successful athletes have anorexia nervosa? Can you win, if your body is not in perfect condition? You will not be any more successful in sports with anorexia than you would be after a serious injury. Your body needs a rest to recover first, and it needs nourishment to cope with the excess demand for energy. Otherwise, you may suffer permanent damage.

You should also bear in mind that anorexia may provide a perfect 'excuse' to stop an activity that has become too stressful. It forces people to re-evaluate previous priorities, so it may signal a desire to change without having to risk feeling a failure. 'Having to stop' competitive sports may come as a secret relief.

Self-induced vomiting

Self-induced vomiting is a dangerous and unpleasant compensatory strategy in anorexia. It is usually associated with intense feelings of guilt, shame, disgust and secrecy. Probably the most important way of helping the sufferer is to break the silence and secrecy. If you are a carer, try to address this by showing care and compassion. A matter-of-fact attitude can reduce shame. You may start by saying:

'I know that sometimes people with anorexia make themselves sick, and I have noticed that you... (disappear to the toilet after mealtimes), which makes me think that this is happening to you. You must feel really anxious about weight gain, if you are having to do this... It can't be very pleasant... I really would like to help you manage this anxiety a different way. What do you think would be helpful?'

Usually, it is helpful to spend some time together after meals, about an hour, or sometimes even longer, in order to be able to break the cycle of vomiting. Doing something together can offer distraction from anorexic urges. It could be anything relaxing that you enjoy doing together, watching telly, playing cards, doing crosswords and so on. This again requires significant change in family routines, and a clear agreement with the sufferer. Otherwise, there is a risk of developing an unhelpful 'cat and mouse game', where the sufferer is trying to hide the compensating behaviours, and the carer is trying to catch him or her out, whilst their relationship is deteriorating. Ultimately, the sufferer will need to learn to take responsibility for this, but a few weeks' support can be helpful as a start.

'Does my bum look big in this?'
'I am too fat!'

Patients often try to seek reassurances about weight and shape from their friends and relatives. The problem is that there is no 'right' answer to this kind of question. Anorexia selectively impairs patients' perception of themselves, so they do not accept reassurances, leading to repetitive questions and resulting arguments. This will just make things worse for everyone. Do not fall into this trap. You can try saying something like: 'I am sorry that anorexia makes you feel that you are fat. This will get better when you recover from the illness. It is not helpful to talk about this all the time. It will just make you more worried. Can we talk about something else?'

Do not try to give false reassurances when the person starts regaining weight. As emphasised before, it takes longer for the body to rebuild muscle, bone and other tissues than to restore fat reserves, so there will be a time during weight restoration when the person does have a relatively bigger tummy or fat percentage than before. This can be seen in starving African children during refeeding, who often have a big tummy and very thin limbs. The solution to the problem is to continue with the weight restoration and gradually build up physical activity. Friends and family can be very helpful in supporting the sufferer, so they do not give in to panic and start losing weight again when this happens. The anorexia sufferer needs to understand that this is a temporary biological response to starvation, and it will resolve after a few months. That timescale can also help him/her to learn to accept and cherish his or her body with its imperfections. This is an important task for recovery. Nobody has (or believes they have) a perfect body. Happiness cannot be found in the mirror.

'You want to make me fat. I hate you!'

All patients with anorexia will use this sentence (in one shape or form) against people who are trying to help them. Whilst it is not nice having to listen to this, it may help you to tolerate these outbursts if you are prepared for them, and do not take them personally. Anyone who is close enough to an anorexic person will get this response from time to time. These outbursts are driven by fear of getting fat, mistrust, and terror of the change that is happening. They do not mean that you are doing anything wrong. In one sense, these outbursts are a good sign; the anorexia sufferer has enough energy to be angry, and has enough trust in the other person that he or she will not be abandoned after the outburst. It should also help to remember that people in the Minnesota study became more irritable during weight restoration. This will pass with time. Try to be patient. Do not respond with panic, and do not give up. Taking the long-term perspective can help everybody to get through.

You need to use your judgement as to how best to manage these situations when they arise, and be prepared to learn from mistakes. It may be helpful to say:

'I am sorry that you feel this way just now. I am trying to help you to recover from anorexia. I understand that it is very difficult for you. It will get better if you persevere.'

Or:

'I am sorry that anorexia makes you so scared and angry. Can we talk about this later, when you have calmed down a bit? We need to find a way to help you through this.'

Do not tolerate physical aggression, or abusive language. Be firm but calm if that happens, and say:

'Stop it. This is unacceptable.'

Ending up in abusive slanging matches can be very damaging, so do not let the situation deteriorate to that level. If it does happen, it may be better to take a break, and sit down together as soon as possible after the incident when you have both calmed down. You both need to be prepared to learn from the incident, and find an agreement on how best to manage distress in the future in a way that is more helpful. One important maintaining factor of anorexia is isolation, and this is often the result of unacceptable behaviours from the patient. Family and friends sometimes give up in the face of sustained hostility and abuse. It is important to bear this in mind, and to find a civilised way of communicating with each other.

However, if the person becomes physically aggressive and you cannot stop her, say that you will call the police, and do so if necessary before someone gets hurt. This may sound like a drastic action, but it is usually very helpful in preventing the aggression from escalating further. Thankfully, this very rarely needs to happen. In the long term, your loved one will appreciate your efforts and determination to help with his or her recovery.

Pitfalls for carers

Blame

Families often search for one explanation and end up blaming themselves or each other for the illness. Mothers are particularly vulnerable to self-blame.[36] Perhaps this is not surprising, as one of the most basic roles of a mother is to feed her child. When the child, regardless of that child's age, does not eat, the mother feels responsible. When trying her best to help does not work, she can easily feel like a failure. As discussed among the factors that maintain anorexia, families are often paralysed with guilt.

Blame can be extremely destructive in a situation that requires trust and dogged effort to change things for the better. It would clearly be an unhelpful waste of time to try and find blame, if someone in your family suffered any other severe illness such as cancer, or an injury. You would need to provide emotional and practical help to survive the crisis, and to help the person recover as much as possible. When reflecting on these examples, it becomes easier to realise that searching for blame in anorexia is unhelpful and futile. It is soul-destroying, leads nowhere, and can draw your energies away from trying to work on getting better.

Do not blame yourself and do not blame the sufferer. Nobody chooses to suffer from anorexia, and nobody can cause it. Sufferers feel extremely guilty anyhow. They feel guilty about eating, about not being able to eat, being greedy, about not being able to achieve their potential, upsetting their loved ones and so on. The last thing they need is to have this guilt confirmed by others blaming them. Tact combined with practical help is a much more useful approach.

Expecting miracles

After the initial denial of the illness, carers often expect some miracle to solve the problem. This could be some new treatment, alternative medicine, homeopathy, finding a famous expert and so on. People sometimes waste a lot of their resources in terms of time, energy and money trying to find a 'miracle' solution. This is a natural reaction. When something bad happens to us, we often wish that a miracle would make the problem go away. If you are religious, praying will help you to keep your strength and hope. The problem is that when the miracles do not happen, people get disheartened, frustrated and angry.

It cannot be emphasised enough that recovery from anorexia takes a long time. It is necessary to complete full weight restoration and to maintain a healthy weight before the anorexic fears can get better. These goals are not easy to achieve. If things do not change quickly, that does not mean that you are doing anything wrong. Just persevere.

Anger

Carers often experience anger. They get cross with the illness, or with themselves, or with the sufferer. Anger is an instinctive reaction arising at a time of crisis, which helps to mobilise the energies needed to protect oneself. Do not beat yourself up about being angry at times.

However, hostility is not helpful for managing anorexia in the long term. It does not solve anything. On the contrary, angry outbursts can contribute to the maintenance of the problems in several ways. They can contribute to the sufferer's poor self-esteem, and reinforce anorexic logic ('Nobody likes me, therefore I must lose more weight'). Angry scenes can also result in the breakdown of personal relationships and increase the sufferer's risk of isolation at a time when family support is crucial. Carers who lose their temper are also more likely to give in to anorexic demands later, in an attempt to repair damaged relationships. Anger also maintains the shame, guilt and secrecy associated with the illness. It can also lead to a breakdown in communication.

This is a particular risk between separated or divorced parents. The chances are that you divorced because you were not happy together for whatever reason. You may both be disappointed about it, but want to move on with your lives and forget about the past, whilst continuing to care for your children. The experience for the children is rather different. Both parents remain important to them. If parents focus their energy on being angry with each other, children end up hurt and rejecting them both, and hence lose the opportunity for family support. Regardless of how hard it is, having a child with anorexia should help you focus on the important things in life and re-evaluate your relationship with your ex-partner as parents. The divorce might have been unfortunate and undesirable, but it did not cause the anorexia. Being angry with each other is not going to solve anything at a time of crisis; you both need to move on. If you can find a way of working together as parents to support your child through recovery from anorexia, this can be tremendously helpful for everyone. Getting a clear and consistent message from both parents is vital.

The first step in learning to manage your anger is to take time and reflect on where this feeling is coming from. If you think about it, you are angry because of the impact of anorexia on your loved one's and your family's life. Anorexia causes immense suffering to the people who have it and to their families. You are angry with the illness and not the sufferer. You would get angry even if you had to cope with any other serious illness, such as cancer. It does not mean that you are angry with the person for being ill.

Try to find ways of managing your anger and frustration, in a way which does not damage your relationship with the sufferer. Family therapists recommend separated family therapy if there is a high level of 'expressed emotion' (angry and critical comments). This provides an opportunity for carers to vent their feelings and help them find alternative solutions without the sufferer having to witness this process. This approach reduces the risk of entering into a vicious circle of anger and blame between family members.

Even if you cannot access this treatment, you can use the same principles, drawing on your own support systems. If you feel angry, it can be helpful to talk to someone about your feelings without the sufferer being present. This could be a family member, such as a grandparent, a friend, professionals, or various self-help groups. In the UK, the B-EAT offers a free telephone helpline for carers.

If you do lose your temper in front of the sufferer, it is better to give yourselves both time to cool down, and reflect on the situation together later. You can say something like this:

'I am sorry that I lost my temper when... It sometimes makes me so angry how anorexia is destroying your life. I was not angry with you, but with the impact of your illness on your life. I want to help you so much so that you can recover. What do you think would be helpful, when...?'

Conflict avoidance and collusion with the illness

Guilt-ridden or frightened family members are often vulnerable to colluding with the illness. This is mainly because they are terrified of upsetting the already upset patient even more by challenging the anorexia. Or, some family members may share the beliefs regarding the importance of a thin or 'fat-free' body. As a result, the anorexic beliefs and behaviours can be reinforced unwittingly. For example, a heated argument about the type of meal, or the size of meal, may result in the family giving in to the patient's wishes just to keep the peace in the short term. Whilst the family may think it is better to have a small amount of food instead of nothing, the person with anorexia interprets their response as being that eating the right amount of food would have been too much, and next time will argue for even less. So avoiding conflict in the short term does not solve anything; it may even make things worse in the long term.

Carers need to be vigilant about potential opportunities for collusion with the illness. Anorexic arguments and behaviours can be deceitful and disguised as something perfectly reasonable. The child may say:

'I had a big lunch at school. I am not hungry.'

Do not fall for this. Remember: anorexia changes people. Even if the person is normally honest and trustworthy, whilst ill with anorexia, food and weight-related behaviours will be driven by the overwhelming desire to lose more weight. It is unwise to trust a person with anorexia about weight-related issues until he or she gets quite well, even if you desperately want to.

The art is to find a way to minimise collusion without getting angry or critical. Joint planning of mealtimes is often the best way to achieve this. It is also helpful to use your support system to find ways of managing the conflict in a helpful way. You can be supportive and challenge anorexia at the same time. It is a question of trial and error and learning from experience, and from each other.

Praise and compliments

Surely praise cannot cause any problems, right? Well, not quite. Carers are often desperate to try to cheer up the sufferer by giving compliments about his or her weight and shape. Do not fall into this trap. This is quite difficult, but important. It is polite and natural to make positive comments about other people's appearance, particularly in the case of young people.

'Oh, you are looking much better!'

'Oh, you have started filling out!'

These comments are perfectly well intended and positive. However, for anorexia sufferers they only confirm their 'enormous' size, and can trigger further dieting and weight loss. It is much better not to comment, or to express, in a calm manner, a concern about their health rather than their weight and shape. Remember, every comment is examined through the anorexic magnifying glass, and will be interpreted differently from how it was intended.

On the other hand, praise of things other than weight and shape can be very helpful. People with anorexia tend to have very poor self-esteem, and a high level of ambivalence towards getting better. So, giving praise about their attempts to tackle their fears by trying new foods, completing meals, meeting friends, or eating out, can encourage them on the way to recovery.

Be careful with praising other achievements though. Many anorexia sufferers become obsessive about achievement and drive themselves to destruction by wanting to be perfect (having top marks, etc) at all times. Saying 'You are the best' to a person struggling with anorexia and poor self-esteem can often backfire. People with anorexia do not feel perfect. Hearing this comment, sufferers, instead of feeling reassured, often respond with increased anxiety believing that they have to be perfect at all times or else people will not love them. If this is a problem in your family, it is better to focus on 'good enough' than perfection, and help the person to find a better balance of fun and achievement in life. We are all imperfect, but that does not mean that we cannot find happiness in our lives.

You can offer praise in a different way, which is more specific: 'I really liked how you...'

Despair and hopelessness

When you try to help someone with anorexia, there will be times when you feel despair and hopelessness. This is often the result of expecting change too quickly, or having to cope with the sufferer's mood swings and hostility during weight restoration.

There are various ways you can cope with this. It is important to learn as much as you can about the nature of the illness and the consequences of starvation, so that you can take the long-term perspective. If you have an expectation of a quick fix, you are more likely to despair when it does not happen. It is also important to avoid isolation, and to use friends and family to support you. You need to look after your own sanity by finding time for fun and positive experiences. You cannot be effective in helping someone with anorexia if you exhaust all of your emotional energy or make unsustainable financial sacrifices (such as giving up a job to become a carer). Sharing the caring role can give you a well-deserved break and an opportunity to recharge your batteries. It is important to give yourself time for this.

Involving professional services can also help. Specialists, who are experienced at working with people suffering from anorexia, can be a useful source of encouragement and advice for carers, who struggle helping their loved ones. Family therapy or carers' support is often part of the treatment on offer.

Martyrdom

It can be difficult to find a balance between providing care and support for your loved one and becoming a martyr, sacrificing your own life and happiness at the altar of anorexia. Martyrdom is more likely to develop if you collude with anorexia, and as a result, both of you end up being trapped in a never-ending vicious circle, becoming increasingly unhappy and resentful.

Think about it. In order to be effective, carers need to lead by example. You need to demonstrate to the sufferer that there is life beyond anorexia. Being able to pursue your dreams and hopes, having fun in your life, including having nice meals, being able to get on with your career, and caring for other family members, all show the person that there are other important things apart from being preoccupied with weight and shape and restricting food intake. Carers need to remain firmly on the ground of reality, and not let themselves be carried away into an abnormal anorexic world.

Martyrdom is difficult to recognise alone; it is usually others who have to draw attention to this problem. It could be a parent, a partner, or even the sufferer, who will tell you that you are trying too hard. Give yourself a break sometimes. You need to remain as calm and strong as possible in order to remain helpful. If you are overwhelmed with worries, it may be useful to seek help for yourself, either from family or self-help groups, or from professionals. Family therapy can be very helpful in addressing this issue if it arises. Remember that allowing the illness to waste your life will not help the sufferer; it will only make the problem worse. It may help to think carefully about how best you can help without sacrificing yourself. This will be dependent on your financial and personal circumstances, and your loved one's age. Looking after a child with anorexia requires very different resources from looking after an adult. With children, providing intensive supervision and clear expectations of change is usually effective, but very time consuming. With adults, the role of the carers is more about improving motivation and offering emotional and financial support. Helping adults can be even more anxiety-provoking than helping children. In either case, you need to think carefully about how you can manage your time and your emotions without getting overwhelmed and exhausted.

Summary

Recovery from anorexia requires determination and commitment from both sufferers and their families. People do not necessarily want to change at first, and unfortunately this is even more likely to be the case if they are seriously unwell due to their starvation. Family and friends can help with providing motivation to change and also with practical support, such as offering joint meals, and staying with the person during and after mealtimes to reduce compensatory behaviours.

There is very limited research on people who do not receive professional help, but population-based epidemiological studies suggest that some people can get better without professional help. Before you make any treatment decision, you need to be aware of the level of risk, and you need to monitor your progress. There are many traps on the way to recovery, but if you are aware of them it is easier to avoid them.

References

1. Ben-Tovim DI, Walker K, Gilchrist P, Freeman R, Kalucy R, Esterman A. Outcome in patients with eating disorders: a 5-year study. *Lancet* 2001; **357(9264)**: 1254-1257.
2. Wade TD, Bergin JL, Tiggemann M, Bulik CM, Fairburn CG. Prevalence and long-term course of lifetime eating disorders in an adult Australian twin cohort. *Australian and New Zealand Journal of Psychiatry* 2006; **40(2)**: 121-128.
3. Woods S. Untreated recovery from eating disorders. *Adolescence* 2004; **39(154)**: 361-371.
4. Keski-Rahkonen A, Hoek HW, Susser ES, Linna MS, Sihvola E, Raevuori A et al. Epidemiology and course of anorexia nervosa in the community. *American Journal of Psychiatry* 2007; **164(8)**: 1259-1265.
5. Nedoschill J, Leiberich P, Popp C, Loew T. www.hungrig-online.de: Results from an online survey in the largest German-speaking internet self-help community for eating disorders. *Praxis der Kinderpsychologie und Kinderpsychiatrie* 2005; **54(9)**: 728-741.
6. Fairburn CG. *Cognitive behaviour therapy and eating disorders.* New York: The Guilford Press; 2008.
7. Mayer LES, Roberto CA, Glasofer DR, Etu SF, Gallagher D, Wang J et al. Does percent body fat predict outcome in anorexia nervosa? *American Journal of Psychiatry* 2007; **164(6)**: 970-972.
8. Hudson JI, Hiripi E, Pope HG, Kessler RC. The prevalence and correlates of eating disorders in the national comorbidity survey replication. *Biological Psychiatry* 2007; 61(3): 348-358.
9. Lesinskiene S, Barkus A, Ranceva N, Dembinskas A. A meta-analysis of heart rate and QT interval alteration in anorexia nervosa. *World Journal of Biological Psychiatry* 2008; **9(2)**: 86-91.
10. Birmingham CL, Gritzner S. Heart failure in anorexia nervosa: Case report and review of the literature. *Eating and*

Weight Disorders – Studies on Anorexia Bulimia and Obesity 2007; **12(1)**: E7-E10.

11. Birmingham CL, Tan AO. Respiratory muscle weakness and anorexia nervosa. *International Journal of Eating Disorders* 2003; **33(2)**: 230-233.

12. Walder A, Baumann P. Increased creatinine kinase and rhabdomyolysis in anorexia nervosa. *International Journal of Eating Disorders* 2008; **41(8)**: 766-767.

13. Birmingham CL, Beumont PJ. *Medical management of eating disorders: A practical hnadbook for healthcare professionals.* Cambridge: Cambridge University Press; 2004.

14. Britt E, Blampied NM, Hudson SM. Motivational interviewing: A review. *Australian Psychologist* 2003; **38(3)**: 193-201.

15. Jones A, Bamford B, Ford H, Schreiber-Kounine C. How important are motivation and initial body mass index for outcome in day therapy services for eating disorders? *European Eating Disorders Review* 2007; **15(4)**: 283-289.

16. Wade TD, Frayne A, Edwards SA, Robertson T, Gilchrist P. Motivational change in an inpatient anorexia nervosa population and implications for treatment. *Australian and New Zealand Journal of Psychiatry* 2009; **43(3)**: 235-243.

17. Prochaska JO, Diclemente CC. Stages and Processes of Self-Change of Smoking – Toward an integrative model of change. *Journal of Consulting and Clinical Psychology* 1983; **51(3)**: 390-395.

18. Nordbo RHS, Psychol C, Gulliksen KS, Psychol C, Espeset EMS, Psychol C et al. Expanding the concept of motivation to change: the content of patients' wish to recover from anorexia nervosa. *International Journal of Eating Disorders* 2008; **41(7)**: 635-642.

19. Treasure J, Smith G, Crane A. *Skill-based learning for caring for a loved one with an eating disorder: The new Maudsley method.* Hove & New York: Routledge; 2007.

20. Dare C, Eisler I, Russell GFM, Szmukler GI. The clinical and

theoretical impact of a controlled trial of family-therapy in anorexia-nervosa. *Journal of Marital and Family Therapy* 1990; **16(1)**: 39-57.

21. Eisler I, Simic M, Russell GF, Dare C. A randomised controlled treatment trial of two forms of family therapy in adolescent anorexia nervosa: a five-year follow-up. *Journal of Child Psychology & Psychiatry* 2007; **48(6)**: 552-560.

22. Eisler I. The empirical and theoretical base of family therapy and multiple family day therapy for adolescent anorexia nervosa. *Journal of Family Therapy* 2005; **27(2)**: 104-131.

23. Anonymous. Anorexia, Maudsley and an impressive recovery: one family's story. *Journal of Paediatrics & Child Health* 2008; **44(1-2)**: 70-73.

24. Eisler I, Dare C, Russell GFM, Szmukler G, leGrange D, Dodge E. Family and individual therapy in anorexia nervosa – A 5-year follow-up. *Archives of General Psychiatry* 1997; **54(11)**: 1025-1030.

25. Treasure J, Sepulveda AR, Whitaker W, Todd G, Lopez C, Whitney J. Collaborative care between professionals and non-professionals in the management of eating disorders: A description of workshops focussed on interpersonal maintaining factors. *European Eating Disorders Review* 2007; **15(1)**: 24-34.

26. Treasure J, Whitaker W, Whitney J, Schmidt U. Working with families of adults with anorexia nervosa. *Journal of Family Therapy* 2005; **27(2)**: 158-170.

27. Keys A, Brozek J, Henschel A, Mickelsen O, Taylor HL. *The biology of human starvation*. Minneapolis: University of Minnesota Press; 1950.

28. Messina V, Melina V, Mangels AR. A new food guide for north American vegetarians. *Canadian Journal of Dietetic Practice and Research* 2003; **64(2)**: 82-86.

29. Couzin J. Women's health – Study yields murky signals on low-fat diets and disease. *Science* 2006; **311(5762)**: 755.

30. Anand RG, Alkadri M, Lavie CJ, Milani RV. The role of fish oil in arrhythmia prevention. *Journal of Cardiopulmonary Rehabilitation and Prevention* 2008; **28(2)**: 92-98.

31. Schebendach JE, Mayer LES, Devlin MJ, Attia E, Contento IR, Wolf RL et al. Dietary energy density and diet variety as predictors of outcome in anorexia nervosa. *American Journal of Clinical Nutrition* 2008; **87(4)**: 810-816.

32. Gu DF, He J, Duan XF, Reynolds K, Wu XG, Chen J et al. Body weight and mortality among men and women in China. *JAMA – Journal of the American Medical Association* 2006; **295(7)**: 776-783.

33. Darmadi I, Horie Y, Wahlqvist ML, Kouris-Blazos A, Horie K, Sugase K et al. Food and nutrient intakes and overall survival of elderly Japanese. *Asia Pacific Journal of Clinical Nutrition* 2000; **9(1)**: 7-11.

34. Visscher TLS, Seidell JC, Menotti A, Blackburn H, Nissinen A, Feskens EJM et al. Underweight and overweight in relation to mortality among men aged 40-59 and 50-69 years – The seven countries study. *American Journal of Epidemiology* 2000; **151(7)**: 660-666.

35. Simopoulos A, Robinson J. *The Omega Diet*. New York: HarperPerennial; 1998.

36. Whitney J, Murray J, Gavan K, Todd G, Whitaker W, Treasure J. Experience of caring for someone with anorexia nervosa: qualitative study. *British Journal of Psychiatry* 2005; **187**: 444-449.

Chapter 7

Treatment options

Asking for help

Asking for professional help is not easy, and in some countries it can also be expensive. If you are a carer, by the time you resort to seeking help, you are probably extremely worried about the health and well-being of your loved one. You will probably have tried various ways to help but without success. You may also be worried that by seeking help you will damage your relationship with your loved one, and that this will just make matters worse. If you are a sufferer, you are probably extremely worried about how professionals might judge you, and what treatment would involve.

Asking for help is easier if you understand the system and have an idea of what might be or should be on offer. By the time patients or their families decide to seek treatment they generally know what the problem is, but the healthcare professionals who meet them for the first time do not. In the UK, health services are organised through general practitioners (GPs), who usually see patients first before referring them on to specialist treatment if this is thought necessary. As mentioned in Chapter 1, individual GPs in the UK do not see many patients with anorexia nervosa and they are able to allocate only a few minutes to each patient. The best way to prevent delay in diagnosis and treatment is to be open and straight with the doctor. Despite the time limitations,

GPs want to be helpful. Therefore, being succinct is important. Perhaps the best way to start is to say simply: 'I believe that I (or my child) am (is) suffering from anorexia nervosa (or an eating disorder).' Then, just explain why you think that this is the case (deliberate weight loss, fear of being fat, changed eating behaviours, physical symptoms, etc), and request a physical examination to assess immediate risk.

It also helps to be aware of the clinical guidelines relevant to your country and these can generally be found on the internet (see Appendix). This should help you to understand what services you can expect when seeking help where you live.

Guidelines: NICE & APA

Several countries have produced guidelines for the assessment and treatment of eating disorders. The most commonly cited are those of the American Psychiatric Association (APA), http://www.psychiatryonline.com/pracGuide/pracGuideChap-Toc_12.aspx and the National Institute of Clinical Excellence (NICE) in the UK, http://guidance.nice.org.uk/CG9/Guidance/pdf/English, but there are also national guidelines in many other countries, including Australia and Finland.

Before reflecting on these, it is important to understand that all guidelines are based on the scientific evidence available at the time the guidelines were published and that they are regularly updated. Unfortunately, the quality of scientific evidence regarding the various treatment options for anorexia nervosa is poor due to a lack of appropriate research studies.[1] The reasons for this are complex.

In modern medicine, 'double-blind randomised controlled trials' are regarded as the gold standard of evidence for treatment effectiveness. This is because in historical times there were far too many harmful practices based on well-intended, but misinformed expert opinions, maintained by respect for medical tradition and charismatic leaders. In recognition of the need for better evidence, by the end of the 20th century, new medications could be introduced only following clinical trials proving that they conveyed more benefit than harm.

The best way to achieve an objective evaluation of a new treatment is to offer two different interventions (one can be a 'placebo' or dummy treatment) to two similar groups of patients, and compare the results. If the groups are the same at the start, then at the end of the trial any difference can be reasonably attributed to the effect of the active treatment. A random allocation of a large number of patients into the groups is the best way to ensure that there are no differences between them to start with.

To avoid bias, ideally neither the patients nor the treating doctors should know who is receiving which intervention. This concealment of the treatment allocation is called the 'blinding' of a clinical trial and it is 'double-blind' when neither the patients nor the treating doctors are aware. Whilst blinding in medication trials is relatively easy, with more complex interventions, such as psychological or inpatient treatments, this is often next to impossible to achieve.

Anorexia nervosa poses additional challenges for clinical trials. Because the risk of mortality is significant, not all patients can be included in randomised trials, as it would be unethical to subject them to additional risk potentially associated with the unknown effects of a new treatment. Furthermore, certain interventions can never be randomised. For example, researchers cannot randomly allocate patients into voluntary and involuntary treatment. This means that there will never be randomised controlled evidence about the pros and cons of starting a treatment against the will of the patient. As a consequence, when making decisions, clinicians have to rely on their judgement of risk, rather than on evidence.

Random allocation of patients can also be undermined if the treatment to be evaluated is widely available. This can be a problem for studies trying to test the benefits of self-help

Chapter 7

materials, or even simple dietary supplements, such as omega-3 fatty acids. Patients randomised to the placebo group in such studies will be tempted to get the active treatment without telling anyone (as they will want to maximise their benefits from participating in the trial), and hence reduce the power of the trial to find a difference.

In addition, anorexia sufferers are often reluctant to participate in trials owing to shame and secrecy concerning their illness. And even if they agree to participate, when things do not turn out as they would like, they may opt out of the randomisation and choose the treatment that is more likely to be successful – or unsuccessful if they are only going through the motions of treatment to appease their families and do not really want to put on weight. Whilst this is understandable, if many participants do this, the ability of the trial to detect any significant differences is undermined. This is what happened in a recent randomised controlled trial that tried to compare the effectiveness of inpatient and outpatient treatments for anorexia (see pages 249-50). Although the researchers were successful in recruiting participants and in persuading them to agree to random allocation, when they were allocated to treatment options they did not like, they changed their minds. Not surprisingly, at the end of the study, the statistical analysis found no difference between the groups, because by that time all groups had had a mixture of treatments.[2]

This research is often quoted as showing that there is no evidence that hospital treatment for anorexia is effective. The truth is not so simple: the trial did not find a difference between outpatient and inpatient treatments because health care professionals, families and patients chose the option that was most appropriate in the individual circumstances, regardless of random allocation, the management of risk being the overriding factor. Having no evidence for a particular treatment is not the same as having evidence of ineffectiveness.

Because anorexia is a rare condition, any randomised controlled trial requires collaboration on a large scale, making this kind of research expensive and time-consuming. Funding for research into anorexia is lagging behind that for more common disorders, such as cancer or heart disease. For these reasons, the number of randomised trials investigating treatment options in anorexia is small, and they tend to have various methodological flaws.[3]

These practical complications explain why the research evidence for anorexia nervosa treatments is so limited.[4] For example, Professor Fairburn's team in Oxford have carried out several large randomised controlled trials regarding the treatment of various eating disorders. However, owing to ethical considerations, patients with anorexia have had to be excluded from most of these studies, so these treatment trials provide evidence mainly for people with bulimia and EDNOS.[5, 6] Some experts have argued that randomised trials are not appropriate for anorexia because of these complications.[3] The only exception is family therapy for young people with anorexia nervosa, which has been tested in several randomised trials.[7, 8]

As a result of these technical difficulties, current clinical guidelines continue to rely on expert opinion based on historical practices in different countries. They therefore differ to some extent. For example, in the US, hospital treatment is recommended if the person is just below 85% weight for height ratio, whilst in the UK, this recommended ratio tends to be much lower.

Most of the other recommendations in the various guidelines are similar. For example, they all emphasise the need for a comprehensive assessment, including information about physical and psychological health, as well as social factors. Weight restoration and psychological interventions are always recommended as part of the treatment. All guidelines advise that parents should be included in the treatment of children and adolescents, and if it is necessary to admit the patient, it needs to be at a commutable distance, so that friendships, education and/or employment can be maintained.

Components of treatment

Assessment

Any treatment plan needs to be based on a thorough assessment of the sufferer's and the carers' specific difficulties and strengths. The NICE guidelines[9] recommend that GPs should take responsibility for the initial assessment and care coordination of patients with anorexia nervosa. This assessment should include physical, psychological and social factors. However, NICE does not comment on the need for additional training and time. The APA guidelines recognise that a full assessment can take several hours, sometimes in more than one setting. This is clearly unrealistic for UK GPs, who generally have 8-10 minutes allocated per individual patient. So the initial assessment can vary a great deal depending on the organisation of healthcare in different countries.

A full *physical* examination can, however, be fitted into 10 minutes, and this can inform you and the doctor about the immediate physical risk, and help you to consider treatment options. The GP should also be able to give you advice regarding the specialist services available where you live. In England, if there are no NHS services available, the GP should also be able to advise you how to access private services. Organisation of healthcare services varies greatly from country to country, and even within the UK, so you need to do your research about the local services on offer. Fortunately, the web is a very useful source of information in this respect (see Appendix).

Weight restoration

The importance of weight restoration is emphasised in all guidelines. Professionals will follow the principles described in Chapter 6 (see page 195). In the UK, it is usually a nurse or dietician who offers detailed help on how to succeed with weight restoration.

Professionals tend to monitor weight re-gain once or twice a week, and the scales will tell them whether or not the dietary intake is sufficient, provided patients are honest and/or not given opportunities for falsifying their progress using concealed weights or water loading. (If falsification is a serious issue, out-patient treatment may not be sufficient.) The rate of expected weight gain is 0.5-1 kg per week, and portion size and types of food need to be adjusted to achieve this. As mentioned earlier, if you are uncertain about the nutritional value of foods, cookbooks or relevant software can be helpful, particularly if you do not have ready access to a dietician.

Dietetic advice is only crucial if the sufferer is severely underweight (for the first few weeks) or has a special diet, such as vegetarianism. It is important that the dietician should be experienced in working with eating disorders, since most specialise in other conditions.

If weight restoration cannot be achieved as a result of out-patient treatment, hospital or day-hospital admission may be necessary.

Psychological interventions

There are three main forms of psychological treatment for eating disorders:
1. individual therapy;
2. family therapy; and
3. group therapy.

In the next sections, I shall focus in the main on individual and family therapy. This is because, although group therapies are widely used in inpatient settings, they tend to vary a great deal. They are also poorly researched, and it is therefore difficult to be certain about the effectiveness of various therapeutic groups. The underlying rationale for group work is that sharing your problems with other people with similar conditions can help to relieve the shame and isolation. However, there is a risk that as a 'side-effect' of group treatment, patients increase their preoccupation with weight and shape due to increased competition within an abnormal peer group. Being part of such a group may also reinforce a pathological identity. This can be seen sometimes with groups designed for alcohol and substance misuse.

Well-designed studies of group treatments are needed in order to explore the balance between the risks and benefits of these therapies. However, it may take years before these studies can be carried out. In the meantime, the best advice for sufferers is that you should use your own judgement concerning the usefulness of group therapy. Some people find it helpful; others do not.

There are various forms of individual therapy used in the treatment of anorexia. The evidence for the effectiveness of any type of individual psychological approach is still limited, although most patients report a preference for talking therapies.[10] Some trials have shown that any psychological intervention is better than nothing at all.[11]

Experts often recommend cognitive behavioural therapy (CBT) or interpersonal therapy (IPT) for adults, on the basis of bulimia nervosa research.[12] However, a recent randomised controlled trial showed that supportive counselling was more effective in anorexia than either of these therapies.[13] There is even less evidence that any specific form of individual therapy in children is effective. Moreover, population-based outcome studies seeking to determine the most effective approach to treatment have found no difference between treated and non-treated patients, and this is a major challenge for specialist services.[14]

However, as I explained before, the lack of evidence for effectiveness is not the same as evidence for lack of effectiveness. As outlined earlier, good quality clinical trials are rare in this patient group. Until further studies are completed, the best advice would be to choose carefully between the available psychological interventions in order to suit your needs.

The US, UK and Australian guidelines differ in the timing and type of psychological interventions they recommend. The APA guidelines recommend 'psychodynamic', or 'psychoanalytic', therapy (see page 236) after weight restoration, whilst the NICE guidelines are non-committal about the type or timing of individual therapy, and emphasise patient or carer preference. The Australian guidelines are upfront, stating that research has not yet unearthed a cure; but, in the main, they recommend supportive counselling or CBT as a second step after nutritional rehabilitation.

If you seek professional help, it is important to discuss with the healthcare provider what options are available for you, and to decide what approach might suit you best. If you feel that the therapy offered is unhelpful, you can discuss it and choose a different approach. I shall explain the various options for individual and family therapy in the next section.

Beware of therapists who 'prefer' to ignore weight and diet when working with people suffering from anorexia. This approach is unlikely to be helpful on its own, as starvation is one of the main sustaining factors of the illness. The chances are that people advocating this approach do not have sufficient experience treating anorexia nervosa. There are also enthusiasts advocating a magic cure for the condition; but bear in mind that there are no quick fixes, so spending time and money on them is wasteful and likely to be disappointing for everyone. If you are uncertain about your therapist's qualifications and experience in helping people with anorexia nervosa, do not be afraid to ask. You would not employ an electrician who lacked appropriate qualifications. The same should apply to mental health professionals.

Individual therapies

As mentioned above, the APA guidelines recommend individual psychotherapy after weight restoration. The main reason for this is that starvation has a negative effect on the brain. People who are severely starved tend to have real difficulty thinking rationally and reflecting on their problems. But while patients are certainly more able to reflect on their illness after weight restoration and to find alternative coping mechanisms, there remains the problem of how best to engage with them during weight restoration. It is important to talk to them in a respectful way, particularly when they are severely malnourished and unable to process information. Most specialists would use supportive counselling at this stage, focusing on building up a therapeutic relationship, and encouraging and praising the patient for the effort he or she is making towards recovery.

It helps you to make informed decisions about your therapy if you understand what is on offer. All individual therapies are based on the principle that talking to a professional about your problem can be helpful. However, the approaches of different schools can be rather different. At present, there is no clear evidence that any particular individual approach is more effective than the others, which explains the differences between various guidelines. Furthermore, there has been little research on how the personal qualities of the therapist, from communication style to gender and personal body size, might affect the success of the therapy. Clinical experience suggests that the quality of the relationship with the therapist is important. And so, if you feel that you are not getting on with a particular therapist, you should seek a change. Far from being rude, it is recognised that a change of therapist can sometimes be helpful. After all, it would be unrealistic to expect to get on with everybody, and experienced therapists understand this.

What is clear is that seeing any properly qualified psycho-therapist consistently is helpful in comparison with seeing a different junior doctor at every visit.[11] If the latter is your experience you should raise this with health services, quoting Dare *et al*'s findings if necessary.

Psycho-education
All guidelines include psycho-education as part of the treatment. This means sharing information about the illness with patients and carers. While this is clearly essential, many patients initially find it difficult to take the information on board, or believe that it does not apply to them. This is partly the result of denial and partly the consequence of the impairment of thinking caused by starvation. Because of this, it is important to revisit the information from time to time. Books can be helpful, as they can be picked up again and again.

As you begin to recover, it will become easier to reflect on the issues relevant to you. It is also crucial to understand what is happening to you, not only in starvation, but also during weight restoration, so that you do not give up before you can start feeling better.

Similarly, carers are in a much better position to help if they are fully aware of the complex issues relating to anorexia. This was confirmed, a few years ago, by a small randomised trial, which found family therapy and family psycho-education to be equally effective in helping young people who have been hospitalised for anorexia nervosa.[15] A larger study (the 'CASIS study') is currently being carried out by Professor Treasure's team at the Maudsley, London, UK, involving carers of patients in all age groups.

Psychodynamic psychotherapy
Psychodynamic (or psychoanalytic) therapy was the first psychological approach to helping people with mental health

problems, and was very popular during the 20th century. This form of therapy is long term and non-directive. Therapists see the patient at least once a week and sometimes up to five times a week. They listen and occasionally offer interpretations of the themes presented by the patient. There is often an emphasis on linking the past and the present, and on learning from patterns of relationships over time (including the relationship with the therapist). Not eating enough is interpreted as a way of communicating distress.

Psychodynamic therapy does not offer any advice regarding eating and dietary intake (hence the US recommendation to use such therapy after weight restoration has been completed). Some adult specialist inpatient services in the UK use a psychodynamic approach in addition to intensive nursing supervision of dietary intake. This is obviously not possible on an outpatient basis. In relation to the treatment of anorexia nervosa, there is some evidence to suggest that, in its effectiveness, psychodynamic psychotherapy is comparable to other psychological treatments.[11] No trial has shown it to be superior to alternative treatments.[16]

Motivational approaches

The importance of motivation was explained in Chapter 6. Motivational interviewing techniques have been promoted as the best way to engage anorexia sufferers with psychological work. This is because they are often reluctant to change. The approach consists of a gentle exploration of the pros and cons of the illness, with the therapist trying to help the patient to recognise the problems and to encourage him or her to make a commitment to change.

Generally, a higher level of motivation is associated with better outcomes.[17] However, with the lack of randomised trials into the clinical effectiveness of motivational therapy for anorexia, it is difficult to know whether this is the result of intervention, or simply because some patients are more motivated to get better than others.

Some studies have shown that anorexia sufferers are more resistant to change than patients with bulimia or EDNOS, possibly due to their low weight and the effects of starvation on the brain.[18, 19]

Despite the lack of robust evidence, motivational enhancement makes instinctive sense, and it is acceptable to sufferers. The few studies available on the subject have reported short-term benefits from motivational work, but further research is needed.[20]

Cognitive behavioural therapy

During the past 10 to 20 years there has been significant research focusing on cognitive behavioural therapy (CBT) for eating disorders, based on its success in bulimia nervosa.[21] CBT is concerned with the factors that maintain the condition once it has become established. By focusing on the link between thoughts, feelings and behaviours, it aims to challenge thoughts and behaviours in order to achieve a positive change in feelings, and therefore break the maintenance cycle.

CBT has been used successfully in the treatment of a number of disorders, including depression, obsessive compulsive disorder (OCD) and various anxiety disorders. Professor Fairburn has recently completed a large randomised controlled trial on the use of focused and enhanced CBT for eating disorders, with positive results. Unfortunately, most patients with anorexia were excluded from this trial (average BMI at the start was 22).[5] However, the treatment was effective for patients with EDNOS or bulimia. Further work on lower-weight patients is under way. In Professor Fairburn's view, CBT is useful for all patients with eating disorders, regardless of the diagnosis. Although the randomised controlled trial evidence is still limited, there is a possibility that this approach will also be helpful in anorexia, as long as patients are well enough to be able to engage in the therapy. The jury is out as to whether starting CBT before weight restoration is complete can be equally effective. My clinical experience is that this is rarely the case, but it can sometimes happen.

Cognitive-analytical therapy

Cognitive-analytical therapy (CAT) is recommended by the NICE guidelines for adult patients with anorexia nervosa. This approach was developed with the aim of combining both cognitive and analytic techniques and was tested about 15 years ago by Professor Treasure's team.[22] The interest in CAT subsided when it was shown to be less effective than psychodynamic or family therapy.[11] There are only a few therapists, mainly in the London area, trained in CAT in the UK.

Interpersonal therapy

Interpersonal therapy (IPT) has a fascinating history. Originally it was developed by Klerman and Weisman's team as a placebo (dummy) treatment for antidepressant medication trials. To their surprise, this 'placebo' turned out to be as effective as some of the well-established antidepressant medications. With hindsight, the team was probably too smart when they devised this 'dummy' treatment. They recognised that happiness is related to the quality of relationships, and that certain life situations are more likely to trigger low mood. These include bereavement, 'role transition' (for example, becoming a carer, or finishing school), role disputes and interpersonal skill deficits.

As depression often occurs with eating disorders, Professor Fairburn included IPT in his early treatment trials of bulimia nervosa. IPT performed well as compared with CBT, particularly when the patients were followed up long term.[23] On the basis of this result, he has also included IPT in his new 'enhanced' CBT of eating disorders.

His recent results show that this form of treatment is necessary for helping people with eating disorders if there is a more complex psychopathology and/or low weight.[5] However, evidence for effectiveness in anorexia nervosa remains limited. Clinical experience suggests that interpersonal therapy can be valuable in patients who are lonely or struggle with difficult relationships (in parallel with or after weight restoration).

Addressing issues around relationships can also improve the patient's motivation to change. While interpersonal therapy does not concentrate on eating disorder behaviours directly, it can powerfully challenge the belief that losing weight will offer a solution to the sufferer's loneliness or unhappiness. The combination of CBT and IPT seems promising in complex eating disorders.[5]

Brief therapy

Brief therapies have been intensively researched for a variety of conditions. While they may be helpful for various anxiety disorders, it is clear that psychological interventions for anorexia nervosa need a longer time in order to be effective. The NICE guidelines recommend that outpatient psychological treatment should be of at least six months duration, and if the patient needs hospital admission, the treatment should be for at least 12 months. So, brief therapy is unlikely to be effective.

Supportive therapy

This is a commonly used non-specific approach that is offered in parallel with weight restoration. Therapists often use a variety of insights and techniques from differing psychotherapeutic traditions that are relevant to the individual's strengths and difficulties. One randomised trial, over a 20-week period of intervention, found this approach superior to IPT and CBT in the treatment of anorexia.[13] This was a surprising result, but at the same time reassuring to most practising clinicians, who frequently use a supportive approach when working with people with anorexia (particularly at the beginning of weight restoration).

Cognitive remediation therapy

Cognitive remediation is a new therapy and still at the experimental stage. It is based on the recognition that most people with anorexia tend to have rigid, obsessional thinking styles, and to get lost in the detail, instead of being able to see the bigger picture. They often have difficulty with switching from one strategy to the next, when circumstances require it. Traditional individual therapies do not address these difficulties, as they focus on *what* patients think and not *how* they think. In the treatment of other psychiatric disorders – for example, schizophrenia – thinking skills addressed by cognitive remediation therapy have been shown to improve working memory, planning skills and flexibility. Dr Tchanturia's[24] team at the Maudsley Hospital has been working on adapting this technique for anorexia nervosa. Here again, the main focus is to improve the style of thinking rather than the content. Time will tell whether it will bring the much-needed breakthrough in psychological therapies.

Family therapy

All guidelines recommend family therapy for children. In contrast with individual and group therapies, family interventions oriented towards eating disorders have been found to be helpful for young people with anorexia nervosa in several randomised controlled trials.[8, 25] Other, exploratory, family therapies have not been researched, and therefore cannot be recommended at present.

In my experience, parents are often worried about participating in family therapy, expecting that professionals will blame them for their child's illness. ('Do they think that there was something wrong with my family to cause the illness?') This is not what modern family therapy should be about. The emphasis is on assisting parents to find ways of helping their child, both with weight restoration and to address underlying emotional difficulties. Professor Treasure's new approach seeks to use these principles for carers of adults too. Her team emphasises the benefits of helping carers to develop new skills to support a loved one with an eating disorder.[26]

In the UK, most Child and Adolescent Mental Health Service (CAMHS) teams can offer some form of family therapy or family work. However, the training of family therapists varies, so it is worth checking whether the treatment team is experienced in offering family therapy specifically for young people with eating disorders. It is important that the therapist does not ignore the importance of eating behaviours and weight changes in sessions. If this does not happen, feel free to refer to the NICE guidelines and to ask for a different approach. Family therapy should be offered for young people regardless of whether they are treated as inpatients or outpatients. In some districts, multifamily therapy (involving more than one family) is also available.

Medication

Medication is not recommended as a sole treatment for anorexia nervosa, because the evidence for its effectiveness is poor.[27] However, 'co-morbidity' in anorexia (that is, another condition also being present, such as underlying depression, or obsessive compulsive disorder) is common. These problems may need to be treated by medication, particularly if there is no response to psychological treatment. Furthermore, specialists sometimes use various medications in an attempt to alleviate severe symptoms associated with anorexia.

The main options include antidepressants, anxiolytics (for relieving anxiety, as the name suggests), and antipsychotics, which have been developed for the relief of symptoms in schizophrenia and related disorders.

Antidepressants

The most frequently studied and prescribed medication in anorexia is fluoxetine (Prozac) and similar antidepressants (serotonin re-uptake inhibitors or 'SSRIs'), such as citalopram (Cipramil) or sertraline (Lustral).[28] Other antidepressants have also been tried.[29]

There is high-quality evidence that Prozac can be effective in bulimia, but evidence of its effectiveness in restrictive-type anorexia is poor. Its use should therefore be limited to those who have severe co-morbid problems, such as depression and obsessive compulsive disorder.

The jury is still out on whether the use of such medications is beneficial when people are malnourished. There is some evidence that it is ineffective in starved patients, but further trials are needed. Furthermore, concerns have been raised that there is an increased risk of self-harm while on these medicines, particularly in adolescents. As with any other medication, the potential side-effects and benefits need to be balanced very carefully before treatment decisions are made. There are websites that give reliable and up-to-date information about these medicines, including that of the Royal College of Psychiatrists: http://www.rcpsych.ac.uk/mentalhealthinfoforall/problems/depression/antidepressants.aspx, and others: http://www.patient.co.uk/pils.asp, and http://www.medicinenet.com/script/main/art.asp?articlekey=12510.

Anxiolytics
The other commonly used medicines are the so-called anxiolytics, such as diazepam and lorazepam. These are often used in hospitals as a temporary measure to manage the high levels of anxiety associated with initial weight restoration. They have never been tested for anorexia in formal clinical trials, but at the same time there is no evidence of harm in the scientific literature. The main risk with anxiolytics is that people often develop a tolerance to and a dependence on these drugs, and so it is generally not a good idea to use them outside of hospital. However, if they are used cautiously, they can be helpful in managing severe anxiety and distress in the short term.

Antipsychotics
Olanzapine and other types of antipsychotic medication are some-

times used if patients are very highly distressed and agitated, or if anorexic beliefs are of an almost delusional intensity and resistant to any rational discussion. Apart from reducing the delusional level of preoccupation, these medications can also help to reduce intense anxiety and mood swings. There is some preliminary evidence to show that olanzapine can be beneficial in these difficult-to-treat cases of anorexia, as part of a comprehensive treatment.[30-32] Its main side effects are drowsiness and low blood pressure, which can result in fainting episodes in some patients. Interestingly, olanzapine can cause increased appetite and associated weight gain in other patient groups, such as those suffering from psychosis or bipolar disorder, but this almost never happens in anorexia. The reason for this is unknown, but this fact should be reassuring for anorexia patients, who are often desperately worried about weight gain as a side effect of medication.

The optimal length of treatment in anorexia is unknown, but it is likely to be several months. In my experience, the main benefit of olanzapine is the reduction in distress associated with severe, uncontrollable anorexic fears. Reduced anxiety can also help patients to use psychotherapies more effectively.

Medication to prevent osteoporosis

Oestrogens or 'the pill' were recommended in the past as an attempt to prevent osteoporosis in chronic anorexia. This approach is no longer recommended as there is no evidence that it is effective. In addition, there are risks associated with the use of artificial oestrogens, including maintaining the denial of malnutrition, and the increased risk of certain cancers.

Other medications to help with osteoporosis have also not been shown to be helpful. The best prevention of osteoporosis is full weight restoration with a nutritionally balanced diet. Some experts recommend the use of vitamin D and calcium supplements. As long as these are not used instead of a balanced diet, they may be helpful.

Supplements

Vitamins and omega-3 supplements are also used by some clinicians. At the beginning of re-feeding, these may be helpful in restoring reserves of essential nutrients in the body, but it is important to recognise that they cannot replace a normal mixed diet.

Recent research about certain dietary supplements has been disappointing: it seems that consuming natural fresh foods is more beneficial than taking supplements, but with a few exceptions, including thiamine and omega-3 fatty acids. Further studies are needed to explore the benefits of omega-3 fatty acids in improving depression and preventing heart rhythm abnormalities in anorexia.

Services for young people and adults

CAMHS and AMHS: what do they do?

In the UK, most general Child and Adolescent Mental Health Services (CAMHS) offer assessment and treatment for young people with anorexia nervosa within the NHS. While the quality of service provision varies from district to district, on average the treatment outcome is comparable to that of specialist services.[2] The upper age limit for patients accepted by CAMHS varies: in some districts it is 16 years, in others it is 18; but it is likely to become 18 universally in the near future owing to changes in national policy.

Most CAMHS offer family therapy combined with individual therapy for the child. Some districts have access to dieticians; others do not. At the time of writing, there are very few dedicated specialist eating disorder services for children and young people within the NHS, and about 80 per cent of the specialist inpatient placements are provided by the private sector. However, recently there has been a new trend of setting up intensive community

NHS CAMHS treatment teams with the intention of reducing the cost of hospital treatment. Most of these teams offer support for young people with eating disorders. The range of treatments on offer varies from district to district. It is uncertain how the economic downturn will influence the funding for these services during the next few years. Your GP or NHS Direct should be able to provide you with local information, and similar support from independent providers and specialist services is to be found on the web.

There is a striking difference between CAMHS and adult services in their approach to treatment, and in whether they involve family members to facilitate change. Whilst CAMHS' main focus is on assisting the family to help the young person with anorexia, adult services emphasise the individual responsibility of the patient, and often there is a reluctance to involve the family at all (with a few notable exceptions, such as Professor Treasure's team). The widespread approach within adult services is based on the assumption that patients choose not to eat of their own free will, and that they can be helped only if they want to be. As we have already shown, to make such an assumption is highly questionable when a patient is in a state of severe malnutrition, and leading experts in the field have publicly challenged this view of eating disorders.[36]

In contrast, CAMHS emphasise parental responsibility for the well-being of the child, and encourage the parents to take control of the child's eating disorder and help him or her through recovery. As we have seen, research evidence shows that this approach is useful for young people, in both the short and long term. Research on using a family approach with adults is much more limited.

In practice, it can be difficult to decide when is the most appropriate time to shift the focus from a family-based approach to one based on the individual. The pace at which young people mature varies. Ideally, there should be a gradual transition, depending on the young person's level of maturity, the quality of their relationships, their social circumstances and so on. Patients and families should be involved in this decision-making process. In practice, funding of NHS services does not always allow this to happen. For example, some CAMHS discharge young people on their 16th birthday. Even worse, in some districts, adult services refuse to accept referrals for young people until after their 18th birthday. If you face this situation, the only option is to make a formal complaint, as the NHS should provide continuity of services for everybody. Fortunately, this is done in most districts.

Unfortunately, most General Adult Mental Health NHS Services in England (AMHS, or CMHT – Community Mental Health Teams) do not have sufficient expertise to treat anorexia nervosa. Over the last 20 years or so, adult mental health services in the UK have been pushed by successive government policies into specialising in the treatment of what they call 'severe and enduring' mental illness, which usually excludes eating disorders such as anorexia, despite the severe and enduring nature of these conditions. On the other hand, many districts have special-ist adult eating disorder services, but provision is patchy. It is important to find out about the size and expertise of your local team. Unfortunately, some of these teams are under-funded or consist of only one person interested in eating disorders. As a consequence, they lack the time to offer sufficiently intensive treatment to everyone who needs it.

If there is no specialist service where you live, you can ask your GP to refer you to a regional centre. There are a number of independent organisations that offer assessment and treatment for eating disorders. If you have private insurance, you should be able to access them. In England, current government policy increasingly emphasises the patient's right to choose a provider, so your primary care trust may agree to fund private assessment and treatment for you or your loved one if specialist services are not available on the NHS where you live. Referring to the

NICE guidelines may be helpful if you need to argue a case for the funding of recommended treatment. Asking for help from B-EAT (www.b-eat.co.uk) regarding treatment options in the UK can also be useful.

Accessing and funding treatment in the US can be even more difficult. The Academy of Eating Disorders' website provides useful information regarding the options available: http://www.aedweb.org/Treatment/1533.htm.

Home or hospital – Outpatient or home treatment?

The majority of patients receiving professional care are treated as outpatients. Ideally, this service should be provided by a specialist team, or at least by a range of experienced professionals.

In the UK, there are usually several professionals involved, and they may work across different organisations. For example, the GP may refer the patient to a paediatrician or physician, as well as to a psychiatrist or a specialist nurse. Many districts (but not all) have local protocols about care pathways and sharing responsibilities. Most CAMHS teams can offer family therapy and some form of individual work for the young person. Adult services usually provide individual or group work as a minimum.

Specialist services may be able to offer CBT or interpersonal therapy. However, funding and capacity are recurrent problems in the NHS, and because of this there may be a problem with the frequency of these appointments. Professor Fairburn's research has shown that having twice-weekly CBT sessions at the beginning of therapy can be helpful in engaging the sufferer and stimulating change. Similarly, multi-family therapy sessions are initially very intensive (starting with several days in the first week). If your service offers only fortnightly or monthly meetings, you should express concern, as this level of intervention is unlikely to be effective. In some districts, home treatment teams are also part of the service.

In other countries, such as the US, the service organisation may be even more confusing. Many insurance companies offer a list of providers, and leave it to the sufferer and the family to explore their options. Using the NICE and APA guidelines can help when you are trying to choose between services available close to your home.

Hospital treatment

Patients and families often dread having to be admitted to hospital for treatment. To make it even more confusing, there are different types of hospitals, and in some countries, including the UK, patients have limited choice as to where they can be admitted. However, recent health policy changes in England have resulted in increased choice for patients. Before you can make an informed choice, you need to understand the options available.

Generally, hospital treatment is discouraged in most countries, partly because of the high cost and partly because the evidence for lasting long-term benefit is at best limited. However, this is often a chicken and egg dilemma. Only the most severely ill patients need hospital admission, so it should not be surprising that positive outcomes are not more frequent. It needs to be borne in mind that the right hospital treatment can be lifesaving. Furthermore, evaluating the long-term benefits of complex interventions, such as hospital treatment, is extremely challenging for researchers. The only randomised controlled trial that attempted to compare the outcomes of hospital and two forms of outpatient treatment was recently carried out by Professor Gowers's team in the North-West of England.[2] They randomly allocated 150 young people with anorexia nervosa into three treatment groups, two of which were administered by outpatient services (general CAMHS and a specialist eating disorder clinic) while the other involved admission to general adolescent units which did not specialise in the treatment of eating disorders. The problem was that despite the random allocation, there was a significant change of treatment between these three groups. This was because parents and patients, having initially consented to random allocation of treatment, subsequently changed their minds according to the patients' needs. So, by the end of the study, almost all participants had received a mixture of all three types of care. Not surprisingly, there were no differences in the outcomes. This work demonstrates the challenges researchers face when trying to compare complex treatment approaches using randomised controlled trials. Long-term follow-up studies are more accurate representations of real-life circumstances.

One such study from Sweden found that a longer hospital stay at first admission resulted in a better outcome.[34] Similar results have been found in studies of CAMHS inpatient services in the UK.[35] The most likely explanation for this is that in anorexia it takes a long time to achieve sustainable change. Other studies have shown that healthy weight on discharge is important in achieving a good outcome.[36] Again, this can be achieved only with sufficient time. At present, there are no studies examining the whole patient care pathway (that is, what happens before and after admission to hospital).

In routine clinical practice, the treatment setting is decided on the basis of the level of risk to the patient, and the services available locally. Hospital admission is usually recommended only if the person is severely underweight, physically unstable, has experienced a lack of response to outpatient treatment, or if there are other risks (such as of severe self-harm or suicide), which are also indicators for hospital admission. However, the definition of risk is to some extent relative. The UK guidelines recommend a 'graded' approach to treatment, leaving hospital admission as the very last resort. The US guidelines, on the other hand, state that it is unlikely that people below 85% weight for height ratio can achieve weight restoration without inpatient treatment. There is, therefore, a striking difference between the two countries. The APA guidelines recommend admission earlier, emphasising that if it is left too late the effectiveness of residential treatment is likely to be compromised. They also recognise that hospital treatment is often necessary when the sufferer is severely ill and consequently unable to recognise the need for change or, indeed, any danger to their life. It should not, therefore, be surprising that this patient group has the worst outcome, because only the most severely ill patients will receive hospital treatment. If sufferers are motivated to change and can accept help from family and friends, they will have a better chance of recovery.

In my own clinical practice, I have found that hospital treatment tends to be more successful and shorter in duration if the patient is admitted relatively early – for example, once there is a clear indication that outpatient treatment is not going to achieve sufficient change – rather than when the patient is extremely ill. This observation is consistent with the US guidelines.

Accident & emergency and medical wards

In the UK, if there is a medical emergency, the first point of access is usually the local casualty department. Here, there is usually 24-hour medical cover, where doctors can check if there is any immediate physical danger. After this initial assessment, if the patient is physically compromised, he or she is usually transferred to a general medical or a paediatric ward for further assessment (such as heart monitoring) or treatment (naso-gastric tube feeding). Most of these wards have very limited experience in treating eating disorders, so the quality of care tends to vary a great deal.[37] The level of nursing staff on general medical or paediatric wards is not usually sufficient to offer intensive supervision of meals and any compensatory behaviour, such as vomiting. It is important to ask whether your local hospital has (or has access to) a specialist who can advise the team on medical or paediatric wards. Sometimes specialists cover a large area, so there may be some waiting time before they can see the patient. If you are concerned whether your loved one will be able to comply with meals on a general medical ward, you should ask whether you can stay there to help. This is usually standard practice on a paediatric ward, and most casualty departments allow this too.

Psychiatric hospitals and mental health units

Psychiatric hospitals can be either general (for all kinds of mental health problems) or specialist units (for eating disorders only). There is a significant difference between adult and child and adolescent inpatient units in this respect: most adult eating disorder units tend to be specialist, whilst the majority of young people are treated within general units in the NHS. The difference is due to geographical variations and historical funding arrangements, and not necessarily patient need. Recent health policy initiatives in England have not encouraged the development of specialist NHS services, so the private sector has stepped in. B-EAT and NICE guidelines emphasise the importance of an experienced team. There are very few services in the NHS for young people where the same team provides both inpatient and outpatient care. This is due to current funding arrangements, which are separate for inpatient and outpatient services, and unfortunately causes significant discontinuity for patients. One can only hope that this will change sometime in the future. This is in contrast with most adult specialist eating disorder services, which provide a range of services including outpatient, day patient and inpatient care.

The main advantage of hospital treatment is that intensive support is available at mealtimes, so weight restoration can be achieved, even when the patient is highly ambivalent about getting better. The main challenge is to maintain a healthy weight and continue with treatment even after discharge. In the past, hospital treatment programmes mainly worked using 'behavioural' interventions. This meant providing and removing privileges depending on the patient's weight gain. These have now gone out of practice, as they were too punitive and degrading, and hence counterproductive.

Modern specialist inpatient treatments usually offer a combination of approaches. These include nutritional rehabilitation, weight restoration, support and supervision at mealtimes, and supervision after meals to prevent compensatory behaviours. In addition, most units offer various group programmes, as well as individual and family therapy, and education for young people. Unfortunately, there are no comparative studies to inform patients and clinicians about the best model of care. This may improve in the future, however, as the UK government has recently introduced an emphasis on treatment outcomes for healthcare providers.

If you need to consider hospital treatment, it is important to find out about the local services available. Most units these days encourage visits prior to admission, so you can meet the team and ask any questions before agreeing to treatment. Private units tend to have good websites with lots of information about the services on offer. Current guidelines emphasise the importance of experienced teams, so feel free to ask questions about the service on offer and the professionals involved. Ideally, there should be a range of disciplines available within the team, including psychiatry, psychology, nursing, dietary and family therapy, and various other professionals such as occupational therapists for adults, teachers for adolescent units, physiotherapists and so on.

The Royal College of Psychiatrists is currently developing standards for inpatient units caring for people with severe eating disorders. Guidance for standards of adult and child psychiatry inpatient services is available on the College's website.

Artificial feeding

What can you do if a person refuses to eat altogether? Until the late 1980s there was disagreement in the UK about whether it was ethical to feed a person who was refusing to eat normally. By now, it has been widely accepted that artificial feeding, if necessary, should be part of the treatment, as starvation maintains the illness.

There are a lot of myths about naso-gastric feeding, some people regarding it as 'horrific' and 'inhumane'. There is nothing inhumane about saving a person's life by whatever means necessary. On the contrary, doctors and nurses would be negligent to leave a person to die of starvation when feeding would help. The overwhelming majority of patients understand that not being able to eat is dangerous, and therefore accept naso-gastric feeding as a helpful medical intervention, just as they would accept other interventions, such as a drip or blood tests. The process simply involves the insertion of a thin tube through the nose to the stomach. Whilst this can be somewhat uncomfortable to insert, once the tube is in place, it is painless. So the intervention is similar to having a drip, but much safer.

There are various methods of using tube feeding. Most pae-diatric units tend to use overnight feeding with a pump, whilst most eating disorder services tend to use several smaller portions of feeds during the day, usually following mealtimes. This latter method allows the body to get used to regular mealtimes. If the team works well with the patient, it is very rare that naso-gastric feeding needs to be administered against the patient's will. Most sufferers understand that this is an intervention to keep them alive, and when severely ill, they may find artificial feeding easier than coping with their anxiety and guilt regarding eating.

In extreme situations, doctors and patients might decide to use a PEG, which is a tube inserted into the stomach through a minor surgical procedure. This is usually used if a person has problems swallowing, or if a patient with anorexia is unable to eat for a long time. Fortunately, this is very rarely necessary. The PEG allows the person to be discharged from hospital, as long as she or he accepts the feed through the PEG voluntarily.

Educational aspects in hospitals

In UK law, hospitals need to provide education for all young people. This is particularly important in the case of hospital treatment of anorexia because the length of stay tends to be several months.

Feel free to clarify details of the education on offer before you agree to hospital treatment. Most inpatient units have a school on site and close links can be maintained with the young person's local school. This offers a healthy structure to the day, allows the young person to keep up with her/his education, and helps her/him develop interests and activities other than anorexia.

Criteria for discharge

Inpatient units vary as to whether discharge occurs after stabilisation of a healthy weight, or prior to reaching a healthy weight, for continued work in the community.[41] If the patient is to be discharged prior to achieving a healthy weight, it is essential that there is an intensive package of care in the community, as relapse following inpatient admission is high. The APA guidelines strongly recommend full weight restoration and stabilisation for relapse prevention before discharge from hospital.

In my own clinical practice, the decision about discharge is always negotiated with the young person and the family, based on the likely response to further outpatient treatment. If the patient is able to complete his or her weight restoration at home, that is fine, but if there is a high level of anxiety or reluctance to do so, it is better to complete weight restoration in hospital where intensive support is available. Otherwise, the risk of relapse would be almost 100%.

Compulsory treatment

What can be done if a person suffering from anorexia is at severe risk, but refuses to accept help? Most countries have a legal framework which allows compulsory treatment of people with mental disorders. This usually means hospital treatment (although the new Mental Health Act in England also allows compulsory treatment at home after discharge). However, there is often confusion about anorexia, as it is sometimes regarded as a personal choice rather than an illness. For this reason, compulsory treatment of severe eating disorders is considered controversial in Western countries,[39–49] but this is not necessarily the case elsewhere. Compulsory treatment raises strong feelings, but it is rarely studied. In England and Wales, the Mental Health Act Commission (MHAC) issued a *Guidance Note on the Treatment of Anorexia Nervosa under the Mental Health Act 1983* to help clinicians with treatment decisions when the patient refuses treatment.[50] This guidance emphasised that in general, 'compulsory measures are unnecessary in the treatment of anorexia nervosa because it may be counterproductive to patient autonomy in the long term'. However, they recognised that in 'rare cases, when the patients' physical health or survival is seriously threatened by food or fluid refusal, compulsory treatment may be necessary'.

It is striking that in this guidance, anorexia nervosa is viewed differently from other mental disorders. The physical risk to the patient is emphasised rather than the general conditions for compulsory treatment such as risk to health, or safety of self or of others. It may be questioned whether there is any theoretical reason to assume that patient autonomy is more important in anorexia nervosa than, for example, in depression or psychosis. The risk of mortality is higher in anorexia nervosa than in other mental disorders, and a significant proportion of sufferers commit suicide rather than die of the consequences of starvation.[51–54] Therefore, the different approach cannot be justified on the basis of the risk to the patient. This attitude was also questioned in the *American Journal of Psychiatry* by Andersen, who stated that 'if a patient's clinical condition meets the criteria for involuntary admission to hospital and treatment, there is no reason the category of eating disorders should be excluded from consideration for life saving treatment.'[55]

In English law, parents can consent to treatment on behalf of a non-consenting child under the age of 16 years. The NICE guidelines underline the importance of a collaborative approach in the treatment of young people with eating disorders, just as with adults. NICE state that 'when feeding against the patient's will becomes necessary, it is recommended that this should only be done in the context of the Mental Health Act (MHA) or the Children Act.' The NICE guidelines stress that although parental consent can be used to override the young person's refusal of treatment, relying 'indefinitely' on parental consent to treatment should be avoided. This reflects a significant shift in the consensus view in the UK. Before the publication of these guidelines, the prevailing view used to be that the use of the Mental Health Act should be avoided in the treatment of anorexia nervosa in young people, because parents can override their children's refusal of treatment. However, there is no definition in the NICE guidelines as to what timescale constitutes 'indefinitely' when relying on parental consent. Therefore individual practices vary a great deal.

The NICE guidelines add that if both the patient with anorexia nervosa and those with parental responsibility refuse treatment, legal advice should be sought in order to consider proceedings under the Children Act.

There is surprisingly little research in this area despite its importance. For ethical reasons, it is not possible to carry out randomised controlled trials on compulsory treatment, and therefore studies rely on case series, or qualitative work. There are a small number of publications from other countries.[56-63] These also tend to emphasise the physical risks to the patient when using compulsory treatment. The only long-term follow-up study was carried out at the Maudsley Hospital.[64] The authors compared the five-year outcome for 80 detained adult patients with anorexia nervosa with that for 80 informal patients. Factors leading to compulsory treatment were a history of childhood sexual or physical abuse, or previous self-harm. Detained patients had also had more previous admissions. The short-term outcome showed benefits, as detained patients had gained as much weight as voluntary patients by the time they were discharged (although the weight gain took longer to achieve). However, at five years after discharge, there were more deaths among compulsory patients than voluntary patients (12% versus 2%). The authors concluded that although in the short term compulsory treatment could be life-saving, patients who were detained had a much higher rate of mortality. However, because of the design of the study, it was possible that the higher mortality rate was due to the more severe condition of detained patients.

Dr Tan worked on this topic using qualitative research methods.[65-67] Her main findings suggest that most families and patients accept that the use of the Mental Health Act may be necessary if the condition is life threatening. However, the way it is used is fundamentally important, so that the compulsory intervention is perceived as something helpful by the patient and the family, rather than punitive and coercive. She also found that the capacity to consent to treatment may be different in anorexia nervosa depending on the *stage* of the illness. Her studies have shown that, although patients with anorexia nervosa have a good understanding, reasoning and appreciation of their illness, this may not be relevant in their decision making about their treatment. She found that anorexic patients' attitudes revealed the relative unimportance of fear of death or disability compared with continuing with their anorexia. This may play a crucial part in treatment refusal and 'yet it is not related to depression and nor is it picked up in standard tests of competence'. This can change over time. With successful treatment, patients developed an overriding wish to live above the importance of the anorexia. This is a very important finding, as it shows that acceptance of treatment and patient autonomy are not static, but it can change with weight restoration.

The work of my team is in agreement with her findings. We systematically evaluated the outcomes of young people treated under parental consent, as opposed to using the Mental Health Act, by a specialist inpatient eating disorder service.[68] In our study, 35 patients under 18 years old were treated under parental consent and 16 were treated under Section 3 of the Mental Health Act. All informal patients were initially treated with their parents' consent. Many of these young people were highly ambivalent about accepting hospital admission, but they accepted their parents' and the doctors' decision, and consequently the use of the Mental Health Act was not necessary. However, some of these patients only partially cooperated with the treatment programme, but not to the extent that they would put themselves at immediate risk. Those patients who had to be detained under the Mental Health Act, because of refusal of treatment, had a high rate of co-morbid depression, and a much higher rate of severe non-accidental self-injury and/or suicidal behaviour on admission. They also had a longer history of the illness, with more previous hospital admissions and more severe clinical symptoms, and they more often needed tube feeding.

All of the physical and psychosocial measures had improved significantly by the time they were discharged, and there was no significant difference between the two groups. By 12 months after discharge, the detained group had a slightly better overall outcome. Notably, 41.4% in the parental consent group discharged themselves prematurely as compared with 15.4% of detained patients. In contrast, all detained patients agreed to continue their treatment informally in the hospital after their condition had improved sufficiently for them to become voluntary again.

In the informal group, sadly two patients died in the next 12 months. Both of these patients had been discharged prematurely at their own request. These tragedies are stark reminders that waiting too long for compulsory treatment (with all the best intentions to honour the patient's wishes) can have tragic consequences, and that compulsory treatment is not the worst thing that can happen to a patient. The use of compulsory treatment may be protective on several counts. It can reduce the patient's guilt about accepting food, nutrition and treatment. It also gives a powerful message to the patient that the condition is serious, and therefore can help in reducing the denial that maintains the illness.[52] It relieves the pressure on the parents, who do not need to feel to blame for the patient being treated against her/his will, and are therefore more likely to be perceived as supportive. Finally, it reduces the risk of premature discharge from treatment.

Our study confirmed that the initial refusal of treatment, and the importance of anorexia to the patient, can change with treatment, and this supports Tan's findings. We did not find evidence that treating the patient against her or his will compromised patient autonomy in the long term, as the readmission and mortality rates were lower at 12 months follow-up in the detained group. The conclusion must be, if you are desperately worried about your loved one, and he or she refuses any treatment, you should feel free to talk to your GP or a specialist about compulsory treatment.

Summary

The treatment of anorexia nervosa usually involves a range of approaches. Apart from weight restoration, there are various forms of individual, group and family therapy. The evidence for the effectiveness of these treatments remains limited, and you should therefore feel free to choose the approach that suits you best. National and international guidelines can help you to make an informed choice.

Decisions about treatment settings are dependent on many factors. These include the age of the sufferer, the level of risk, and the services available in your locality. The majority of people can be treated as outpatients. This usually includes a combination of approaches, such as dietetic advice, and individual and family therapy. In the UK, there is a significant difference in approach between services for young people (CAMHS) and those for adults (AMHS), the former strengthening the family's role in helping the young person's recovery, whilst the latter emphasises individual responsibility. Transition between these services can be difficult and confusing, so mind the gap!

Inpatient treatment should be reserved for those at serious medical and/or psychiatric risk or in situations where appropriate treatment in the community has failed. If the sufferer is at high risk and is unwilling to be admitted to hospital, compulsory admission will need to be considered to prevent tragedy.

References

1. Le Grange D, Lock J. The dearth of psychological treatment studies for anorexia nervosa. *International Journal of Eating Disorders* 2005; **37(2)**: 79-91.
2. Gowers SG, Clark A, Roberts C, Griffiths A, Edwards V, Bryan C et al. Clinical effectiveness of treatments for anorexia nervosa in adolescents – Randomised controlled trial. *British Journal of Psychiatry* 2007; **191**: 427-435.
3. Treasure J, Kordy H. Evidence-based care of eating disorders: Beware the glitter of the randomised controlled trial. *European Eating Disorders Review* 1998; **6(2)**: 85-95.
4. Agras WS, Brandt HA, Bulik CM, Dolan-Sewell R, Fairburn CG, Halmi KA et al. Report of the National Institutes of Health Workshop on overcoming barriers to treatment research in anorexia nervosa. *International Journal of Eating Disorders* 2004; **35(4)**: 509-521.
5. Fairburn CG, Cooper Z, Doll HA, O'Connor ME, Bohn K,

Hawker DM et al. Transdiagnostic cognitive-behavioral therapy for patients with eating disorders: A two-site trial with 60-week follow-up. *American Journal of Psychiatry* 2009; **166(3)**: 311-319.

6. Wilson GT, Fairburn CC, Agras WS, Walsh BT, Kraemer H. Cognitive-behavioral therapy for bulimia nervosa: Time course and mechanisms of change. *Journal of Consulting and Clinical Psychology* 2002; **70(2)**: 267-274.

7. Le Grange D, Eisler I. Family interventions in adolescent anorexia nervosa. *Child and Adolescent Psychiatric Clinics of North America* 2009; **18(1)**: 159.

8. Eisler I, Simic M, Russell GFM, Dare C. A randomised controlled treatment trial of two forms of family therapy in adolescent anorexia nervosa: a five-year follow-up. *Journal of Child Psychology and Psychiatry* 2007; **48(6)**: 552-560.

9. National Institute for Clinical Excellence. Core interventions for the treatment and management of anorexia nervosa, bulimia nervosa and related eating disorders. *NICE Clinical Guideline* no 9, 2004.

10. Keel PK, Haedt A. Evidence-based psychosocial treatments for eating problems and eating disorders. *Journal of Clinical Child and Adolescent Psychology* 2008; **37(1)**: 39-61.

11. Dare C, Eisler I, Russell G, Treasure J, Dodge L. Psychological therapies for adults with anorexia nervosa – Randomised controlled trial of out-patient treatments. *British Journal of Psychiatry* 2001; **178**: 216-221.

12. Agras WS, Robinson AH. Forty years of progress in the treatment of the eating disorders. *Nordic Journal of Psychiatry* 2008; **62**: 19-24.

13. McIntosh VVW, Jordan J, Carter FA, Luty SE, McKenzie JM, Bulik CM et al. Three psychotherapies for anorexia nervosa: A randomized, controlled trial. *American Journal of Psychiatry* 2005; **162(4)**: 741-747.

14. Ben-Tovim DI, Walker K, Gilchrist P, Freeman R, Kalucy R,

Esterman A. Outcome in patients with eating disorders: a 5-year study. *The Lancet* 2001; **357(9264)**: 1254-1257.

15. Geist R, Heinmaa M, Stephens D, Davis R, Katzman DK. Comparison of family therapy and family group psychoeducation in adolescents with anorexia nervosa. *Canadian Journal of Psychiatry – Revue Canadienne de Psychiatrie* 2000; **45(2)**: 173-178.

16. Fonagy P, Roth A, Higgitt A. The outcome of psychodynamic psychotherapy for psychological disorders. *Clinical Neuroscience Research* 2005; **4(5-6)**: 367-377.

17. Bewell CV, Carter JC. Readiness to change mediates the impact of eating disorder symptomatology on treatment outcome in anorexia nervosa. *International Journal of Eating Disorders* 2008; **41(4)**: 368-371.

18. Casasnovas C, Fernandez-Aranda F, Granero R, Krug I, Jimenez-Murcia S, Bulik CM et al. Motivation to change in eating disorders: Clinical and therapeutic implications. *European Eating Disorders Review* 2007; **15(6)**: 449-456.

19. Geller J, Cassin SE, Brown KE, Srikameswaran S. Factors associated with improvements in readiness for change: Low vs. normal BMI eating disorders. *International Journal of Eating Disorders* 2009; **42(1)**: 40-46.

20. Wade TD, Frayne A, Edwards SA, Robertson T, Gilchrist P. Motivational change in an inpatient anorexia nervosa population and implications for treatment. *Australian and New Zealand Journal of Psychiatry* 2009; **43(3)**: 235-243.

21. Fairburn CG, Jones R, Peveler RC, Carr SJ, Solomon RA, Oconnor ME et al. 3 Psychological Treatments for Bulimia-Nervosa – A Comparative Trial. *Archives of General Psychiatry* 1991; **48(5)**: 463-469.

22. Treasure J, Todd G, Brolly M, Tiller J, Nehmed A, Denman F. A pilot-study of a randomized trial of cognitive analytical therapy vs educational behavioral-therapy for adult anorexia-nervosa. *Behaviour Research and Therapy* 1995; **33(4)**: 363-367.

23. Fairburn CG, Jones R, Peveler RC, Hope RA, O'Connor M. Psychotherapy and bulimia-nervosa – Longer-term effects of interpersonal psychotherapy, behavior-therapy, and cognitive-behavior therapy. *Archives of General Psychiatry* 1993; **50(6)**: 419-428.

24. Tchanturia K, Davies H, Campbell I. Cognitive remediation therapy for patients with anorexia nervosa: preliminary findings. *Annals of General Psychiatry* 2007; **6(1)**: 14.

25. Loeb KL, Walsh BT, Lock J, Le Grange D, Jones J, Marcus S et al. Open trial of family-based treatment for full and partial anorexia nervosa in adolescence: Evidence of successful dissemination. *Journal of the American Academy of Child and Adolescent Psychiatry* 2007; **46(7)**: 792-800.

26. Treasure J, Smith G, Crane A. *Skill-based learning for caring for a loved one with an eating disorder: The new Maudsley method.* Hove & New York: Routledge; 2007.

27. Crow SJ, Mitchell JE, Roerig JD, Steffen K. What potential role is there for medication treatment in anorexia nervosa? *International Journal of Eating Disorders* 2009; **42(1)**: 1-8.

28. Kaye WH, Nagata T, Weltzin TE, Hsu LG, Sokol MS, McConaha C et al. Double-blind placebo-controlled administration of fluoxetine in restricting- and restricting-purging-type anorexia nervosa. *Biological Psychiatry* 2001; **49(7)**: 644-652.

29. Claudino AM, Hay P, Lima MS, Bacaltchuk J, Schmidt U, Treasure J. Antidepressants for anorexia nervosa. *Cochrane Database of Systematic Reviews* 2006; **(1)**.

30. Bissada H, Tasca GA, Barber AM, Bradwejn J. Olanzapine in the treatment of low body weight and obsessive thinking in women with anorexia nervosa: A randomized, double-blind, placebo-controlled trial. *American Journal of Psychiatry* 2008; **165(10)**: 1281-1288.

31. Hodge MAR, Siciliano D, Withey P, Moss B, Moore G, Judd G et al. A randomized controlled trial of cognitive remediation

in schizophrenia. *Schizophrenia Bulletin* 2010; **36(2)**: 419-427.

32. McKnight RF, Park RJ. Atypical antipsychotics and anorexia nervosa: a review. *European Eating Disorders Review* 2010; **18(1)**: 10-21.

33. Klump KL, Bulik CM, Kaye WH, Treasure J, Tyson E. Academy for Eating Disorders Position Paper: Eating disorders are serious mental illnesses. *International Journal of Eating Disorders* 2009; **42(2)**: 97-103.

34. Papadopoulos FC, Ekbom A, Brandt L, Ekselius L. Excess mortality, causes of death and prognostic factors in anorexia nervosa. *British Journal of Psychiatry* 2009; **194(1)**: 10-17.

35. Green J, Jacobs B, Beecham J, Dunn G, Kroll L, Tobias C et al. Inpatient treatment in child and adolescent psychiatry – a prospective study of health gain and costs. *Journal of Child Psychology and Psychiatry* 2007; **48(12)**: 1259-1267.

36. Steinhausen HC, Grigoroiu-Serbanescu M, Boyadjieva S, Neumarker KJ, Metzke CW. The relevance of body weight in the medium-term to long-term course of adolescent anorexia nervosa. Findings from a multisite study. *International Journal of Eating Disorders* 2009; **42(1)**: 19-25.

37. Robinson P. *MARSIPAN: Management of Really Sick Patients with Anorexia Nervosa*. College Report CR162. http://www.rcpsych.ac.uk/publications/collegereports/cr/cr162.aspx 2010. London, Royal College of Psychiatrists and Royal College of Physicians.

38. Roots P, Hawker J, Gowers S. The use of target weights in the inpatient treatment of adolescent anorexia nervosa. *European Eating Disorders Review* 2006; **14(5)**: 323-328.

39. Draper H. Anorexia nervosa and refusal of naso-gastric treatment: a reply to Simona Giordano. *Bioethics* 2003; **17(3)**: 279-289.

40. Giordano S. Anorexia nervosa and refusal of naso-gastric treatment: a response to Heather Draper. *Bioethics* 2003; **17(3)**: 261-278.

41. Draper H. Anorexia nervosa and respecting a refusal of life-prolonging therapy: a limited justification. *Bioethics* 2000; **14(2)**: 120-133.

42. Melamed Y, Mester R, Margolin J, Kalian M. Involuntary treatment of anorexia nervosa. *International Journal of Law & Psychiatry* 2003; **26(6):** 617-626.

43. Mitrany E, Melamed Y. Compulsory treatment of anorexia nervosa. *Israel Journal of Psychiatry & Related Science* 2005; **42(3)**: 185-190.

44. Webster P, Schmidt U, Treasure J. 'Reforming the Mental Health Act': Implications of the Government's white paper for the management of patients with eating disorders. *Psychiatric Bulletin* 2003; **27(10)**: 01.

45. Tiller J, Schmidt U, Treasure J. Compulsory treatment for anorexia nervosa: Compassion or coercion? *British Journal of Psychiatry* 1993; **162(May)**.

46. Newton JT, Patel H, Shah S, Sturmey P. Perceptions of the use of compulsory detention in treatment of people with eating disorders. *Psychology Reports* 2005; **96(3 Pt 1)**: 701-706.

47. Dyer C. High Court detains girl with anorexia. [Miscellaneous]. *British Medical Journal* 1997; **314(7084)**: 850.

48. Edwards L. The right to consent and the right to refuse: more problems with minors and medical consent. *Jurid Review* 1993; **Part 1**: 52-73.

49. Russell GFM. Involuntary treatment in anorexia nervosa. *Psychiatric Clinics of North America* 2001; **24(2):** 337.

50. The Mental Health Act Commission. *Guidance Note on the Treatment of Anorexia Nervosa under the Mental Health Act 1983*. Nottingham, UK: The Mental Health Act Commission; 2006.

51. Keel PK, Dorer DJ, Eddy KT, Franko D, Charatan DL, Herzog DB. Predictors of mortality in eating disorders. *Archives of General Psychiatry* 2003; **60(2)**: 179-183.

52. Moller-Madsen S, Nystrup J, Nielsen S. Mortality in anorexia

nervosa in Denmark during the period 1970-1987. *Acta Psychiatrica Scandinavica* 1996; **94(6)**: 454-459.

53. Soomro GM, Crisp AH, Lynch D, Tran D, Joughin N. Anorexia nervosa in 'non-white' populations. *British Journal of Psychiatry* 1995; **167(3)**: 385-389.

54. Crisp AH, Callender JS, Halek C, Hsu LK. Long-term mortality in anorexia nervosa. A 20-year follow-up of the St George's and Aberdeen cohorts. *British Journal of Psychiatry* 1992; **161**: 104-107.

55. Andersen AE. Eating disorders and coercion. *American Journal of Psychiatry* 2007; **164(1)**: 9.

56. Lehmkuhl G, Schmidt MH. [How voluntary can treatment of adolescent patients with anorexia nervosa be?]. [German]. *Psychiatrische Praxis* 1986; **13(6)**: 236-241.

57. Surgenor LJ. Treatment coercion: Listening carefully to client and clinician experiences. *International Journal of Law & Psychiatry* 2003; **26(6):** 709-712.

58. Xavier B. Eating disorders may warrant compulsory hospital admission. *The Lancet* 1999; **353(9157)**: 993.

59. Carney T, Tait D, Saunders D, Touyz S, Beumont P. Institutional options in management of coercion in anorexia treatment: The antipodean experiment? *International Journal of Law & Psychiatry* 2003; **26(6):** 647-675.

60. Geist R, Katzman DK, Colangelo JJ. The Consent to Treatment Act and an adolescent with anorexia nervosa. *Health Law Canada* 1996; **16(4)**: 110-114.

61. Dobrzynska E, Frydecka D, Kiejna A. Coercion in the treatment of anorexia nervosa. *Polski Merkuriusz Lekarski* 2006; **20(116):** 245-248.

62. Appelbaum PS, Rumpf T. Civil commitment of the anorexic patient. *General Hospital Psychiatry* 1998; **20(4)**.

63. Guarda AS, Pinto AM, Coughlin JW, Hussain S, Haug NA, Heinberg LJ. Perceived coercion and change in perceived need for admission in patients hospitalized for eating

disorders. *American Journal of Psychiatry* 2007; **164(1)**: 108-114.

64. Ramsay R, Ward A, Treasure J, Russell GFM. Compulsory treatment in anorexia nervosa – Short-term benefits and long-term mortality. *British Journal of Psychiatry* 1999; **175**: 147-153.

65. Tan JOA, Hope T, Stewart A, Fitzpatrick R. Control and compulsory treatment in anorexia nervosa: The views of patients and parents. *International Journal of Law & Psychiatry* 2003; **26(6)**: 627-645.

66. Tan J, Hope T, Stewart A. Competence to refuse treatment in anorexia nervosa. *International Journal of Law & Psychiatry* 2003; **26(6)**: 697-707.

67. Tan JO, Hope T, Stewart A. Anorexia nervosa and personal identity: The accounts of patients and their parents. *International Journal of Law & Psychiatry* 2003; **26(5)**: 533-548.

68. Ayton A, Keen C, Lask B. Pros and cons of using the Mental Health Act for severe eating disorders in adolescents. *European Eating Disorders Review* 2009; **17(1)**: 14-23.

Chapter 8

Prevention of relapse and life without anorexia nervosa

Carers who experience anorexia nervosa for the first time often expect that the associated problems will magically disappear when the patient starts eating, or as a result of some therapy. Sufferers, on the other hand, often struggle to imagine that life can ever exist without anorexia. The truth lies somewhere in between. The Minnesota study has shown us that even psychologically healthy people will become preoccupied with food, weight and shape if they starve themselves for long enough, and that recovery takes several months after weight restoration. This knowledge should help you to prepare yourself for a realistic timescale for recovery. Even if you are successful with weight restoration, the anorexic fears and preoccupations will not disappear straight away. The risk of relapse will remain high for the first year or so, and gradually subsides thereafter. In some studies, 30-50% of patients relapse after hospital treatment.[1-4] There is limited research to advise us how best to prevent this.[5] However, we can learn from clinical experience and from the stories of people who are able to move on with their lives.

Weight maintenance, nutrition and exercise

The few studies that have been done consistently show that people who remain chronically underweight have a worse overall outcome.[6, 7] This includes their physical and mental health, and their general ability to achieve their potential. If people are mal-nourished they continue being preoccupied with food and weight and shape, and everything else is put on hold. Therefore, the only way to prevent relapse is to ensure that your weight remains within a healthy normal range (BMI 20-25 for adults). Anorexia may tell you that absolute thinness brings happiness, but in reality, staying at a healthy weight is essential if you are aiming to recover from the illness. A healthy mind is dependent on a healthy body.

It does not mean that you cannot be slim and healthy. For women, the best indicator of the minimum personal healthy weight is the return of regular periods (there are very few excep-tions to this). There is a common myth (even among some pro-fessionals) that the return of periods takes several months after weight restoration. This is not the case. Most young women start having their periods if their BMI is somewhere between 20 and 22. Only a few will have regular periods below this level (those who are constitutionally thinner than usual, like some oriental ethnic groups, or some younger girls). It can be helpful to make a note for yourself of the weight that allows the return of your periods, and make sure that your weight remains above this for the rest of your life (with adolescents, normal growth and development obviously need to be taken into consideration). This should help you when you need to start using the contraceptive pill, which will cause you to have periods regardless of your weight. For men, it is more difficult to establish the minimum healthy weight, but as a rule of thumb, most would also need to be between a BMI of 20 and 25. The return of libido and sexual interest is a good indicator of the return to healthy weight in both sexes.

After weight restoration, there will be a long period of time when you will continue to feel the desire to lose weight again. It is important to be aware of this, so that you do not give up before recovery can take place. Recovery will happen, but it takes a long time. However, you need to make sure that you find a diet that suits your lifestyle without resulting in a negative energy balance.

Otherwise, relapse is inevitable. Family members or friends can be very helpful in keeping you on the right track. As I discussed before, for most sedentary women, 2000 kcal daily intake is necessary to maintain weight, whilst men need about 2500 kcal per day. If you are more active, your energy requirement will be higher. If you are worried about your weight and shape, it is more helpful to introduce extra activities than to restrict your diet. Most current healthy lifestyle guidelines recommend at least 30-60 minutes of aerobic activity a day. However, it is essential that any exercise should be enjoyable rather than repetitive and anorexia driven, as the latter would maintain the illness. Solitary exercise is generally unhelpful, as is any other exercise that focuses on weight and shape, such as ballet or dancing on the stage. Outdoor activities, if possible, are preferable to indoor sports. Being out in the fresh air, enjoying the sunshine and nature improves people's mood and reduces stress levels, both of which are important when you are trying to recover from anorexia. However, compulsive exercise of any kind will maintain anorexia, so be mindful. You also need to be aware that general daily activities can consume a large amount of energy – for example, just cleaning the house can use up about 500 kcal per hour!

As the Minnesota study has shown, after weight restoration, some people experience excessive hunger for some months, and this can result in binges. This can be a very frightening change for a sufferer who has spent a long time restricting his or her diet. It is helpful to understand that some types of foods are more likely to trigger bingeing than others. Generally, foods with high glycaemic index (GI) are more likely to disturb your insulin regulation and result in insulin overproduction, causing low blood sugar levels and intensive hunger a few hours after a meal. These are usually foods with high sugar and carbohydrate content, or high levels of caffeine. A low-fat, low-protein and high carbohydrate diet, which many sufferers regard as 'safe', is more likely to trigger bingeing. If this develops, it is important to review your diet and change your food choices to low GI foods. Research is still in its infancy about this issue, but there are lots of good recipe books that can help you. It is also important to maintain a regular pattern of meals and snacks, as you will be much more likely to binge if you starve yourself. Keeping a record can be helpful for you to recognise any unhelpful patterns of diet or behaviours. Reflecting on changes over time is a useful way of learning from experiences and it is often used as a tool as part of cognitive behavioural therapy.

The best way to keep an eye on how things are going is to check your weight weekly or fortnightly. If you are in treatment, most services will offer this, but it is also easy to do this at home. Do not weigh yourself on a daily basis, as this will just increase your preoccupations. It is usually useful to keep a graph of any weight fluctuations, so that you can look at changes from a bird's eye perspective. Remember, it is the trend over time that is important, and 2-3 kg fluctuations are entirely normal.

It is crucial to increase the variation and flexibility of your diet, and to continue challenging yourself until your anxieties entirely subside. People on restricted and repetitive diets have a much higher risk of relapse, as these are impossible to fit into normal life. Being able to be flexible is essential to freeing yourself from the tyranny of anorexia. It is important to learn to manage meals and exercise in a way that does not interfere with you getting on with your life. Can you eat a snack with other people at work or school? Having a Kit-Kat or a small packet of nuts is much better than having a prescription supplement. Can you have a meal out with friends and family on the spur of the moment when you are out and about? Are you able to have new or unexpected things on holiday, without becoming overwhelmed with anxiety about food? Are you able to have the right amount of food to maintain your lifestyle and development? All of these can be achieved by trial and error and learning from experience. After enough practice, the body's natural appetite regulation will return to normal, but this takes a long time. The NICE guidelines recommend a minimum of 12 months' outpatient treatment after hospital weight restoration. This is because clinical experience shows that it takes a long time for people to accept having a normal weight after suffering from anorexia. But until that happens, you need to be careful not to start cutting down on food, because that would restart the vicious anorexic circle. Even short-term dietary restriction can trigger the cycle again. It is important that you don't panic if this happens. You can get back on track if you reinstate regular meals and snacks. Practice and patience will get results.

Relationships

Anorexia is often triggered by relationship problems, and then maintained by the false logic that thinness will bring love and happiness. Therefore, one of the main tasks for relapse prevention is to rethink and review your relationships. This is often difficult and it takes considerable time. Some people can achieve this by themselves through talking to friends and family; others need professional help. As discussed before, it is easier to benefit from psychological therapies when you are not malnourished any more.[8, 9] This is the other reason why the guidelines recommend long-term treatment after weight restoration and/or hospital treatment.

The process of weight restoration usually results in significant re-negotiation of relationships. Most people with anorexia find it very difficult to express their views when very ill, and during weight restoration they may become angry and hostile. By the end of this process, the mood of both patient and family usually improves. There is often an enormous sense of achievement and success that brings people together. Paradoxically, this can sometimes also maintain anorexia: 'Shall we still remain close if eating is not a problem any more?' You and your family need to find a solution that works for you. Young people often need to become more independent after recovery from anorexia, and this can be scary at times. Meeting old friends or making new ones can be challenging, as much as moving away from home, trying to find love and succeeding in work or education. It is important to have friends who do not have eating disorders. This should help you to accept that life can go on without constantly worrying about weight or shape and food.

For most of us, being able to find love is crucial for personal happiness. For this to happen, you do not need to be perfect, but you need to be well enough. As we have seen in the Minnesota study, sexual feelings disappear during starvation, and this has been confirmed in everyday clinical experience and modern studies.[10] If you are unable to have romantic feelings because you are malnourished, romance will not happen. You also need to be able to think about someone else rather than your weight and shape for any relationship to last. Many patients report that having a happy relationship helps them to recover from anorexia. Give yourself a chance.

Fun

I sometimes say to patients and families that I would like to prescribe fun for them. People are often surprised to hear this, as they expect a doctor to be always serious, and to offer medication to solve problems. While medication may be necessary if there is a severe co-existing mental health problem, it cannot bring happiness. As we have seen, anorexia is often maintained by anxiety and depression. People's mood can be profoundly influenced by their experiences, and it is easy to forget about fun when you are overwhelmed with worries, or when you are trying to achieve some impossible standard.

Think about activities that make you happy and help you forget about anorexia. Use your imagination. What did you used to enjoy before the tyranny of anorexia? Can you do a bit more of that? Your friends and family can be very helpful with this task, and all of you will benefit. Being able to find enjoyment will protect you from relapse and from the risk of developing other mental health problems.

School or work

Many people with anorexia are highly driven or highly anxious to be the 'best'. They are also often very talented, so can perform exceptionally well in work or school. The problem is to know when to stop. Ask yourself from time to time: 'Am I happy about doing all this work? Has it stopped me having relationships or just having fun?' You may need to learn not to give yourself such a hard time. Sometimes being second best is happier and healthier than the person who is 'perfect' but lonely and miserable.

Returning to school or work after an episode of hospital treatment is not easy. Young people are often worried about insensitive questions or comments from peers; adults may worry about losing their job if they have been unable to perform due to their illness. Some professions require occupational health certificates before allowing someone to return to work. This is particularly important if you work in a job where you are responsible for others. It is not unreasonable to ask that you should be able to look after yourself before you look after other people.

Certain environments may interfere with recovery: these include the fashion industry, competitive aesthetic sports, all-girls' schools and so on. You may need to consider a change to find something less stressful and more enjoyable, rather than risk relapse. Often anorexia forces people to rethink their priorities, so try to use the adversity of the illness to your advantage. Think what is really important for you in your life, something that makes you happy.

Children

Most people who suffer from anorexia want to have children eventually, and this desire often motivates them to work on recovery from the illness. However, the timing of having children is very important. You need to be well enough, both physically and emotionally. Having a loving and committed relationship is necessary, but not sufficient. Ongoing anorexia harms the unborn child, and increases the complications in both the mother and the baby, even if you are able to conceive. There is a higher risk of developmental abnormalities and long-term consequences in the child, and also a higher risk of post-natal depression in the mother.[11-13] Before planning a pregnancy, ask yourself: 'Am I ready for this? Will I be able to "eat enough for two"? Will I be able to cope with my body getting bigger? Will I be able to breast-feed my baby? Will I be able to feed my child without worrying about it getting fat?'

I would strongly advise against fertility treatment if you cannot conceive naturally. The chances are that your body is lacking sufficient energy to conceive and support a successful pregnancy. Fertility treatments only provide the genetic material, but not the energy that is required for the development of a healthy baby. Would you forgive yourself if your child was born prematurely due to your malnutrition and suffered lifelong consequences, such as brain damage? If you are not ready, it is better to wait until your anorexia is safely behind you. This will be worthwhile for everyone in the long term. Before you can be certain that you are ready, it is important to use contraception so that you do not end up having an unexpected and unwanted pregnancy and the resulting heartache.

Summary

Maintaining a healthy weight is essential if you want to remain well, and avoid relapse. This is usually a body mass index (BMI) of between 20 and 25 for people of Caucasian origin. For women, the return of regular periods is a good indicator of minimal healthy weight.

The most challenging time is probably the first year after weight restoration, or during stressful life events. It is important to continue working on flexibility and variety of diets, and to become at ease with eating in company, challenging anorexia until it does not interfere with your life any more.

You need to learn to adjust your diet to your energy expenditure, so that your life is not restricted because of anorexia. Healthy energy intake is likely to be between 2000 and 3000 kcal per day depending on your gender and activity levels.

Developing or rebuilding relationships is protective and can bring you happiness that anorexia never would. Be patient: recovery from anorexia takes a long time, but it can happen. Good luck!

Reference

1. Treat TA, Mccabe EB, Gaskill JA, Marcus MD. Treatment of anorexia nervosa in a specialty care continuum. *International Journal of Eating Disorders* 2008; **41(6)**: 564-572.
2. Vandereycken W. The place of inpatient care in the treatment of anorexia nervosa: Questions to be answered. *International Journal of Eating Disorders* 2003; **34(4)**: 409-422.
3. Fennig S, Fennig S, Roe D. Physical recovery in anorexia nervosa: Is this the sole purpose of a child and adolescent medical-psychiatric unit? *General Hospital Psychiatry* 2002; **24(2)**: 87-92.
4. Gowers SG, Weetman J, Shore A, Hossain F, Elvins R. Impact of hospitalisation on the outcome of adolescent anorexia nervosa. *British Journal of Psychiatry* 2000; **176**: 138-141.
5. Federici A, Kaplan AS. The patient's account of relapse and recovery in anorexia nervosa: A qualitative study. *European*

Eating Disorders Review 2008; **16(1)**: 1-10.

6. Steinhausen HC, Grigoroiu-Serbanescu M, Boyadjieva S, Neumarker KJ, Metzke CW. The relevance of body weight in the medium-term to long-term course of adolescent anorexia nervosa. Findings from a multisite study. *International Journal of Eating Disorders* 2009; **42(1)**: 19-25.

7. Mayer LES, Roberto CA, Glasofer DR, Etu SF, Gallagher D, Wang J et al. Does percent body fat predict outcome in anorexia nervosa? *American Journal of Psychiatry* 2007; **164(6)**: 970-972.

8. Pike KM, Walsh BT, Vitousek K, Wilson GT, Bauer J. Cognitive behavior therapy in the posthospitalization treatment of anorexia nervosa. *American Journal of Psychiatry* 2003; **160(11)**: 2046-2049.

9. Carter JC, McFarlane TL, Bewell C, Olmsted MP, Woodside DB, Kaplan AS et al. Maintenance treatment for anorexia nervosa: A comparison of cognitive behavior therapy and treatment as usual. *International Journal of Eating Disorders* 2009; **42(3)**: 202-207.

10. Pinheiro AP, Raney TJ, Thornton LM, Fichter MM, Berrettini WH, Goldman D et al. Sexual functioning in women with eating disorders. *International Journal of Eating Disorders* 2010; **43(2)**:123-129.

11. Micali N, Simonoff E, Treasure J. Infant feeding and weight in the first year of life in babies of women with eating disorders. *Journal of Pediatrics* 2009; **154(1)**: 55-60.

12. Bulik CM, von Holle A, Siega-Riz AM, Torgersen L, Lie KK, Hamer RM et al. Birth outcomes in women with eating disorders in the Norwegian Mother and Child Cohort Study (MoBa). *International Journal of Eating Disorders* 2009; **42(1)**: 9-18.

13. Manzato E, Zanetti T, Gualandi M. Pregnancy in severe anorexia nervosa. *International Journal of Eating Disorders* 2009; **42(1)**: 84-86.

Appendices

Sample menu plans

Weight restoration – first stage: 1000 kcal menu plan

This menu represents a very low dietary intake and it should be used only for a few days at the very beginning of weight restoration, and only if the person concerned is severely underweight and has been consuming less than 1000 kcal per day for some weeks. In this case, the sufferer is severely starved and is likely to experience significant negative consequences (such as feeling unwell, faint, cold, and irritable). It is highly likely that he or she will need help to re-establish a normal eating routine, and children and young people will need to be supervised at mealtimes. During this early stage of weight restoration it is important to preserve energy: the person should be kept warm and remain sedentary during the day. The overall fluid intake (water, and non-caffeine tea) should be around 1500-2000 ml (depending on the size of the person: children need smaller amounts). Having at least two cups of milk during the day is important, to ensure sufficient calcium and phosphate intake. If the person is lactose intolerant, fortified soy milk may be an alternative, but it is helpful to consult a dietician if a special diet is needed for any reason.

1. Breakfast: 1 cup (250 ml) semi-skimmed milk and 20 g cereals (e.g. Cheerios, Rice Krispies)

2. Morning snack: 1 small apple or other fresh fruit

3. Lunch: 1 cup of chicken vegetable soup (or any other soups – but no diet products) with ½ bread roll with butter

4. Afternoon snack: 100 ml fresh fruit juice

5. Evening meal: 3 oz (85 g) steamed white fish, ½ cup (90 g) boiled rice or mashed potatoes, ½ cup (90 g) green peas

6. Late snack: 1 cup of hot chocolate with semi-skimmed milk

This sample diet is usually well tolerated by patients. It can be varied by using different kind of cereals, yoghurt instead of milk, different types of soup and fruit juices.

Weight restoration – second stage: 1500 kcal menu plan

After a few days, it is important to increase the diet to 1500 kcal per day. Some dieticians like to increase the diet very slowly, but in my experience this is rarely necessary, and a delay can result in prolonged anxiety and further weight loss for the patient. A 500 kcal increase does not cause any physical complications and it is necessary for stabilisation. Severely malnourished patients may be able to start their weight restoration with this dietary intake (but only until their metabolic rate returns to normal; they will then need a higher intake).

The increase can be achieved by small changes during the day, as demonstrated here by building on the previous 1000 kcal diet.

Appendices

1. Breakfast: 1 cup (250 ml) semi-skimmed milk and 30 g cereals (e.g. Cheerios, Rice Krispies)

2. Morning snack: 1 large apple or other fresh fruit

3. Lunch: 1 cup of chicken vegetable soup (or other soups – no diet products) with 1 bread roll with butter, 1 cup of fresh juice

4. Afternoon snack: 1 small pot of Greek yoghurt with honey (150 g) or 1 biscuit with 100 ml of fruit juice

5. Evening meal: 3 oz (85 g) steamed fish, 1 cup (180 g) boiled rice, ½ cup (90 g) green peas, 1 tbsp olive oil (or butter)

6. Late snack: 1 cup of hot chocolate with semi-skimmed milk

It is important to introduce dietary fats early on, as this helps to challenge prolonged fat phobia. This should include butter or spread on bread, and olive oil or vegetable oil in food. Diet foods, such as non-fat yoghurts can maintain anorexic fears, so they are best avoided. They are usually packed with sugars and preservatives, so they tend to be nutritionally inferior anyhow. There are lots of options for flexibility in this menu plan: you can change the lunch to various sandwiches, or pasta salads, or the evening meal with the usual family meals (just smaller portions). It is important to avoid special cooking for the sufferer: it adds to the stress and the isolation, and it often creates conflict. Introduce the family's usual meals as early as possible during weight restoration, as this is much more likely to be maintained in the long term.

It is important to remember that a 1500 kcal diet is a weight loss diet for a normal person. However, a severely malnourished person may be able to gain weight on this diet until his/her body returns to its normal metabolic rate (that is, the resting or 'basal' rate). If the 1500 kcal diet results in weight restoration of 0.5-1 kg per week, it can continue for a few weeks, but sooner or later the diet will need to increase again as the person's basal metabolic rate goes up. The best way to decide when to increase the diet is monitoring weekly weight gain: if it slows down, the body needs more energy.

Weight restoration and maintenance: 2000 kcal diet

The next increase can be achieved by increasing portion sizes to normal and adding a piece of toast at breakfast, and some light puddings, such as ice cream and various fruit salads at main meals, or more energy dense snacks, such as biscuits, a small packets of nuts or small chocolate or muesli bars. It is also important to increase protein intake, by including eggs, a range of meats and seafood. For vegetarians it is important to seek advice from a qualified dietician, so that essential nutrients are not missed out.

This level of dietary intake offers lots of flexibility, and it is important to choose a menu plan that fits in with the person's usual lifestyle, so I will not offer a detailed plan here. However, for those wishing to build on the menu plans already given, the next step up is shown below. If you need more comprehensive help, there is plenty of information on the web (see website and book suggestions below), and there are many useful applications available for smart phones. It is important to keep the regular rhythm of the three main meals and snacks, as this helps prevent a return to the vicious circle of restriction and binges.

1. Breakfast: 1 cup (250 ml) of semi-skimmed milk and 30 g cereals (e.g. Cheerios, Rice Krispies), 1 slice of toast with butter and one slice of cheese (cheddar or similar) or 1 slice of meat or a boiled egg, and 1 cup of orange juice

2. Morning snack: 1 large apple or other fresh fruit or a cereal bar or a cup of fruit juice

3. Lunch: 1 cup of soup (no diet products) with a sandwich (e.g. prawn and mayonnaise, or ham, or turkey), and a small dessert such as ice cream or a cupcake
   - Options instead of the sandwich: pasta salads, various wraps
   - Eating out: most light meals in restaurants are also appropriate at this stage and can help address fears regarding social eating

4. Afternoon snack: 1 small pot of Greek yoghurt (150 g) or
   - 1 biscuit with a cup of fruit juice, or
   - a small piece of chocolate (e.g. Kit-Kat), or
   - a small packet of nuts

5. Evening meal: 3 oz (85 g) steamed fish, 1 cup boiled rice, 1 cup green peas, 1 tbsp olive oil (or butter), fruit salad with ice cream
   - At this stage the evening meal can be varied according to the family's taste, and it is important to return to the usual family meals that fit your tradition and lifestyle

6. Late snack: 1 cup of hot chocolate with semi-skimmed milk

The 2000 kcal diet is usually sufficient for maintaining the weight of sedentary women whose weight is normal, but it is also often adequate for weight restoration in a starved person. The only way to be sure is to monitor weight restoration once or twice a week. During weight maintenance this dietary intake maybe sufficient, but you may need more depending on your level of activity and lifestyle.

Completing weight restoration: 2500-3000 kcal diet

The increase to 2500 or 3000 kcal is often necessary to complete weight restoration if it slows down after a few weeks on 2000 kcal. This is usually a challenging task for the patient, who has to cope with the fear of weight gain and the embarrassment of having to eat more than some other family members. However, most physically active men or boys eat more than this, so the amounts are not excessive.

There are different ways of achieving this dietary intake when trying to recover from anorexia. Some experts (including Professor Fairburn) advocate the use of medically prescribed supplements such as Fortisip, Ensure, and ProSure. The reasoning is that these can be regarded as medicine by the patient and therefore help to manage the guilt related to eating. They are also easy to discontinue when weight restoration has been completed. However, in my experience, for many patients, this is not so simple, and the use of supplements often leads to the temptation to cut food out. Furthermore, having to have medical supplements instead of food can reinforce the anorexic identity, and it is also difficult to have them in school or in the workplace. If at all possible, it is better to use food. With persuasion, many patients accept that having more food is necessary during weight restoration, and the additional food can be cut out after weight restoration has been completed. Energy-dense snacks are also helpful: these include smoothies, nut-based snacks and cakes. This example shows how to build on the previous menu. Again, feel free to use your own preferred foods instead to suit your lifestyle.

7. Breakfast: 1 cup (250 ml) of semi-skimmed milk and 30 g cereals (e.g. Cheerios, Rice Krispies), 2 slices of toast with butter and jam, and 1 cup of orange juice

8. Morning snack: 1 large apple or other fresh fruit with 1 biscuit

9. Lunch: 1 cup of chicken vegetable soup (or other soups – no diet products) with a sandwich (e.g. tuna mayonnaise), 1 cup of fresh juice

10. Afternoon snack: 1 small pot of Greek yoghurt (150 g) or 1 biscuit with a cup of fruit juice

11. Evening meal: 3 oz (85 g) steamed fish, 1 cup boiled rice, 1 cup green peas, 1 tbsp olive oil (or butter), fruit salad with ice cream

12. Late snack: 1 cup of hot chocolate with semi-skimmed milk

Useful websites and organisations

Guidelines

NICE Guidelines (UK):
http://guidance.nice.org.uk/CG9/PublicInfo/pdf/English

APA Guidelines (US):
http://www.psychiatryonline.com/pracGuide/pracGuideTopic_12.aspx

Royal College of Psychiatrists (UK) guidance:
The nutritional management of anorexia nervosa:
http://www.rcpsych.ac.uk/files/pdfversion/cr130.pdf

The management of really sick patients with anorexia nervosa (MARSIPAN report):
http://www.rcpsych.ac.uk/files/pdfversion/CR162.pdf

The Royal Australian and New Zealand College of Psychiatrists:
http://www.ranzcp.org/images/stories/ranzcp-attachments/
Resources/Publications/CPG/Australian_Versions/AUS_
Anorexia_nervosa.pdf

Self-help organisations

Beating Eating Disorders, or B-EAT (UK charity, previously
known as the Eating Disorders Association). It provides a variety
of help, including telephone advice and local support groups.
http://www.b-eat.co.uk/Home

Eating Disorders Association Australia
http://www.eda.org.au/

Eating Disorders Association New Zealand
http://www.ed.org.nz/

Something Fishy: is a well respected US based website
http://www.something-fishy.org/

National Eating Disorder Information Centre Canada:
http://www.nedic.ca/

Professional organisations

The Academy for Eating Disorders (AED) is a global, multidisci-
plinary professional organization
http://www.aedweb.org//AM/Template.cfm?Section=Home

Institute of Psychiatry Eating Disorders Research Team
http://www.iop.kcl.ac.uk/sites/edu/?id=131

Australian and New Zealand Academy of Eating Disorders
http://www.anzaed.org.au/

Useful websites regarding healthy eating and weight restoration

A word of warning: most of these websites aim to reach the majority of the population who are overweight, so the language may be unhelpful for patients with anorexia. However, they offer objective information about healthy eating and exercise levels, which can be useful in challenging extreme anorexic beliefs.

UK:
http://www.eatwell.gov.uk/

US:
http://www.mypyramid.gov/

Canada:
http://www.hc-sc.gc.ca/fn-an/food-guide-aliment/index-eng.php

Australia:
http://www.nhmrc.gov.au/publications/synopses/dietsyn.html

Nutritional software

Most of these programmes are aimed at adults, but can be used for adolescents too.

Tap & track: This is an excellent software for smart-phones. It includes an extensive food database (mainly US-based), and monitors exercise, weight and BMI changes:
http://nanobitsoftware.com/?cat=4

Weight by date: This is for the desktop. The only problem with it is the language (aimed at people who are obese, so need to lose

weight), but otherwise excellent for up to 10 people in the family. The company is planning to release a mobile version soon.
http://www.weightbydate.com/dietsoftware/index.
htm?c1=Google&source=AdGrp_DietSoftware&kw=diet_
exercise_software&gclid=CM3ZoovBj6UCFYFH4wodjGXaNA

Growth and weight charts

As I explained in chapter 1, children's healthy weight and BMI significantly change during normal development. If you are uncertain whether your child is developing normally, ask your GP or a paediatrician. Some websites or smart-phone applications can be informative:
http://www.childrenchart.com/index.php
http://www.medcalc.com/growth/
http://itunes.apple.com/us/app/stat-growthcharts-lite/
id324489815?mt=8

Useful books

Self-help books

Alexander J, Le Grange D. *My kid is back: empowering parents to beat anorexia nervosa*. Routledge; 2010.

Bryant-Waugh R, Lask B. *Eating disorders: a parents' guide*. Revised edition. Brunner-Routledge; 2004.

Freeman C. *Overcoming anorexia nervosa*. New York: New York University Press; 2002.

Lock J, Le Grange D. *Help your teenager beat an eating disorder*. The Guilford Press; 2005.

Treasure J, Smith G, Crane A. *Skill-based learning for caring for a loved one with an eating disorder: the new Maudsley method*. Hove & New York: Routledge; 2007.

Books to help with healthy diet and meal planning

There are many useful books to help you devise meal plans and a healthy, nutritionally balanced diet for weight restoration and maintenance. It is best to choose according to your family's traditions and personal taste, so that everyone can eat together. Books about nutrition can also be useful for challenging anorexic misconceptions about healthy eating.

Blake S. *5-a-day menu planner: More than half a million delicious recipe combinations to ensure you and your family get all the fruit and vegetables you need*. Duncan Baird; 2008.

Oliver J. *Jamie's 30-minute meals*. London: Michael Joseph; 2010.

Simopoulos AP, Robinson J. *The omega diet*. New York: Harper Collins; 1999.

Wills J. *The food bible: the ultimate reference book for food and your health*. Revised edition. London: Quadrille Publishing Ltd; 2007.

Index

Index

Index

Index

Index

deficits, 71–72, 130
digestive system and, 148
gastric emptying and, 148
supplementation/inclusion in
diet, 109, 194, 201, 206,
229, 245
with lipid abnormalities,
154
omega-6 fatty acids, 70, 71, 74
deficits, 71
onset, age of *see* age of onset
oral contraceptive pills, 15
osteoporosis (brittle bones), 15, 43,
130, 131, 154–155
medication preventing, 244–245
outcome in anorexia nervosa,
158–160
length of hospital stay related
to, 250
outpatient treatment, 248–249
after weight restoration, 273
ovarian atrophy, 150
overweight *see* obesity

partners, helping your, 189–190
paternal parent *see* father
patience, lack of, 119
see also perseverance
peer relationships, 77, 113–115
PEG (percutaneous endoscopic
gastrostomy), 255
percutaneous endoscopic
gastrostomy (PEG), 255
perfectionism, 64, 87, 105–107, 187,
188
perseverance, 202
carer, 112, 119
see also patience
phobia *see* fear
phospholipids, brain, 156
physical activity *see* exercise
physical aggression, 213
physical examination, full, xi, 26,
231
skin abnormalities, 147

physical health, positive
consequences of anorexia
nervosa, 140–141
physical illness (medical disorders)
assessing risk of, 174–179
evolutionary advantage, 79
starvation/fasting causing, 9,
118, 119, 142–158
long-term effects, 160–162,
177
males, 45
males, in Minnesota study,
125, 142, 144, 146, 147,
150, 152, 153, 155, 156,
158, 160
as triggering factor, 76–77
pituitary gland atrophy, 149
placebos in trials, 228, 229
planning
meals, 201, 204, 218
for recovery, 179–180
point prevalence, 38
polyunsaturated fatty acids
(PUFAs), 70–75
deficiencies, 70, 71, 72
liver problems, 148
skin problems, 146
zinc and, 76
see also omega-3 fatty acids;
omega-6 fatty acids
portion size, 192, 194, 204, 206,
206–207, 207, 217, 232
`positive' things about anorexia
nervosa, 137–141, 162
praise, 218–219
precipitating factors, 76–78
pre-contemplation (stage of
change), 182
predisposing factors, 59–76
pregnancy planning, 276
prevalence
non-European countries and
ethnic groups, 41
Western/European countries,
38, 39, 40

Index

Index

Notes

Notes

Other Hammersmith Press titles

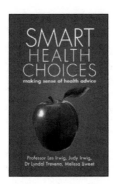

Smart Health Choices

Making sense of health advice
By Professor Les Irwig, Judy Irwig, Dr Lyndal Trevena, Melissa Sweet
242 pp £12.99
ISBN: 978-1-905140-17-6

Smart Health Choices provides the tools for assessing health advice, whether it comes from a specialist, general practitioner, complementary therapist, the media, the internet, or a friend. It shows how to take an active role in your healthcare, and how to make the best decisions for you and your loved ones, based on your personal preferences and the best available evidence.

> *'I wish all my patients would read this book. It encourages a sceptical but positive attitude to medical care, and encourages patients to be wise consumers. Read it, find a doctor you can work with, and together make the best of your healthcare.'*

Dr Paul Glasziou (Professor of Evidence-Based Medicine, University of Oxford, UK)

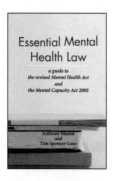

Essential Mental Health Law

a guide to the revised Mental Health Act and the Mental Capacity Act 2005
By Anthony Maden and Tim Spencer-Lane
230 pp £24.99
ISBN: 978-1-905140-29-9

This practical guide provides understanding of what recent changes in
mental health legislation mean for the individual clinician when making
decisions about the care of individual patients. Neutral on the wrongs and
rights of the changes, it focuses on helping psychiatrists, clinical psycholo-
gists, mental health nurses and social workers - especially those in training
- with the day to day application of the law in clinical practice. Non-
specialist doctors and lawyers will also find it invaluable, and it provides a
clear, user-friendly resource for patients and their families who may want
to understand the legislative framework themselves.